Unheard Voices

UNHEARD VOICES

Labor and Economic Policy in a Competitive World

RAY MARSHALL

Basic Books, Inc., Publishers   New York

Library of Congress Cataloging-in-Publication Data

Marshall, F. Ray.
  Unheard voices.

  Bibliography: p. 319
  Includes index.
    1. Industrial management—United States—Employee
participation. 2. Employee ownership—United States.
3. Collective bargaining—United States. 4. Industrial
management—Japan. 5. Competition, International.
I. Title.
HD5660.U5M36 1987   338.6   83–46084
ISBN 0–465–08869–4

This book is dedicated to
Jill, Susan, John, Christopher, and Sarah

CONTENTS

Contents

PREFACE

THE main impetus for this book grew out of my professional work as a labor economist and my responsibilities as secretary of labor from 1977 to 1981. The main functions of the secretary of labor are to serve as the president's chief labor adviser and to administer the Department of Labor—whose mandate is to protect and promote the interests of American wage earners. In carrying out these responsibilities, I participated in economic policy processes in the United States and in such international organizations as the International Labor Organization and the Organization for Economic Cooperation and Development (OECD). My colleagues in the Department of Labor and I were also involved in the successful completion of the "Tokyo Round" of trade negotiations. We likewise established formal bilateral relationships with the ministries of labor from about eighteen countries to work jointly on common problems. One of my most fruitful relationships was with the OECD labor ministers in the "Copenhagen Group," which met periodically to discuss labor and economic problems. We soon discovered that we had very similar points of view with respect to priorities in economic policy and the danger of allowing economic policy to be dominated by business or financial interests or, which usually comes to the same thing, orthodox economic analysis. We tended to support the proposition that those countries that incorporated labor concerns into economic policy were more successful than those that did not. We also generally supported the need for consensus mechanisms such as those discussed in this book. The labor ministers, in addition, were likely to emphasize the importance of human resource development and full employment as the major goals of economic policy; and we tended to regard selective labor market, anti-inflation, and industrial policies as necessary supplements to macroeconomic policies in achieving those objectives. We all felt, moreover, that the OECD countries in general gave inadequate attention to labor matters in international economic affairs, though in most of them (except the United States) *unions* had much greater participation in policy making, through labor parties or formal consensus-building processes. In fact, one of the main reasons we organized the Copenhagen Group within the OECD was to gain greater participation by labor ministries in the economic policy work of that organization.

Many of the ideas in this book were developed in connection with my activities as secretary of labor—usually as briefing materials for domestic economic policy purposes or in support of my participation in international discussions. I owe particular debts to many valuable discussions with the Copenhagen Group and my colleagues in the Department of Labor and the Carter administration —especially the Economic Policy Group. I am particularly indebted to Arnie Packer, assistant secretary of labor for policy, evaluation, and research; Howard Samuel, deputy undersecretary of labor for international labor affairs; my special assistant, Chuck Knapp; and Janet Norwood, commissioner of labor statistics. I am also indebted to my Labor Department colleagues, Mike Aho, Jodie Allen, Nancy Barrett, Nik Edes, Paul Jensen, and Don Nichols, for their assistance with economic policy matters. All of these dedicated people and their staffs helped prepare me for economic policy discussions and congressional testimony.

The preparation of this book has also benefited from the work of my students in the Economics Department and at the Lyndon B. Johnson School of Public Affairs at the University of Texas and my colleagues, both at the LBJ School and the Economic Policy Council of the United Nations Association. I am indebted to my LBJ School colleague Norman Glickman for helpful and thoughtful comments on an earlier draft of this manuscript and to Jeanette Paxson for editorial help. I gratefully acknowledge financial support for this book from the Ford Foundation, the Rockefeller Foundation, and the American Income Life Insurance Company.

Finally, there is no way I can adequately express my gratitude to Cheryl McVay for her efficient and cheerful work in the preparation of several drafts of this manuscript.

Unheard Voices

Introduction

THE BASIC PREMISE of this book is that improved U.S. economic performance and competitiveness require greater worker participation.* Indeed, a major conclusion is that American business is losing its competitive position in the world economy at least in part because inadequate worker involvement has resulted in misguided and uncoordinated management and economic policies, which have placed our producers at a serious competitive disadvantage.

That is why we must look at these problems from a labor perspective. American economic policy today is dominated by politicians, economists, and financial interests. The perspectives of these groups often neglect some matters of great importance to workers that also happen to be significant determinants of personal welfare and national economic strength, including employment, real wages and family incomes, labor standards, human resource development, employment security, and equity.

---

*As used here, "worker participation" means worker involvement in economic policy and workplace management decisions, as well as an equitable sharing of the benefits and costs of change.

Orthodox economists and financial experts are also likely to stress short-run financial considerations while giving inadequate attention to global strategies, technological innovation, productivity, and the need for *negotiated,* enforceable rules of national and international economic conduct. In their stress on consumer sovereignty over national productive potential, moreover, many mainstream economists seem to lose sight of the reality that national power and real income growth are more likely to be determined by the ability to produce than by the ability to consume. A healthy economy requires participation and cooperation by all major economic interests as producers *and* consumers.

This book therefore considers greater worker participation important for both economic and political reasons. In fact, the rationale for political democracy is very similar to the justification for industrial democracy (worker participation in workplace decisions) and economic democracy (worker ownership). The conviction is growing in the United States and elsewhere that participatory systems are more viable than the traditional authoritarian management systems that historically have characterized most of American industry. Of course, industrial relations experts long have known the advantages of industrial democracy, but the inability of many American companies to compete with more participatory European and Japanese management systems (derived, ironically, from American industrial relations thought) has attracted worldwide attention to the consensus model.

In the United States, these newer, more cooperative worker involvement processes have clashed with collective bargaining, a more adversarial form of worker participation. Indeed, in this country such noncollective bargaining forms of worker involvement are unique in having been instigated mainly by employers—often as part of a union avoidance strategy—which explains why quality of worklife (QWL) and other worker involvement schemes have so often been viewed with suspicion by American union leaders, who until quite recently regarded collective bargaining as the only dependable form of worker involvement in workplace decisions. During the 1980s, however, some American unions have cautiously embraced alternate forms of worker participation, including worker ownership and membership on corporate boards of directors. Increasingly, union policy makers have come to believe that these more cooperative forms of workplace involvement are necessary to the competitiveness of American industry and the protection of American workers' jobs and working conditions.

Still, there is less understanding in the United States than among our strongest competitors of the importance of worker participation when it comes to national economic policy decisions beyond the workplace. This is surprising, because the same logic applies: in a democratic society the most effective policies are those that balance the major economic interests. Moreover, ideas about workplace democracy are derived from theories of political democracy. Indeed, industrial democracy emerged in part because of the incongruity of making workers full and equal participants in political matters while treating them like children on the job. But effective participation means more than participating as individuals: effective participation also requires the ability to have organized representation in arenas where national policies are formulated. Indeed, economic democracy without organizations would be like political democracy without political parties.

Organized representation by workers is important because policies that merely reflect financial or business interests will be incomplete and unstable. Workers are by far the largest economic interest group, and human capital is by far the most important source of productivity growth—several times as important, according to many studies, as physical capital. Despite this evidence, the development of physical capital has received much higher priority in national economic policy making. By contrast, countries like Japan and Germany, which are gaining competitively relative to the United States, place more emphasis on human resource development.

Input from the worker on public policy needs to be increased for equity as well as economic reasons. In an internationalized economy, financial and business interests (at least among large international corporations) can protect their interests by shifting resources to places with the highest economic returns—which often means the lowest wages. Corporations in some countries, such as Japan, derive sufficient special benefits from their governments that there is no need to worry about whether their global activities contribute to the national welfare. Their governments have adopted consensus-based policies to ensure that companies operating in their countries further national objectives. This is not true of American companies, which derive few special benefits not generally available to foreign companies operating here. Indeed, even military procurement in the United States is increasingly dependent on foreign producers, especially the Japanese. American companies are increasingly transnational corporations, so that there is no direct relationship between their economic health and that of their American workers, the American government, or the communities in which their firms operate. What this means is that public policy should be particularly concerned about *people,* who have a long-run interest in the country and whose fate is inextricably bound up with the national welfare. What is good for General Motors may not necessarily be good for the country, but what is good for American workers and their families is almost certainly good for the country.

The other main theme of this book is that worker participation, whether in the workplace or in economic policy decisions, must be considered in the context of the

American economy's evolution in the 1980s and beyond. Thus the internationalization of the American economy and the information revolution have transformed traditional management and industrial relations systems in ways that often nullify or impair the effectiveness of traditional economic policies. The following chapters will show that these changes make greater worker participation in national policy making and workplace decisions even more important.

The first three chapters provide the economic context for participatory public and private systems. Chapter 1 analyzes the implications of the internationalization of formerly more isolated national economies. Internationalization and technological changes are universal imperatives that have greatly altered the effectiveness of national economic policies and management and industrial relations systems. Chapter 2 discusses the problems created by these changes and demonstrates the inability of traditional nonconsensus-based policies, especially monetarism and supply side economics, to deal with these problems. Chapter 3 discusses the declining competitiveness of American industry because of defective public and private policies.

The next three chapters analyze the impact of various forms of worker participation on economic performance at the enterprise and industry levels. Chapter 7 demonstrates the use of consensus mechanisms for public policy making in Europe and the United States. Chapter 8 outlines the uses Japan has made of consensus processes to put together a very competitive economic system. The Japanese system is contrasted with the ineffectiveness of American policies, by outlining specifically how Japanese public and business strategies have increased their market share at the expense of U.S. companies even in high-tech industries, where the Americans have strong technological advantages. My conclusions and recommendations are presented in chapter 9.

Chapter I

The Context:
The Global
Information World

IN ORDER TO SHOW how worker participation can improve management and economic policy making, it is necessary to consider the economic context of those decisions and policies. Some recent economic and technological trends have impaired the effectiveness of traditional management, industrial relations, and economic policies. The nature of this new era—which is most appropriately called the global information society—makes consensus-based management and more participatory economic policies even more important than they were in the goods-producing economy of the 1940s and 1950s.

The Social Compact of 1945 to 1965

To understand fully the causes of our present state of economic instability and uncertainty, we need to consider the basic characteristics of what economic historians are likely to regard as America's Golden Age, roughly from 1945 to 1965. During this period, a combination of Keynesian economic policies, a mixed free-enterprise economy in which workers participated through strong free labor movements and collective bargaining, and the international economic system developed after World War II produced relatively low levels of inflation and high growth in productivity and real incomes.

The system that prevailed during this Golden Age produced easy growth and a more equitable sharing of that growth by workers than was true of the more competitive, laissez-faire policies that both preceded and followed it. Because the United States dominated the international economy in the immediate postwar period, it was easy for us to promote free-trade policies to govern our relatively limited involvement in the rapidly growing global economy. Although international trade grew rapidly, most production was still for the American market, where limited competition enabled large enterprises to reach an accommodation to share rewards with workers in exchange for stable production and labor peace. By taking labor out of competition, collective bargaining thus helped regulate both product and labor markets. Labor peace was further enhanced by union acceptance of both the capitalist system and the very narrow job assignments dictated by "scientific management." Growing worldwide demand, augmented by federal monetary and fiscal policies, allowed companies to prosper despite relatively inflexible and authoritarian management systems. Average productivity growth for the economy as a whole was enhanced by the shift of workers out of low-productivity agriculture into higher-productivity manufacturing, the exploitation of technology developed during World War II, relatively low levels of unemployment, stable growth, and the rising education levels made possible by both government policies and higher real incomes. Collective bargaining raised wages and forced management to improve productivity in order to be able to pay those higher wages. In this environment, there was general support for legally mandated worker benefits such as collective bargaining, minimum wages, social security, and unemployment compensation as ways to sustain purchasing power and therefore promote economic growth and prosperity. Along with recall rights under collective bargaining contracts, safety nets like unemployment compensation enabled corporations to retain their workers during the layoffs dictated both by their inflexible pricing practices and by business cycles. In this period of easy growth, real wages could increase and workers could improve their conditions through participation in collective bargaining and through pressure group politics.

Unfortunately, the arrangements that produced easy growth between 1945 and 1965 became less effective during the sixties and seventies. It soon became obvious, for example, that the United States could not pursue large-scale international ventures, like the Vietnam War, and simultaneously deal with the nation's pressing domestic problems without generating inflationary pressures. Indeed, the problems of the sixties exposed some important economic realities that had been minimized or ignored by traditional American macroeconomic policies; these included efficiency, productivity, resources, and technology. Moreover, it became clear that traditional macroeconomic policies had built-in inflationary biases that had been concealed by prosperity, fast-growing productivity, and favorable exchange rates and terms of trade. The

Keynesians also tended to minimize sectoral differences and structural problems within the economy as a whole, which made it very difficult to solve economic problems by monetary and fiscal policies alone.

The growth of the fifties and sixties was also slowed by the realization that progress carried with it some very important social costs: environmental pollution; damage to workers' safety and health; discrimination against people because of race, sex, or other characteristics unrelated to merit and productivity; and injustice for the economically disadvantaged. These costs have always had to be borne by somebody, but until the sixties and seventies, when strong public demands were made that these costs be internalized to businesses, they were generally shifted from business enterprises to individuals or to society as a whole. Unfortunately, our nonconsensus-based economic policies caused these new protective regulations to be formulated with inadequate attention to either their effectiveness or their economic impact. Regulations largely shaped by consensus, as they are in most other industrialized democracies, would have been less burdensome and more effective. These and other developments changed the economic outlook from one of certainty and optimism to one of confusion and pessimism. The confusion was caused by a growing realization that the old policies and institutions—of firms, industries, and the economy in general—were no longer as effective as they had been, but it was not at all clear what should replace them.

Internationalization

Perhaps what has brought this change home to the American public has been, more than any other factor, the internationalization of the U.S. economy and the globalization of markets. International transactions accounted for 9 percent of the U.S. gross national product in 1950 and about 25 percent in 1980. In the eighties, from a third to a half of all profits for major American corporations come from overseas, and international trade accounts for a third of all U.S. crops (indeed, more U.S. than Japanese land was used to feed the Japanese), a fourth of farm income, and a sixth of all jobs. Today, about 70 percent of all goods manufactured in the United States compete with imports. Similarly, at least 15 to 20 percent of the growth in the U.S. work force during the seventies probably came from immigrants (legal and illegal) and refugees.

These aggregate statistics actually understate the extent to which the American economy has been integrated into the world economy. Trade has been particularly important in the manufacturing sector. Exports increased from 9 percent of U.S. manufacturing production in 1960 to 19 percent in 1980; during the same period, imports increased from 5 percent of domestic production to about 23 percent. A New York Stock Exchange study found that imports increased proportionally against domestic production in twenty-eight out of forty industries between 1972 and 1982.[1] These industries accounted for roughly 70 percent of total U.S. production in 1977.

The internationalization of the U.S. economy was accelerated by the nation's dominant role in the international economy, which made it possible for our interests to prevail in a relatively free, open, and expanding global economy. The United States provided almost half of the world's industrial output in 1950. Our economy had actually been strengthened during World War II when our major competitors had been devastated, and we emerged with a backlog of technology that provided the basis for the unprecedented growth in productivity and total output. The dollar became the currency of international commerce, and English the language of international transactions. The theory of the trading process was that the welfare of the whole world was enlarged through a competitive free-trade, open-market system in which each country concentrated on producing the goods it could make and sell most efficiently. Exceptions were acknowledged only for developing countries with "infant industries," and for national security reasons.

Cohesion in the international economy was provided by multinational companies, whose activities were greatly strengthened by improved information and transportation technologies, the deregulation of markets, and shrinking barriers to the movement of capital and goods. Such corporations have become dominant international entities because they face no effective countervailing organization. They have evolved into "large transnational entities, not limited by constraints of domestic market size or costs of inputs, but, on the contrary, availing themselves of the most advantageous conditions in labor, capital, and goods markets."[2]

The emergence of international corporations, joint ventures, and consortia during the seventies and eighties complicates the concept of competitiveness among nations. Indeed, sharing production between countries in certain products, such as automobiles, makes it very difficult to identify an "American" product—its components may be produced in a number of different countries. International companies are locating not only marketing and sales activities overseas, but also production and, to a lesser extent, research and development. They are arranged according to a variety of contractual forms: wholly or partially owned subsidiaries, joint ventures, licensing agreements, and others.* These transnational organizations operate on a global basis to maximize benefits for the corporation, not to serve the welfare of either the

---

*From now on, I shall use the term "multinational corporation" to mean one headquartered in one country and operating in several others; a "transnational corporation" has diverse ownership and contractual arrangements between companies in different countries.

country in which the organization's ownership is based or the employees.

Consequences of Internationalization

The internationalization of markets has had important implications, both good and bad, for the conduct of national economic policy. On the positive side, international economic integration has promoted much greater efficiency in the use of the world's physical and financial resources; expanded managerial skills, knowledge, and technology in the developing countries; and allowed higher standards of living for many of the world's people.

But internationalization has also brought with it many problems. One of the most important has been the loss of national control over economic policies and domestic economies. Moreover, the structure of the information economy has changed to such an extent that international economic rules that appeared to be effective in the fifties and sixties no longer seem to work in the eighties. The internationalization of markets causes a ballooning effect for countries that are relatively open to the influx of goods and people. When, for example, European countries limited their imports of Japanese automobiles, the excess was diverted to the United States and other relatively open market countries. The integration of world markets has, in addition, tended to neutralize efforts by countries to have bilateral relations with other countries. When the United States tried to embargo wheat or pipeline equipment sales to the Soviet Union, our efforts failed because of the fungible nature of world markets: we sold the wheat to other countries and they sold it to the Russians. And when the U.S. government ordered an embargo of equipment sales to the Russian–Western European gas pipeline project, Caterpillar's chief rival, Komatsu, was quite willing to sell equipment to the Soviets.

Perhaps the most important aspect of global economic

interdependence is the way it has changed domestic policy making. As the experience of the United States in the late seventies has shown, traditional Keynesian policies directed at stimulating demand for goods are weakened by international leakages: stimulus when most major economies are depressed tends to limit domestic economic expansion by accelerating foreign imports. This problem was particularly serious for the United States in the recovery from the 1981–1982 recession, when foreign imports offset a large part of the increased demand. Imports were especially important for American capital-goods markets during the 1981–1984 business cycle, when almost all (95 percent) of the growth in final demand was met by imports.[3]

Global interdependence produces, in addition, serious boomerang effects from U.S. policies. For example, the 1981 U.S. tax cut and the ensuing recession created huge budget deficits, greatly increasing the federal demand for money. The fact that the federal government's borrowing requirements offset most of the net private domestic savings put strong pressure on real interest rates to rise. High real interest rates attracted foreign capital, which greatly increased net foreign debt. Since debts must ultimately be repaid in goods and services, future American living standards will have to be reduced to pay for the extent to which our present consumption exceeds our production. Inflationary pressures are moderated by an expensive dollar, which reduces the cost of imports; but this process was reversed when the dollar was devalued late in 1985, and the inflation exported during the early eighties will be brought back into the United States in the form of more expensive imports.*

Macroeconomic anti-inflation policy is also changed by

*In fact, the main factors preventing the declining dollar in 1985 and 1986 from reigniting inflationary fires were high levels of unemployment, tremendous reductions in oil prices, and very low agricultural prices—none of which could be sustained in the long run and all of which spelled very serious problems for farmers, workers, and the oil industry.

internationalization and floating exchange rates, which greatly intensify the restrictive effects of anti-inflation monetary policies. Moreover, such policies have negative repercussions in other countries, which boomerang back to the United States. For example, the Reagan administration's use of restrictive monetary policy and very stimulative fiscal policy during the early eighties caused serious trouble for European countries, which were forced to tolerate higher interest rates and unemployment levels because lower interest rates would have accelerated the flight of capital to the United States. Rising European unemployment, in turn, diminished European demand for American exports.

Similarly, American economic policies and the workings of the international banking system have created serious financial problems for Third World countries, with the same boomerang effect. During the late seventies, when the international banking system was awash in petrodollars and real interest rates were very low or even negative, the developing countries were encouraged to borrow heavily to finance development. The abundance of cheap credit encouraged wasteful practices by the developing countries and unwise policies by the banks. However, with higher real interest rates in the early eighties, the developing countries were unable to earn enough on their exports to pay interest on their loans, which had to be restructured by the International Monetary Fund and international banks in a way that threatens the economic (and political) future of those nations. The non-oil-developing countries were forced to adopt austerity measures that diminished already low standards of living. They greatly restricted their imports and increased their exports. These measures were possible for developing countries because of the expanding American economy, which absorbed more than half of the increase in global exports in 1983 and 1984. However, serious risks are created for the American and world economies by the growing American trade deficit (Third World countries bought about 40 percent of our exports in the late seventies) and by the fact that Third World non-oil-exporting countries have become net exporters of capital, greatly restricting their economic development, which is a prerequisite for their political and social stability. The exposure of many of our leading banks to high-risk Third World loans could also jeopardize U.S. economic health.

International Trade

Internationalization and the emergence of multinational corporations have led workers and companies increasingly to question free trade theories based on the competitive assumption that trade necessarily benefits all parties involved. In reality, competition alone does not govern international markets. Governments, transnational oligopolistic companies, state-owned enterprises, and cartels are heavily involved in international markets. Almost all governments except the United States have active trade policies to support national economic objectives. The United States, by contrast, has passive trade policies that are not directed toward any coherent national objective but merely react to the actions of other countries. Following the Japanese practice, many countries have adopted the theory of dynamic comparative advantage: they pursue strategies to create an advantage over foreign competitors and improve industry mix rather than simply allowing whatever comparative advantage they might naturally have to be revealed by markets. Economic activity is based on national and enterprise strategies, not just on the interplay of short-run market forces and profit maximizing. Free trade is usually justified in the United States on the basis of maximizing short-run profits and consumer satisfaction; Japan and the "little Japans" are more interested in strengthening national power, productive capacity, and market share than in maximizing short-run profit. In the internationalized information world change is not gradual, and trade is not just in goods: whole factories and technologies are exported. The consequence of these changes for the United States and other high-wage industrialized countries is that jobs are lost and wages and working conditions are reduced by international competition. In short, an open trading system can cause some countries to gain at the expense of others. At the same time, market forces within the framework of enforceable consensus-based rules can cause an open international trading system to benefit people in most countries.

Unfortunately, the international trade and finance system created largely under U.S. leadership after World War II is no longer adequate. Indeed, the problems caused by uncoordinated national economic policies dominated by business and financial interests and justified by antiquated laissez-faire economic ideas threaten the international trading system by encouraging competitive trade restrictions or even trade wars. Uncoordinated policies also create confusion, which obscures the fact that many international trading problems are caused by macroeconomic policy failures, not by trade practices themselves.*

The unemployment and competitiveness problems created by the overvalued dollar, the dynamic policies of

---

*In the eighties, for example, the overvalued dollar has caused more damage to the American economy than trade practices of other countries. For example, a 1985 study by Data Resources, Inc. (DRI) found that the more expensive dollar accounted for 55 percent of the deterioration in net U.S. exports between 1980 and 1984. The remaining 45 percent was due to such factors as the stronger economic growth in the United States, the Third World debt problem, and the other competitiveness problems of American industry to be discussed in chapter 2. Except for the higher dollar, the real gross national product would have been 15 percent higher in 1984 than it actually was; employment was 1.4 percent higher and the consumer price index 1.2 percentage points higher.[4]

other countries, and the passive American response to those policies all generate pressure to restrict trade. Trade restrictions in an interdependent world, however, could exacerbate our economic problems not only through the boomerang effect but also by inspiring retaliation. For example, restricting imports from Third World countries will make it more difficult for them to keep up payments on their foreign debts and would limit their ability to import from the United States, which contributes to a degenerating system that damages developing and industrialized countries alike. The United States and the world therefore have a big stake in developing consensus-based rules that permit an open and expanding trading system.

A trade union's ability to protect and promote its members' interests through collective bargaining is directly related to its ability to represent the entire labor market. Thus internationalization diminishes the power of national trade unions. The greater mobility of capital strengthens the relative power of large multinational or transnational corporations, which have become the dominant organizing entities in international markets. Unions, governments, and international organizations have not yet developed countervailing mechanisms to offset the multinationals' power. So internationalization creates the threat of international wages and working conditions set at the lowest common level. Because of Third World population pressures and the much lower rates of population growth in the more developed countries, the developing countries and multinationals would be the clear winners of any strategy based on wage competition alone. It is commonly believed that traditional American management and industrial relations systems have been rendered obsolete by the so-called Japanese management system (examined in detail in chapter 4) which, among other things, emphasizes worker participation and cooperative labor–management and government–private relations.

The Information Revolution

Technological change, especially the information revolution, has been the second major universal imperative affecting American industry. It has had important effects on traditional American management practices and has led to pressures for greater worker participation in the development and use of technology and in its economic benefits.

There is nothing new about the interaction between technology and social and economic institutions; technology always has been a revolutionary force in human history. It determines what kinds of work people do, how they learn, their living conditions, their workplaces, and the power relationships between nations as well as between the participants in industrial relations systems. Technology—especially the information revolution—was a major factor in the internationalization of global economies. It is also a force for dynamic change in economic affairs, creating some industries and occupations, destroying others, and affecting the optimal size and profitability of enterprises. Technology will be an important determinant of the long-term competitiveness of American industry. If companies in the United States lose their organizational and technological edge, they will be forced to compete mainly on the basis of wages and prices—a competition they surely will lose.

The efficient use of information technology will require much greater worker participation in the development and use of that technology. Technology—together with an increasingly dynamic and competitive environment—will require much greater attention to human resource development. Clearly, human resource development programs are not likely to be very effective unless they reflect the interests and concerns of workers (learners), as well as managers, teachers, and the public.

The information revolution has been associated with a great decline in the proportion of American workers producing goods, from about two-thirds of all workers in 1950 to one-fourth in 1983. Most of the employment increase in the service sector has been in the information occupations: from about 17 percent of total employment in 1950 to about 60 percent in 1985 (the number varies depending on the definition of information occupation). Information innovations have various effects: they greatly facilitate the work of multinational corporations; they decentralize economic activity from large urban and industrialized areas into rural areas and the Third World; they change skill requirements for work and rearrange the work itself; they alter power relations between labor and management within enterprises; and they reduce the optimal size of producing units.

Most of the job growth during the seventies was in plants with twenty or fewer employees. At the same time, innovations in information and communication have facilitated the integration of world commodity, financial, product, and labor markets. Thus the paradox arises that the information revolution tends simultaneously to reduce the size of enterprises producing many goods and services while facilitating greater control of economic activity through large multinational corporations.

Information technology has changed the nature of the work process itself: by facilitating highly automated processes, information systems make it possible to reprogram machines for new tasks rather than buy new machines. These processes also make possible more custom-tailored precision work that requires sophisticated skills and a great deal of teamwork; they likewise demand the integration of such previously separate functions as engineering, design, manufacturing, distribution, marketing, and sales. The most important characteristics of automated production processes are that they require sophisticated skills and worker cooperation and that they are not easily governed by traditional authoritarian management systems. Greater flexibility is necessary because workers must deal with diverse and fluid work situations that cannot be standardized or anticipated and that require broad training, as contrasted with the highly specialized training typical of traditional mass production and manufacturing operations. Clearly the monitoring and evaluation of workers who function in cooperative teams is very difficult, and cannot be accomplished by the methods used to evaluate employees who produce standardized, mass-produced goods. The new systems based on information technology demand different kinds of management systems.

Economists have always recognized the pervasive and sometimes revolutionary impact of technological change on economic activity. The technology that led to the industrial revolution, for instance, made balancing production and consumption difficult. The balance was maintained because the new technology made labor indispensable and therefore gave workers and their organizations the power to demand the wages they needed to buy the output of industry. The breakdown of this balance between aggregate demand and aggregate supply during the 1930s led to the Keynesian economic policies that served the United States and other industrialized markets very well until the sixties and seventies. Some analysts believe the new information technology creates the need for new forms of governance or demand management based on flexible manufacturing.[5] If flexible manufacturing enabled more production to be on a custom-order basis, for example, there would be more balance between production and consumption, which would reduce the impact of imbalances between demand and supply that became major causes of business cycles in earlier mass-production systems. There can be no imbalance between demand and supply in a custom-order system because products are sold before they are made.

The prospect of returning to a custom-order economy is intriguing, but economies of scale will continue to be very important for a long time. Moreover, the scale is now in an international context and is related more to the need to recoup the development costs of sophisticated technology than to spread the fixed costs of expensive, single-purpose equipment over larger outputs.

Because of technology's importance, there has been much discussion of its net effect on the workplace. Analysts are divided as to whether the net outcome of the information revolution will be negative or positive for workers. Those who stress the negatives emphasize technological unemployment and such possibilities as fragmentation of the work, boredom and fatigue, health hazards, and the management control difficulties generated by the new technology. Those who stress the positives emphasize increased productivity and competitiveness, higher living standards, and safer, more interesting and creative work made possible by information technology.

High Tech and Employment

There is likewise considerable disagreement among the experts over the net employment effects of "high-tech" industries. Indeed, even the term "high tech" means different things to different people. To some it means the changes associated with microelectronics, but there are other closely related developments that justify the use of the term "revolution" to describe what is happening; these include advances in automation, energy and raw materials, agricultural and biological engineering, lasers, robotics, microelectronics, and the development of synthetic materials, which, taken collectively, are causing really monumental economic and social changes.

There are similar disagreements over the identification of high-tech industries. Some analysts define high tech as those industries with larger proportions of scientists, engineers, and technicians in their work forces; others refer to industries with higher proportions of research and development spending; and still others use some combination of these concepts. In general, however, high-tech industries are those in which technological innovation and development play a central role and firms have above-average expenditures for research and development.[6] In quantitative terms, high-tech jobs represent a relatively small fraction of the work force—3 to 6 million in 1984, compared with 19 million for manufacturing and 103 million overall. The U.S. Bureau of Labor Statistics estimated that 3 percent of U.S. jobs could be considered "high tech" in 1985. Although their number will double over the next decade, by 1992 high-tech employment will still constitute only about 6 percent of the U.S. work force.

In some sense, the distinction between high-tech and "smokestack" industries is an artificial one. Given the exigencies of intensified domestic and international competition, information technology will be used extensively in those smokestack industries that survive. It is, therefore, useful to distinguish the employment effects of high-tech industries themselves from the broader and more important impact of the information technology on all industries. Clearly, while there will be relatively rapid growth in the high-tech industries, they will not create very many jobs. At the same time, the technology itself will be used throughout the economy, so it will cause much more pervasive changes. Indeed, information technology has become the new economic infrastructure, every bit as important in the contemporary economy as highways, railroads, telegraph lines, and telephones were in earlier times.

Many futurists and information specialists believe that information technology, especially computers, will replace energy and basic industries as the fundamental source of national power. Automated factories and processes are made possible by computers, which clearly have significant military, scientific, and industrial applications. That is why many believe that the country with the best supercomputer will have the key to world leadership in the twenty-first century.[7] Whatever our assessment of this conclusion, the impact of the new technologies will probably be at least as great as that of the first industrial revolution. In fact, in the minds of some experts the changes currently under way are sufficiently great that "The 1990s will differ from the 1970s as profoundly as the 19th century from the 18th."[8]

The Japanese have developed a national economic strategy based on knowledge-intensive and high-value-added industries, which is basically the application of human capital. Japan has kept unemployment under 3 percent as workers shift into new jobs when their old jobs are replaced by robots and automation. In 1983, the Japanese had about sixty unmanned and semiautomatic factories operated by flexible manufacturing systems, which consist of computer-linked machine tools, automatic conveyors, robots, and automatic inspection equipment. There were many fewer such systems in the United States.

The information revolution has had several other important consequences. First of all, the substitution of knowledge and information for physical resources are major factors in increased productivity. Second, the information revolution, along with international competition, has contributed to the decentralization of work. Economic activity has also shifted from the industrial heartland of the North and East to the so-called Sunbelt, in the South and West. Finally, technological change has been a factor in what is probably the most important labor market development of this century—the increased participation of women in the labor force. In 1950 about 70 percent of American households were headed by a man whose salary was the sole source of income; today less than 15 percent of American households fit this description. The greater participation of women was facilitated by developing technology—birth control, mechanization of household work, and the creation of new jobs, especially in information occupations, filled mainly by women.

Employment Effects

What will be the employment effects of high tech? Before attempting to answer this question, it is useful to contrast the arguments of the pessimists with those of the optimists.

The optimists argue that the new technology will create more jobs than it displaces and that the new jobs will be better jobs. They reason as follows: first, they believe that high technology protects jobs from international competition. Firms faced with low-cost foreign competition can either automate, move some or all of their operations overseas, reduce domestic labor costs, close down, or seek protection from foreign competition. Assuming a relatively open international trading system, in the long run firms must be competitive or go out of business. In order to remain in the United States, many firms will automate because robots can compete with Third World workers in many jobs while some blue-collar workers cannot. Also, high tech is an export industry. During the seventies, when the United States was losing some of its basic industries, it was able to maintain a reasonable net trade balance because of a comparative advantage in high-tech exports.

The optimists also hold that high tech will lead to a net increase in jobs because higher productivity leads to lower prices, greater competitiveness, higher sales, and therefore more employment. By increasing total wealth, high tech creates more jobs than it displaces.

They point out that the introduction of high tech will improve the quality of work life, because robots will do any hot, dirty, or dangerous work and workers will have an intelligent consultant—the computer. As the machines do more of the physical work, workers are freed to be more creative and to participate more effectively in production (and even management) decisions. The machines are most likely to eliminate simple, monotonous tasks like spot welding, spray painting, and handling of material. Workers will be required to have more general knowledge, with a premium on problem solving, communicating, and handling workplace emergencies. In addition, each worker will have greater discretion to determine quality and productivity and will control significantly more capital. To be most effective, future workers will have to be literate, educated, and creative as well as skilled, and workers in automated workplaces are likely to require much less direct supervision than is needed in conventional factories.

Agriculture provides an example of technology's advantages. Although American agriculture uses no more physical resources than it did in the 1920s, there has been a great increase in productivity, and the workers displaced from agriculture have been absorbed in other industries, usually at higher real wages. According to Ed Shuh, an agricultural specialist at the University of Minnesota, "all of the agricultural output from the mid-1920s to the mid-

1970s was accomplished with *no increase in the stock of physical resources.* It was all due to increased productivity, with most of that due to *new knowledge or information.*"[9] In 1923 one farm worker supplied 8.9 people; by 1984 one farm worker supplied 79.1 people. Since the turn of the century, farmers have declined from 40 percent of the work force to 2.8 percent. According to the optimists, farmers are better off because the technology increased their income. The same thing is likely to happen in manufacturing: workers will be displaced, but they will be absorbed in other industries, and total output will continue to increase as employment declines, making everybody better off. An example often cited is that of the Bell System: in 1910 121,310 employees handled an average of 57 telephone calls each. By 1981, 874,000 Bell System employees handled an average of 239,000 calls each.

Some optimists also discount pessimistic predictions about large-scale displacement because those predictions are based on the new technology's long-run physical possibilities rather than short-run realities and economic probabilities. In this view, the market will limit the introduction of labor-displacing technology.[10] For example, the Japanese use more robots than Americans because Japanese capital costs have been relatively low and labor costs have been rising, whereas in the United States real labor costs have been declining relative to capital costs, making it less profitable to substitute capital for labor. Relative factor costs also explain the greater growth in employment in the United States during the 1970s than in either Japan or Western Europe. Lastly, the optimists point out that advanced automated systems—like computer-integrated manufacturing—are still in very rudimentary stages of development and therefore will take a long time to perfect, so their short-term impact is limited.

The pessimists, by contrast, argue that the new technology will displace more workers than it employs and will reduce the quality of life for workers on the job and off. In their view, high-tech industries usually create a few good jobs for engineers, scientists, and managers, but most jobs are marginal, low paying, and require limited levels of education and training. Moreover, according to the pessimists, the new technology makes people more complete appendages to machines—it increases mechanical thought and the "calculative mind" at the expense of other intellectual qualities such as intuition and creativity; it minimizes the importance of individual experience and emphasizes speed over thinking. As one expert put it: "People are going to die in triviality measured to the fourth decimal point. How marvelous!"[11] The quality of work life could also suffer because eliminating the need for the workers to intervene actively in the production process could lead to boredom and stress. Stress could also result from a lack of autonomy at work and the pressure to keep expensive equipment running around the clock. Employees in large word-processing pools or centers are the office equivalent of the factory assembly line; employees are removed from the context of their work and operate in an atmosphere of repetition, boredom, and lack of human interaction. Moreover, many of the high-tech manufacturing processes involve above-average exposure to toxic substances that pose serious health hazards.[12] In addition, the technology greatly increases both management's *control* over workers and the possibilities for manipulation. The pessimists point out that management almost always introduces technology to reduce labor costs, not to improve the quality of work.

They contend additionally that high tech will join with other forces (declining union strength, international trade, the regressiveness of government tax and fiscal policies, higher birth rates among low-income people, and rising worldwide unemployment) to accelerate displacement of middle-income workers and the growing polarization of society into a relatively few wealthy and a great majority of poor people.

Second, pessimists contend that high tech, though growing rapidly in percentage terms, will not create very many jobs in the aggregate. For example, during the next decade, more than three times as many jobs will be created for janitors (779,000) as for computer analysts (200,000), even though the number of computer analysts will grow by 85 percent.

Labor displacement will be pervasive because the new technology is ubiquitous. Thus, in the pessimistic view, the agricultural analogy is seriously flawed: agricultural technology was more industry-specific, whereas the new information technology has pervasive applications; agricultural displacement came at a time of relatively rapid growth in productivity and total output, making it possible for the economy to absorb the displaced workers more easily; the displaced agricultural workers could move to higher productivity manufacturing jobs, whereas displaced manufacturing workers usually move to lower productivity and lower wage service industries; moreover, farmers could improve their conditions because they owned the physical resources (technology and land), whereas workers remaining in manufacturing do not ordinarily own the technology and other physical resources.

Finally, high tech is different from earlier technology, they argue, in that it displaces mental as well as physical work—in fact, the greatest future displacement is likely to be of white-collar office workers, where women are heavily concentrated.*

One widely noted contribution to the pessimistic line of thought is by economics Nobel laureate Wassily Leontief.

---

*This argument is convincing because automated factory technology is in a much more rudimentary state of development and is much more expensive. Robots cost $50,000 and up and mainframe computers $1 million or more. Word processors and personal computers that are revolutionizing office work cost as little as $1,500.

Leontief raises the prospect that the new technology will upset the socioeconomic balance that made it possible for industrialized market economies significantly to improve real incomes for most people. The technology of the first industrial revolution raised labor productivity and therefore enhanced the bargaining power of indispensable workers. These early economic conditions were, in addition, conducive to the formation of labor organizations that strengthened the workers' ability to use their political and economic power to gain greater participation in the system.

The new technology, however, is very different:

> Whereas the harnessing of mechanical power practically eliminated muscular effort as a significant element in the human contribution to production of various goods and services, the electronic chip is proving capable of performing more and more complex "mental" functions that until recently had to be carried out by the human mind.

> As soon as not only the physical but also the controlling "mental" functions involved in the production of goods and services can be performed without the participation of human labor, labor's role as an indispensable "factor of production" will progressively diminish.[13]

Leontief therefore raises the specter that involuntary technological unemployment (technological unemployment so far has been mainly a "voluntary" shortening of hours) will be a serious problem, upsetting the balance between production and distribution and thus making it more difficult to sustain economic growth; in other words, rising unemployment and limited incomes make it more difficult to sustain the economic system. Moreover, the new technology and its accompanying economic trends not only make labor more expendable but also weaken the ability of labor organizations to protect workers in the highly competitive internationalized information world.

Technology and Worker Participation

The pessimistic predictions about the impact of technology are based on the assumption that traditional American "scientific management" practices will prevail. The American system was established between the Civil War and World War I, for a mass-production manufacturing system using expensive and special-purpose capital assets and relying mainly on unskilled and uneducated workers. "Scientific management" was systematized by Frederick Winslow Taylor, who was concerned that the skilled workers' accumulated knowledge gave them control over the work process and permitted "soldiering" or malingering on the job.[14] In order to gain control of the work, "it became the duty and also the pleasure of . . . management not only to replace [the workers'] rule of thumb, but also to teach . . . the workmen . . . under them the quickest ways of working."[15] Taylor felt that fragmenting the work into the "one best way" it could be done and then teaching this way to relatively unskilled workers motivated by piece rates would give management control of the work. The full potential of this system would be realized when "almost all of the machines in the shop are run by men who are of smaller caliber and attainments, and who are therefore cheaper than those required under the old system."[16]

Although Taylor's ideas were very influential, especially in the automobile industry, they were not universally adopted. Opposition came from those managers whose authority might be subordinated to engineering departments and from workers, who "quickly develop" a distaste "for highly routinized and regimented jobs. . . . The social fallout from Taylorism is absenteeism, high turnover rates, shoddy workmanship, and even sabotage." Taylorism faced, in addition, a "technical limit," which "arises from the impossibility of fully eliminating skill and control from the organization of work alone."[17] This technical limitation, derived from the complexity of work processes, gave workers on the shop floor substantial power. However, as *Iron Age* has pointed out, this power can be reduced by computerized automation, which "is more than a means of controlling a machine. It is a system, a method of manufacturing. It embodies much of what the father of scientific management, Frederick Winslow Taylor, sought back in 1890. . . . 'Our original objective,' Mr. Taylor wrote, 'was that of taking control of the machine shop out of the hands of many workmen, and placing it completely in the hands of management.' "[18]

Harley Shaiken, an expert on technology and a former machinist, provides some important insights into the tension between management's conflicting objectives in the introduction of computer-controlled machine tools. He notes that management has many choices in the use of technology, but Taylorism "calls for designs that reduce skill requirements, transfer decisionmaking off the shop floor, and exert tighter control over the workers who remain. The result can be more boring and stressful work in a more tightly controlled work environment." Developing automation in this way can be costly for society as a whole:

> In fact, there is a fundamental contradiction between the potential of computerization to enrich working life and increase productivity and the development of technology in pursuit of authoritarian social goals. The moral cost is that people's lives become diminished through degrading their work. The productivity loss stems from the inability of systems that reduce the input of workers to fully utilize the skill,

talent, experience, and creativity that only human beings can provide. Moreover, in seeking to bypass human input at almost any price, new systems often achieve a breathtaking complexity that is prone to breakdown and consequently requires greater human input. Ironically, the drive to eliminate any dependence on workers who operate machines can result in a new greater dependence on those who repair the equipment.[19]

Efforts to restrict human involvement might have only limited success. "If a machine's reliability is questionable or if the manufacturing process is unusually varied and complex, a need for sustained worker input may arise regardless of the design goals."[20] Similarly, the workers' power to influence the process in either negative or positive ways will limit the adoption of high-tech machinery. The amount of leverage workers have depends on their indispensability in the work process and on their unity.

Some Predictions

What conclusions can be drawn from these conflicting claims? Mainly, that nobody knows what the net effect of the new technology will be. The impact is too pervasive and will be conditioned by a very complex constellation of forces. Moreover, while the new technology has acquired a life of its own, people can have a lot to say about what its effects will be: they can tilt it either toward the optimistic or the pessimistic scenarios.

Despite these uncertainties, several conclusions are supportable. First, it seems clear that emerging technologies will produce rapid changes, placing a premium on adaptable organizations, institutions, individuals, and policies. The inflexible will continue to have great trouble. As I will demonstrate more fully in chapters 6 and 7, consensus-based policies that permit full participation by workers greatly improve flexibility.

The second main conclusion about information technology is that it opens up a wide array of options for society and for enterprise management. Technology can relieve a wide range of human problems—including those caused by the technology itself. It therefore places a high premium on improving public and private policy development, strategic planning, and management systems. It makes the human element a more, not less, critical variable.

Third, the influence of high tech on employment will depend heavily on improved national policies and more effective private management systems. The critical assumption behind the optimistic view is that national and world economic growth will absorb workers who are displaced by technology and that markets or other processes will make it possible for resources to be shifted into alternative employment as workers are displaced. Current policies and trends (explored later) make it doubtful that this smooth adaptation can take place. However, a consensus-based, full employment strategy that takes workers' concerns into account (as outlined in chapter 9) has the best chance to make maximum effective use of the emerging technology.

The importance of a consensus-based system is suggested by the fact that robots and automated systems have been much more readily accepted by Japanese than American workers. American workers not only fear that robots will displace them but are also concerned about the loss of skills and job control. Japanese workers and their unions, by contrast, generally welcome the introduction of technology. The Japanese government maintains economic policies to promote low levels of unemployment and inflation and optimal growth in productivity, national income, real wages, and living standards. These measures include a relatively successful strategy to develop human resources and technology and to facilitate the orderly, efficient, and equitable shifting of resources out of non-competitive into more competitive sectors.

Japanese workers and their unions (which represent about 30 percent of Japanese workers and a majority in the larger companies) welcome the introduction of technology because they participate fully in the development of technology, and the Japanese compensation systems enable workers to benefit directly from the resulting increased production. Regular Japanese workers in major companies not only have lifetime employment but also receive perhaps one-third of their annual compensation from a bonus paid twice a year based on overall company performance. This compensation system tends to increase flexibility and personal savings and to minimize the workers' resistance to change. Japanese workers not only benefit directly and clearly from the introduction of new technology; they and their unions are also involved in the planning decisions that lead to the installation of robots and other systems. American workers, by contrast, do not ordinarily participate in such decisions, which usually are made unilaterally and in secret by management.

In view of these differences, it is not surprising that many American firms make much less effective use of information technology than their Japanese competitors. American workers see little relationship between productivity improvements and their personal welfare. A 1983 *Public Agenda* study of American and Japanese workers found that 93 percent of the Japanese but only 9 percent of the Americans thought they would benefit from higher productivity. Less than 25 percent of the Americans said they were working at full capacity, and 73 percent saw no connection between their compensation and how hard they worked.[21]

Two universal imperatives—internationalization and technological change—are transforming the American and world economies. These developments have greatly changed the nature of economic activity and therefore require changes in traditional management and economic policies. Keynesian economic policies provided greater worker participation in the making (and the benefits) of policy than the laissez-faire policies that preceded and succeeded the period of their greatest efficacy, 1935 to 1965. As will be emphasized in chapter 3, the declining competitiveness of American industry relative to the more participative Japanese system casts doubt on the economic viability of both the authoritarian American management system and the less participatory, more elitist policies that have been proposed as replacements for the Keynesian ones. This question will be examined at length in chapters 4 through 6.

Chapter II

The Problem: Adapting to International Competition

THE CLOSELY RELATED POLICIES and institutions developed during the 1930s and 1940s helped produce the longest period of economic prosperity in U.S. history, in part because those policies were based on the democratic principle that sustained prosperity required participation by all major groups in the benefits of growth. Unfortunately, the inability of the Keynesian policies to deal very effectively with the economic problems of the 1970s provided the intellectual and political opening for the combination of monetarism and supply side policies adopted by the Reagan administration. Reaganomics is based on the "trickle down" theory that economic progress requires a dismantling or weakening of participatory policies and institutions. Collective bargaining was deliberately weakened, as were political and governmental mechanisms to provide wide participation in economic growth through full employment and worker protections. The Reagan administration favored market mechanisms, automatic increases in the money supply, and high unemployment in order to check inflation, instead of balanced monetary and fiscal policies supplemented by direct job creation to achieve full employment. In addition, little or no effort was made to involve workers or their representatives in economic policy processes.

In the following pages I will set forth the economic problems now confronting policy makers, discuss the debate over possible solutions, and evaluate the elitist, nonparticipatory policies developed by the Reagan administration to deal with what some economists considered the fundamental flaws of the more democratic Keynesian policies.

New Economic Problems of the Seventies

Before evaluating the Reagan administration policies, we must examine the economic problems these policies were supposed to solve. These included the deceleration in productivity growth that started in the sixties and intensified in the seventies; the emergence of higher levels of both unemployment and inflation or "stagflation"; economic uncertainty because internationalization and stagflation reduced the effectiveness of traditional macroeconomic policies; and the decline in American industry's competitiveness, explored in chapter 3.

Rising unemployment was particularly troublesome,

because of its great material and human costs and because
the U.S. and other industrialized market economies appeared to have brought this problem under control in the
fifties and sixties. But joblessness again became a major
problem in the seventies and eighties in almost all countries, except Japan and smaller countries such as Austria
and Sweden.

Comparing labor market developments in the United
States, Europe, and Japan between 1973 and 1983 reveals
three main trends: first, steady increases in European
unemployment; second, sharp fluctuations in U.S. unemployment; and third, virtual stability in Japanese unemployment. It is interesting to note that although U.S.
unemployment rates increased during the late seventies,
the difference between U.S. and European rates narrowed
considerably (see figure 2.1). Furthermore, long-term
unemployment has increased dramatically in Europe and,
to a lesser extent, in the United States, which suggests
that employment opportunities have undergone structural realignments in advanced industrial nations (see
figure 2.2).

Despite the higher compensation costs in the United
States, American manufacturing employment and unemployment held up better than in most other countries
except Japan, where manufacturing employment increased by almost 5 percent between 1977 and 1984. Japanese manufacturing output also increased by over 80 percent during that time compared with only .5 percent in the
United States. In 1984, the unemployment rate in the
ten-nation European community was 11 percent, some
four points higher than in the United States. Moreover,
manufacturing employment in this eight-year period remained relatively steady in the United States but declined
as follows in other countries: in Belgium by about 19
percent, in France by more than 14 percent, in West Germany by 10 percent, in Italy and Sweden by more than

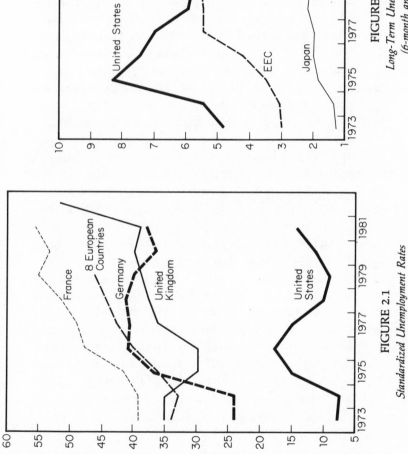

FIGURE 2.1
Standardized Unemployment Rates

FIGURE 2.2
*Long-Term Unemployment
(6-month and over)
As a percentage of total unemployment*

Source: *OECD Economic Outlook* (December 1982):36, 38.

11 percent, and in the United Kingdom by nearly 24 percent.

The reasons for the greater growth in long-term or structural unemployment in Europe are not known, but some factors clearly contributed. The U.S. labor force grew faster than the European during the seventies; in OECD Europe* there was a growth of about seven jobs for each ten additions to the work force, whereas in the United States there was a growth of nine jobs for each ten labor-force additions. Despite rapid job growth, therefore, the United States has not been able to avoid rising unemployment—from an average of 4.8 percent in the sixties and 6.3 percent in the seventies to 8 percent in the first half of the eighties. Second, stronger, more centralized collective bargaining in Europe and more elaborate job and income security systems have caused less wage and employment flexibility than in the United States. The Europeans maintained real wages better than in the United States but had greater difficulty avoiding the growth in long-term unemployment. The growth of real wages in Europe (figure 2.3) encouraged the growth of investment, while rising capital costs in the United States relative to real wages encouraged greater employment growth. Thus European countries on the whole had less flexibility in adjusting to the external shocks of the seventies. Japanese systems permitted greater flexibility than either American or European ones. Moreover, the Japanese kept unemployment low by matching job and labor force growth. Unemployment would have been even higher in Germany and other European countries if they had not been able to export foreign workers.

*The Organization for Economic Cooperation and Development (OECD) was originally a European organization devoted to the cooperative development of the world economy and international trade, as well as the promotion of their national economic interests. There are eighteen European members: Austria, Belgium, Denmark, Finland, France, Greece, Iceland, Ireland, Italy, Luxembourg, the Netherlands, Norway, Portugal, Spain, Sweden, Switzerland, the United Kingdom, and West Germany. The newer, non-European, members are Australia, Canada, Japan, Turkey, and the United States.

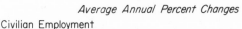

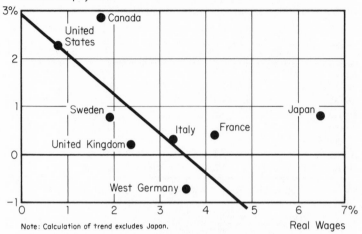

FIGURE 2.3

Changes in Real Wages and Employment in Eight Countries, 1970–1978

SOURCE: New York Stock Exchange Office of Economic Research, pamphlet entitled "U.S. Economic Performance in a Global Perspective" (February 1981), p. 44.

Another way to compare the position of the United States with that of other countries is through a composite economic performance index (see tables 2.1 and 2.2). This index is obtained by dividing real growth rates by the sum of unemployment plus inflation. As measured by this index, only Italy and the United Kingdom performed worse than the United States between 1973 and 1980. Japan and Germany had decisive superiority in terms of this measure during the same period.

Table 2.2 is an update in the economic performance index (EPI) for the United States, Japan, and Germany, showing a deterioration in American and German performance relative to Japan after 1980.

What caused our problems? There is no agreement on all of the factors responsible for the deteriorating position of the United States in the international economy, but some factors can be pointed out. A major problem has

TABLE 2.1

Economic Performance Index*
1960–1973 and 1974–1980

	1974–1980		1960–1973
Japan	37.8	Japan	145.9
West Germany	29.0	West Germany	123.9
France	18.0	France	85.5
Canada	16.5	Italy	67.7
Sweden	15.3	Canada	64.2
United States	15.2	Sweden	55.6
Italy	13.4	United States	50.4
United Kingdom	2.2	United Kingdom	43.1

SOURCE: New York Stock Exchange, Office of Economic Research, pamphlet entitled "U.S. Economic Performance in a Global Perspective" (February 1981), p. 11.

$$^*EPI = \frac{\text{real economic growth rate}}{\text{unemployment rate} + \text{inflation rate}}$$

been the decline in productivity growth, which is also the most important factor in the slower pace of economic growth since about the mid-sixties. Because of these conditions, increases in total output were possible only because we used more resources, especially a much larger work force.

Other obvious causes of our inflation and unemployment problems during the seventies were the energy price shocks of 1973–1974 and 1979. The quadrupling of energy prices in 1973–1974 and the further doubling in 1979 had a dramatic impact on American and other world economies. The inflation that had started with the deficit financing of the Vietnam War, during a time of relatively full employment, was accelerated by the food price increases and the devaluation of the dollar in the early seventies. The drastic energy price increases intensified inflationary pressures. With little increase in productivity, the only way to pay more in real terms for imported oil was to take a cut in real incomes. Since the United States

TABLE 2.2

Economic Performance Index*
(Percent)

	1977	1978	1979	1980	1981	1982	1983	1984	Average 1977–1984
Japan	68.8	75.0	110.6	100.0	81.6	80.5	100.0	181.3	99.75
West Germany	37.3	42.5	54.8	24.1	−2.2	−9.6	11.4	26.0	23.04
United States	43.0	37.0	19.2	−1.8	14.5	−13.4	27.6	60.2	23.29

SOURCE: Calculated from International Monetary Fund, *World Economic Outlook* (April 1985), pp. 206, 209, and 212.

*EPI = $\dfrac{\text{real economic growth rate}}{\text{unemployment rate} + \text{inflation rate}}$

had no consensus-based mechanism to achieve the required reduction in real incomes, we used inflation—the only means available to us. We also had no effective means other than recession and unemployment to deal with that inflation. Thus, as people attempted to sustain their real incomes after the huge oil price hikes, they simply forced prices up. These disruptions also led to unemployment because of the shifts in the patterns of demand caused by higher energy prices and inflation. These developments produced global economic disruption; growth in demand for goods and services fell internationally from an average of 8 percent a year during the sixties to 6 percent in the seventies and 1.8 percent in 1981.

The Economic Policy Debate

Disagreement over how to address the economic problems of an internationalized information world has caused serious problems for the American economy. Without a new consensus it will be very difficult to develop coherent policies. The economy will continue to swing back and forth between high levels of inflation and unemployment, or, worse yet, manage to have both simultaneously. The only stability we are likely to achieve is stagflation at high levels of unemployment, based on the barbaric idea that massive unemployment is the only means to control inflation.[1] If this happens, the competitiveness of the American economy will continue to deteriorate, along with the international power of the United States and the standard of living for most Americans.

Despite the earlier appearance of consensus, confirmed

when even Richard Nixon proclaimed, "We are all Keynesians now," there were always critics of demand-management policies. Conservatives objected to the role the Keynesians assigned to active government intervention. They also considered the Keynesian tendency to minimize the importance of unbalanced budgets contrary to sound fiscal policy. The monetarists criticized Keynesian demand-management policy for interfering with the market system and for its basis on the belief that it was possible to maintain full employment by monetary and fiscal fine-tuning. The monetarists argued that attempts to reduce unemployment below its "natural rate" would be self-defeating and would simply lead to inflation. According to them, inflation was caused mainly by increases in the money supply, and therefore the best macroeconomic policy was to match increases in the money supply with the economy's long-term real growth potential. With this monetary policy and free markets, the natural unemployment rate could be sustained. They objected to the substitution of more participatory processes and collective bargaining for "free market" forces.

Most critics of Keynesian economics were conservatives (though there were significant differences among the conservatives), but there were also critics who thought the Keynesians—and all macroeconomists—gave inadequate attention to those structural and sectoral differences within the economy that made it difficult to achieve anti-inflation, unemployment, growth, and productivity objectives through general macroeconomic policies alone. Some of the critics were "micro," or structural, supply siders, who were particularly concerned that the Keynesians had given inadequate attention to such matters as productivity, resources, technology, efficiency, and inflation.

The structuralists tended to accept Keynesian macroeconomic policies but believed those policies must be supplemented by more targeted approaches to address

specific inflation, unemployment, or productivity problems that cannot be resolved very efficiently or equitably
by pursuing macroeconomic policies alone. Currently
they are also the main advocates of consensus-based industrial policies, to make the economy more competitive
by addressing the opportunities and problems in particular industries or sectors (see chapters 7 and 8). Both the
Keynesians, or "neo-Keynesians," and the monetarists
are critical of these specific interventions, as well as of
collective bargaining, which they regard as inferior to free
market forces, operating within the framework of their
specific macroeconomic policies to deal with microeco-
nomic problems. Structuralists believe selective interventions and collective bargaining are needed to overcome
market imperfections and to make the economy perform
better, as well as to ensure equity.

The first serious political challenge to traditional demand-management policies was Reaganomics, a combination of monetarism and macro supply side ideas. While
they never produced a coherent body of thought, the
supply siders, as their name implies, emphasized the need
to maintain high levels of aggregate output by stimulating
savings and investment. The supply siders, like the neo-
Keynesians, are critical of collective bargaining, participatory policy mechanisms, and market regulations; they
favor free market forces.

Reaganomics

Supply siders emphasize radical tax and budget cuts to
increase savings and investment which, in turn, are supposed to increase supply or production. Supply siders

advocate stimulating the economy by shifting resources from the government and middle- and low-income groups to what they regard as more productive higher-income people.

The supply siders believe (or at least they did at the beginning of the Reagan administration) that curing our inflation, unemployment, and productivity problems could be painless if policy makers had the nerve to make radical tax and budget cuts. They reject the ideas of traditional conservatives who argued that inflation could only be cured by unemployment and recession and who, like Federal Reserve Board Chairman Paul Volcker, argued that deep tax reductions unmatched by spending cuts would generate large budget deficits, causing serious economic problems. These conservatives emphasized the adverse impacts of large deficits and urged the administration to cut spending *before* reducing taxes. The Reagan administration, of course, rejected this advice.

The supply siders' tax policy was based on the assumption that high marginal tax rates had discouraged incentives to work and invest. At first they predicted that by 1984 the greater savings, investment, and work resulting from their tax cuts would, in turn, increase productivity and growth, reduce unemployment and inflation, and balance the budget by increasing tax collections enough to offset both the revenue losses from the tax cuts and increased defense spending.

The early optimism about Reaganomics soon faded as unemployment and budget deficits mounted and real interest rates more than tripled.* Confidence in the administration's policies was shaken by the growing realization that there was a fundamental inconsistency in

---

*During the years 1982–1984, real interest rates reached unprecedented levels. In 1984, short-term real interest rates were 5 to 6 percent, compared with a 1950–1980 average of 1.3 percent. The long-term real rate, based on thirty-year government bond rates, was about 8 percent, contrasted with about 1 percent when the Reagan administration took office.

Reaganomics: huge tax cuts and increases in defense spending tended to stimulate the economy, while the limitations on the money supply prescribed by monetarism (urged on a willing Federal Reserve Board by the administration) tended to restrict growth. It soon became obvious that the administration's deep tax cuts would not generate enough economic stimulus to restore federal revenues. Large and increasing budget deficits kept real interest rates high, which choked off the economic recovery that had begun before the administration took office and plunged the country into the longest and deepest recession since the Great Depression.

Huge budget deficits and high real interest rates created other serious problems for the U.S. and world economies. Since we had the highest real interest rates of any major industrial country, foreigners raised the price of the dollar in order to take advantage of favorable American rates. This overvalued dollar was like a 30–40 percent tax on American exports and a larger subsidy on imports; huge trade deficits resulted, reaching $173 billion in 1986 and costing more than three million American jobs. High real interest rates not only blocked productive investments in the United States but, in the boomerang effect already discussed, also caused problems for other countries.* Most seriously, the United States financed its budget and trade deficits through heavy borrowing, much of it from abroad. As a consequence, in four years the U.S. reversed the net foreign investment position it had accumulated since World War II and, in 1985, became a net debtor nation. Americans will have to reduce their living standards in the future in order to service these debts.

Reaganomics generated, far from the promised economic "miracle," a deep recession, crippling budget deficits, and much higher government spending. Congres-

---

*A 1 percent increase in U.S. interest rates raises the debt service costs of the non-oil-developing countries by $4 billion.

sional Budget Office studies concluded that if the policies in effect when the Reagan administration took office had continued, the budget would have been balanced in 1983, while the actual deficit that year was $195 billion and growing. Federal spending during the first four years of the Reagan administration averaged about 24 percent of the gross national product, contrasted with 21 percent during the Carter administration. The difference was somewhat higher defense spending and significantly greater net interest costs: from 1.4 percent of the GNP in 1985 ($62 billion) without the Reagan policies to 3.2 percent of the GNP ($125 billion) with those policies. These interest payments will become even greater in subsequent years, despite the 1982 and 1984 tax increases.

Savings, Taxes, and Investments

There was very little evidence that taxes had impeded investment between 1965 and 1980, as the supply siders argued. As I and other analysts predicted, the 1981 tax cuts did not increase savings and investment.[2] Rather, capital spending declined during the years 1981 through 1983.[3] Consumer spending relative to the GNP increased from 63 percent in 1980 to 66.5 percent in 1982, and personal savings declined as a percentage of disposable income to 5.8 percent in 1982 and 4 percent in the second quarter of 1983.[4] Personal savings rates for other periods have been considerably higher, according to the *Economic Report of the President* (February 1982): 6.4 percent from 1943 to 1965, 7.5 percent from 1966 to 1973, and 6.8 percent from 1974 to 1981.

The main justification for supply side tax cuts was the need to increase savings and investment. A common contention by conservatives—and even some others—is that a shortage of investment was a major reason for our declining productivity growth during the seventies. Accord-

TABLE 2.3

Savings and Investment Shares of the Gross National Product, 1951–1982

Average annual percentage share

Period	Private Saving		Government Saving			Investment		
	Total	Personal	Total	Federal	State and Local	Nonresidential	Residential	Net Foreign
1951–1960	16.2	4.7	-0.3	-0.2	-0.2	10.4	5.2	0.3
1961–1970	16.3	4.7	-0.4	-0.5	0.1	11.1	4.3	0.5
1971–1975	17.2	5.6	-1.2	-1.8	0.6	11.1	4.6	0.3
1976–1980	17.1	4.2	-0.7	-2.0	1.2	11.9	4.6	-0.2
1981	17.1	4.4	-1.0	-2.0	1.1	12.5	3.6	0.1
1982	17.4	4.6	-3.8	-4.9	1.0	10.6	3.1	-0.2

Net Saving and Investment*

Period	Private Saving	Private Investment	Capital Consumption
1951–1960	8.0	7.3	8.9
1961–1970	8.6	7.6	8.4
1971–1975	8.7	7.0	9.3
1976–1980	7.4	6.7	10.5
1981	6.6	5.4	11.2
1982	6.5	2.4	11.6

SOURCE: U.S. Department of Commerce, *National Income and Product Accounts of the U.S.* (1983).

*Percent of Net National Product.

ing to this view, a major reason for the relative success of countries like Japan was their much higher savings rates. Indeed, many economists favor either consumption or flat-rate taxes in order to overcome this perceived defect. But the evidence raises serious questions about the extent to which private investment was a problem in the seventies and early eighties and, consequently, about the need to shift resources from the public sector to the private. The argument that personal savings were a problem is especially questionable because in the United States the largest source of savings is not personal savings but retained business earnings. In fact, three sources of savings —personal, business, and government—have retained relatively constant shares of the GNP since World War II: personal savings between 4.5 and 5.1 percent; business savings between 11.4 and 12.4 percent; and government savings between 0.0 and −1.1 percent between 1948 and 1981.

Thus, it is difficult to accept the argument that a decline in the rate of private capital investment was responsible for the nation's economic problems in the seventies and early eighties. There was no such decline: the investment ratio (nonresidential fixed investment as a percent of the GNP) was 9.3 percent in 1950, 9.1 percent in 1960, 10.5 percent in 1970, and 10.7 percent in 1980; moreover, for 1977–1980 the ratio averaged 10.7 percent (see table 2.3).

Because savings and investment are identical from an economic perspective, there was no decline in savings relative to the GNP. Furthermore, the main reason for the slower rate of growth in capital stock was a decline in the rate of economic growth. In other words, savings and investment are more likely to increase if real GNP increases, not the other way around.

It might be argued that *net* capital formation had declined by 1980. Depending on the definition of "net," this was probably true, but again the slowdown in productivity growth and total output was the culprit. One could argue that there was a need to increase investment because it now took more capital to produce the same output, but it is not clear why the productivity of capital had declined. I will demonstrate that a much more important source of productivity growth has been *human capital* investment, which the administration reduced in its unsuccessful attempt to increase physical capital.

The 1981 tax cuts were also based on the assumption that the major reasons for America's disadvantageous position relative to Japan and other countries were the higher rates of savings and investment in those countries. It is hard to assess this argument because international comparisons are hampered by different levels of development and different institutions. The United States, for example, has a greater pool of capital than other countries, and, until the advent of Reaganomics, probably had lower capital costs for equipment as well as higher average productivity. Comparisons are also complicated by the fact that most countries include government capital spending as a part of investment, while the United States does not. According to a study for the Federal Reserve Board, the U.S. gross savings rate would increase to 24.5 percent, instead of 16 percent, for the 1948–1977 period if government saving and consumer durable expenditures were included.[5]

Of course, the important point about investment is not its trend or its ratio to the GNP in the United States or to that of other countries; it is whether the amount of capital is optimal with respect to other resources and investment opportunities. In this connection, a 1981 study for the Federal Reserve Board noted the constant rate of investment relative to the GNP and concluded that the investment rate was "optimal" at that time.[6] It is not clear, however, whether the rate of savings relative to the GNP was optimal in the 1980s. The United States clearly has a lower rate of savings than other countries, mainly because our institutions and policies have all been designed to increase consumption in order to sustain a high mass-production economy. The United States needs to put less emphasis on consumption and more on production and savings. This can be done by growth policies and by tax and other policies to create more incentives to save and disincentives to consume. We certainly should not continue tax policies, like the deductibility of consumer credit for income tax purposes, that encourage consumption. It should be noted, however, that our international trade policies also encourage consumption at the expense of production by overemphasis on the importance of short-term price competition regardless of the effects on long-term productive potential. What comparisons with other countries reveal above all is that savings are determined by forces deeply embedded in social policies and therefore will not be changed much by tax cuts alone. The Reaganomics experience demonstrates that savings and investment certainly will not be increased by "trickle down" economics.

The particularly significant declines in the share of investment relative to the GNP were in *public* outlays for human resources and infrastructure, which hardly supports the argument for a shift of resources from the public to the private sector. Government fixed investment in areas other than defense declined from about 4 percent of the GNP in the sixties to about 2 percent in 1981; there were wide fluctuations in private residential fixed investment, but these, too, declined in the seventies.[7]

While placing its hope in a form of economic magic, the administration failed to see the real causes of inflation. Inflation is not due mainly to the federal government and therefore will not be eliminated simply by making government smaller, controlling the money supply, or relying on market forces. The problem is much more complicated.

The underlying rate of inflation increased from about 1 percent during the sixties to 10.2 percent in the fourth quarter of 1980. The inflation of the seventies originated in the way the Vietnam War was financed and was greatly accelerated by such external shocks as oil price increases. It was prolonged by the ongoing spiral that resulted from the inflationary biases in wage and price determining institutions. The moderation of inflationary pressures after 1981 to less than 4 percent was primarily due to the recession, lower energy and food prices, lower housing costs, and lower costs of imports because of an overvalued dollar.* The Reagan administration's main contribution was to make the recession deeper, though most of the action to reduce inflation was taken by the Federal Reserve, not the administration. It must be conceded, however, that the Federal Reserve was able to develop restrictive monetary policies to check inflation because Congress and the Carter administration had failed to develop an effective alternative anti-inflation policy.

Unemployment: The Price Is Too High

The best answer to inflation is not to generate very costly recessions, but to adopt consensus-based policies that deal with inflation's specific causes. The supply siders, as well as traditional conservatives, give inadequate attention to the human and material costs of unemployment. They often argue that the unemployment figures are overstated anyway, that workers are unemployed because their wages are too high, or that high unemployment is "worth it" to reduce inflationary pressures. These attitudes ignore the real losses from unemployment, which are truly staggering. The late Arthur Okun es-

---

*The Congressional Budget Office estimated that over 93 percent of the reduction in the consumer price index during 1982 was due to lower costs of energy (31 percent), food (22 percent), and housing (40 percent).

timated the costs of trying to reduce inflation through recessions at $200 billion in lost output for each percentage point of lower inflation.[8] He concluded that "A $1 trillion cure for chronic inflation is unthinkable." It was an unthinkable price to pay, but we paid it.

The Reagan administration's unprecedented budget deficits have greatly crippled the fiscal power of the federal government. These deficits combined with the administration's hostility to nondefense federal spending to force deep cuts in human resource programs. Moreover, despite the administration's assurances about preserving the safety nets for the "truly needy," the record suggests that in various ways many low-income people have been seriously damaged by the budget cuts. Seventy percent of the 1982 budget cuts and 90 percent of those for 1983 affected the poor. With unemployment at the highest level since the Great Depression, public-service jobs were eliminated, the relatively successful Job Corps was cut, and in 1982 the employment service, which was already understaffed, was cut to one-half of its 1981 level. The deepening recession forced a partial restoration of some of these cuts, but not to the 1981 levels in real terms. Medicaid was weakened, along with Aid to Families with Dependent Children (15 percent cut in 1982, 30 percent in 1983); food stamps for elderly and disabled families were cut an average of 25 percent, child nutrition by 15 percent.

Redistribution of power to the rich and powerful was what the Reagan economic program was all about. The major fault that Reagan and his followers found with the social legislation since the New Deal was not that there was "waste, fraud, and abuse" or inefficiency in government; any objective analysis would show that these programs largely succeeded.[9] The problem was that human resource programs did not further the administration's mainly political and class-oriented purpose. So the Reagan administration has reversed a long series of policies that were based on the assumption that in an advanced industrial, highly interdependent global information society, the nation's sense of community, sharing, and helping those who, for whatever reason, were not able to make it on their own, was mainly expressed through the government. These social programs not only were based on a sense of justice but were also assumed to be "public investments" that would yield social dividends, an inheritance from the democratic New Deal belief that we could not have enduring prosperity unless all major groups shared in that prosperity. The safety nets (social security, unemployment compensation, agricultural price support, deposit insurance for banks, the progressive income tax, the encouragement of collective bargaining) that allowed greater worker participation in policy making and in the fruits of the economy were not just to catch those who were falling out of the market system, but also to sustain that system itself—to provide purchasing power and to strengthen support for America as a just and humane society. This philosophy countered the extreme individualism and power imbalances that contributed to the Great Depression. The Reagan administration's belief that these programs are bad for the country and that we should return to the social Darwinism of the nineteenth century, disguised as "supply side economics," is radical and reactionary. It will fail because extreme laissez-faire and the law of the jungle are inadequate blueprints for a viable, prosperous, equitable, and humane society. An equitable economy is not justified merely for moral reasons; it is justified on the basis of social efficiency, apparently incomprehensible to the administration's elitist inclinations and extreme individualism. A major flaw in supply side arguments is the implication that inequality is necessary for economic efficiency. There is no justification for this idea in the United States or elsewhere. Indeed, among the industrialized countries only France has a more unequal distribution of income. The gap between the highest and lowest 10 percent of income recipients is eleven to one in the United States, five to one in Japan, and seven to one in Germany, and both of these countries are doing very well economically.

Did Reaganomics Work?

It was predictable that supporters of Reaganomics would declare victory at the first signs of economic recovery from the deep 1981–1982 recession. In light of such declarations, it is useful to recall the administration's original reasoning and forecasts: that large tax cuts heavily tilted to high-income groups would stimulate savings and investment and therefore lead us out of the recession, and that monetarism would produce a painless solution for inflation.

The administration also predicted that a shift of resources from the unproductive public sector to the productive private one would so stimulate economic activity that added tax collections would offset the revenue losses and balance the budget by fiscal 1984. On the basis of this plan, administration economists predicted that there would be no recession, a lower inflation rate, and an increase in investment; that real economic growth would pick up late in 1981 and continue through 1982; and that after a slight rise, unemployment would decline to 7 percent by the end of 1982. These predictions were not realized. In particular, investments declined instead of increasing; real interest rates rose to more than double their 1980 level and remained there; growth stagnated; unemployment rose to 10.8 percent instead of the predicted 7 percent in December 1982; and budget deficits rocketed to new absolute and relative highs and promise to remain there for most of the eighties. Finally, government spending relative to the gross national product increased above what it would have been without the administration's policies.

Recovery started only after a justifiably alarmed Federal Reserve Board changed its policies during the summer of 1982. Abandonment of monetarist restrictions did not lead to a surge in inflationary expectations, as the monetarists had predicted. It is true that inflation was down, but the decline in the consumer price index reflected lower oil and food prices and the recession rather than the triumph of Reaganomics, which had promised to bring inflation under control without a deep recession. There is nothing new or magical about checking inflation with a depression; that was the prescription of traditional conservatives, not of the monetarists and supply siders.

It is true that a tax cut was needed in 1981: the Keynesians were right after all, as the Reagan policies demonstrated. But a smaller, less regressive, more targeted tax cut and a tax credit only for job-creating investments would have avoided much of the subsequent uncertainty and unbalanced budgets, and could have made the tax structure more equitable. The administration's policies have made the tax system more regressive, not only by making income taxes less socially progressive but also by substituting federal excise, payroll, state and local property, and sales taxes for the federal income tax. Moreover, across-the-board reductions further distort the tax system and encourage such unproductive use of resources as conglomerate mergers and speculation.

The Problems Remain

Despite the recovery that started in 1982, there are numerous obstacles to sustained economic growth (many of them erected by Reaganomics). Among them is the chronic Third World debt, which will limit both economic development there and imports from the United States. Another problem is the still high level of unemployment, which will not only act as a drag on recovery but also intensify protectionist pressures, threatening the world trading system. Also, servicing federal debts from high structural budget deficits will absorb so much of net savings that increases in private demand for credit will push interest rates too high. We are seeing unprecedented trade deficits, which weaken economic recovery in the United States and create uncertainty in product and financial markets. Finally, the absence of an effective U.S. anti-inflation policy—other than unemployment—makes the Federal Reserve Board reluctant to allow adequate monetary growth and afraid to move to combat inflation in a timely fashion.

The economy improved in 1983 and 1984 not because of Reaganomics, but because monetarism and supply side economics had been abandoned and the recession had run its course, as recessions always do. Indeed, there is a danger that the recovery merely allows us to ignore the serious problems we face. The most important problems—the lack of international economic cooperation, inflation, unemployment, and low productivity growth—remain unresolved and threaten any long-term recovery. All macroeconomic approaches give inadequate attention to the development of cooperative mechanisms to bring governmental and private economic forces together to develop policies that can improve productivity and stimulate growth. The evidence is very strong that without some such mechanism, along with selective programs to deal with particular problems, the American economy will continue to swing erratically back and forth between high unemployment levels and inflation, if not stagnation at high levels of unemployment.

Chapter III

People: The Key to Competitiveness

AS I HAVE DEMONSTRATED, the powerful U.S. institutions developed mainly to produce goods for the American market have become less competitive in the internationalized information world. This loss involves a decline in world leadership and lower living standards. As measured by such indicators as profitability of U.S.-based enterprises, market shares, trade balances, and real wages, U.S. companies have been losing ground to foreign competitors in a broad range of industries since the 1960s.

Two important indicators of the American economy's ability to compete are shares of world output and trade. The big gainers in world output have been the Japanese and the developing countries; the main losers have been the United States and Europe. The other developed and the Communist countries' relative shares have remained unchanged. Between 1960 and 1980 the United States declined from a 26-percent share to 21.5 percent, while Europe declined from 26 percent to 22.5; Japan grew from

5 percent to 9 and developing countries from 11 percent to 15; and the other developed and Communist countries remained at 10 and 22 percent, respectively.[1]

Similarly, the U.S. share of world trade declined from 14.5 percent in 1965 to 10.3 percent in 1983 (table 3.1), and its world share of exported manufactured goods declined from 26 percent in 1960 to 18 percent in 1980. Again, the main loser was the U.S. and the main gainer was Japan, whose share of world trade more than doubled between 1960 and 1983. A third, especially significant indicator of declining competitiveness is the long-run slowdown in productivity growth. In fact, both productivity growth and real wages were lower in 1985 than in 1965.

Our competitiveness problems have been confirmed by a number of thoughtful studies and reports. The President's Commission on Industrial Competitiveness (PCIC)—the Reagan administration's answer to Democratic calls for industrial policy—concluded in 1985 that the ability of American business to compete in world markets had been slipping for twenty years or more, even in high-tech industries.[2] According to the commission, technical superiority has allowed the United States to remain a world industrial leader, but with "world leadership at stake," America is "floundering" in virtually every other major area. Even in high tech, there were setbacks in seven out of ten industries. This finding was confirmed by Harvard Business School (HBS) studies, which found that American firms held market share during the seventies only by reducing prices, with a consequent loss in profitability and real wages. According to HBS's Bruce Scott, net after-tax earnings for nonagricultural workers fell 17 percent between 1972 and 1981, and the return on business assets failed to keep up with the rising cost of capital: "roughly from 1975 onward U.S. manufacturers would have earned more on their assets investing them in corporate bonds than in production of goods."[3] It is not true, as some argue, that our competitive advantages in high-tech exports offset our disadvantages in basic manufacturing. Scott has shown that "the United States was not shifting its comparative advantage toward high-technology areas" between 1965 and 1980, "but [was] building on advantages it had had for years."[4]

The United States, unlike other countries—especially Germany and Japan—was not able to compensate for negative trade balances in energy with a growing surplus in manufacturing, despite a large dollar devaluation, which lowered our prices to foreigners during the seventies. The U.S. merchandise trade balance, which had been positive every year from 1893 to 1970, became negative in 1971; except for 1973 and 1975, this balance has been negative ever since. The large appreciation of the dollar after 1981

TABLE 3.1

Shares of World Trade

	1960	1965	1970	1975	1980	1982	1983
United States	16	14.5	13.7	12.2	10.7	11.0	10.3
European community	34	34.3	36.1	33.9	32.4	30.7	31.4
Japan	3	4.5	6.1	6.3	6.3	7.2	7.6
Other developed countries	14	15.1	15.8	13.5	12.3	13.0	13.7
Developing countries ↓	22	19.4	17.2	23.7	28.4	26.4	24.6
(of which OPEC)	(6)	(5.4)	(5.3)	(12.8)	(14.4)	(10.8)	(8.8)
Communist countries	11	12.2	11.1	10.3	9.8	11.6	12.3

SOURCES: Council of Economic Advisors, *Economic Report of the President* (February 1984), p. 338; 1960 figures, U.S. Department of Commerce, International Trade Administration, *U.S. Competitiveness in the International Economy* (October 1981).

has contributed to a rapidly widening trade deficit, which hit $148.5 billion in 1985 and $173 billion in 1986.*

Detailed studies by Data Resources, Inc. (DRI) in 1984 and 1985 confirmed the competitiveness problems of American industry.[6] The DRI studies show the United States to face massive disadvantages in labor costs, productivity, capital costs, and other key factors when compared with Japan and other industrial countries, not just in steel and autos but in practically every industry. Some analysts argue that these market-share statistics are no cause for alarm because it was inevitable that the United States would lose ground as other countries developed in the postwar period.[7] There is some truth in this argument, of course; but a careful reading of the evidence suggests that government policies and the inadequacies of some of our management and industrial relations systems, rather than natural forces, helped foreign producers gain at the expense of American firms. The prevailing view among some economists that there is nothing to worry about is based on a static view of the economy, which sees no strategic importance for the long term in what is done this year. According to analysts at the Berkeley Roundtable on the International Economy (BRIE), though, declining market shares could signify more serious problems:

> a loss of the capacity to compete in future products and future markets, not just the industrial catch up of our partners. In semiconductors, for example, Japanese world market share has been built on an expansion of sales in the United

*It makes some difference, however, whether trade figures are measured in constant or current dollars. A study for the New York Stock Exchange suggests that in constant price and volume terms, our proportion of the world's exports remained virtually unchanged between 1962 (14.8 percent) and 1980 (14.7 percent).[5] (However, the U.S. share had declined to 12.3 percent by the end of 1982.) What this means is that despite substantial depreciation of the dollar between 1977 and 1980, the United States was unable to regain its relative share of the *value* of manufactured trade, and that the United States had to give up greater exports in order to secure the same imports.

States and Europe, while imports as a share of the Japanese
national market have remained constant. The declining U.S.
world market share suggests a growing Japanese competitive
strength. Indeed, Japanese market positions are providing the
base for further capital and R&D investment with Japanese
investment running at 45 percent of gross sales. In sum, our
national shift into technology intensive sectors is not as secure as it may at first seem.[8]

Similarly, much of the structural damage to the economy will not be reversed very easily. The BRIE group
concludes:

In many industries, market share itself, once gained, confers
cost advantages with respect to distribution and production.
Accordingly, it may take U.S. firms considerable time to lose
sales when the dollar rises, but once lost, a market position
is difficult and expensive to rebuild. In short, in many markets the U.S. may be in the process of ceding first-mover
advantages to others.[9]

DRI's founder, the late Otto Eckstein, agrees:

The trade deficits are real and will lead to further damage in
our industries. The capital flows that will be needed to offset
these trade deficits will generate future interest payments
that will be a burden. . . .

A nation that casually surrenders leading industrial positions
through neglect will find it difficult to stage a comeback,
particularly if the period of non-competitiveness stretches
for more than a few years. . . .

The danger lies in too slow an adjustment process. If the
present situation is allowed to continue, more markets will
be lost and the damage to our trade position will become
irretrievable. The present problems will not keep: in the ab-

sence of improvements in the current decade they will become insoluble in the next.[10]

Does manufacturing matter? Some economists argue that the decline of America's manufacturing industries is no cause for concern because services are growing as manufacturing declines.[11] Indeed, it is considered "natural" for mature economies to shift from goods to services. Rich countries will naturally buy more services as they satisfy their demand for goods, according to this position. There is some truth in this argument, but there are also reasons to be concerned about our loss of competitiveness in many manufacturing sectors. First of all, increased service exports will not compensate for our merchandise trade deficits. Services are a very small part of total trade and encounter even stiffer trade barriers than manufactured goods, and there is no evidence that the United States is likely to be any more competitive in services than in manufacturing. Second, high value-added service industries are closely related to high value-added manufacturing. If we lose manufacturing, we will lose the consulting, insurance, transportation, computer software, and advertising businesses that go with that manufacturing. Third, technological innovations are embodied in manufactured products. There are, moreover, close synergistic and cumulative learning advantages associated with expanding market shares in manufactured products. A loss of market share implies a loss of technological advantage, and whoever controls the technology controls the market. Fourth, although there are some high-productivity service industries and activities, on the average productivity and wages in services are lower than in manufacturing. Not all manufacturing is equally important, of course; some industries have important links to others. Indeed, some industries (such as telecommunications and microelectronics) have become as important to our infrastructure as highways and transportation systems are.

What Makes an Economy Competitive?

Worker participation and human resource development must play an important role in restoring the ability of American enterprises to sustain profitability and high real wages in a global information world. In general, competitiveness may be based on quality, price, product differentiation, service of the product after it is sold, innovations and new product development, or dependability of supplies. Some products are competitive only because of government assistance, because labor costs are low, or because they are based on standardized, easily adapted technologies. Government promotion can be in the form of various export subsidies or import restrictions that give domestic producers a guaranteed home market of sufficient size to enable domestic companies to develop low-cost production on a large enough scale for export to be possible. Government can also help domestic companies become more competitive by creating an environment that helps stabilize costs and prices and ensures dependable supplies of quality human and physical resources and technology at favorable costs. Government economic policies—taxes, expenditures, control of money supplies —support for research and technology, human resource development strategies, and the strengthening of appropriate consensus-building processes, adaptive economic enterprises, and labor organizations are all important to economic viability.

As an economy becomes more advanced, competitiveness depends increasingly on the quality of human resources. Well-educated, well-trained people will insist on participation in matters affecting their interests. And their participation in every stage of the production process, including the policies of government, will be required to achieve quality output at competitive prices.

The importance of worker participation can be illustrated by an examination of the major sources of competitiveness. First, there are marginal, low-wage industries that use standardized manufacturing techniques, where competitiveness is based mainly on wages. The only way to compensate for a wage disadvantage is to increase productivity, which can be done to some extent through superior management and advanced technology. If both technology and management practices are standardized, the edge can come from innovation, product differentiation, and wages. Thus, the ability of a high-wage country like the United States to compete in low-wage manufacturing industries such as textiles and garments depends on its producing products that cannot readily be copied in low-wage countries.

Superior performance in complex manufacturing processes can also lend an advantage. Products in this category are the more expensive but standardized durable consumer and capital goods—automobiles, machine tools, aircraft, and more sophisticated consumer electronics. In these industries, competitiveness depends not primarily on wages but on management systems, the quality and speed of product innovation, production systems, dependability and timeliness of deliveries, and the quality of service after delivery. In complex, standardized manufacturing the most important factors are likely to be quality and product differentiation. In most of these activities quality is as important as price, and perceptions of quality have a longer-lasting effect because they do not change very quickly. If product differentiation has developed, most of the relatively advanced countries competing in those products will export their specialties and import the specialties of other countries. Most of the advanced industrial countries both export and import in the same industries; but, as the BRIE analysts emphasize, Japan is a major exception to this principle:

> Japan ... comparatively tends to export but not import these goods. Increases in intra-industry trade based on product specialization—the Germans buying French Renaults and the French buying BMWs—have limited the costly displacement across industry lines—for example, the movement of labor from steel or textiles into communications—that inter-industry competition among the advanced industrial countries would require.[12]

This practice has important consequences for competition with Japan—trade is likely to be based not mainly on product specialization, but on the price of a product of a given quality. "As a consequence, the pattern of intra-industry trade based on product specialization tends to give way to a pattern of trade in which competition from Japan displaces producers in other advanced industrial countries and is not matched by equivalent growth in exports into Japan."[13]

The third source of competitiveness is in high-tech industries, where the ability to compete depends heavily on the quality of human resources, manufacturing capabilities, and research and development. Here, sustained product innovation and a sophisticated manufacturing capability are needed. There are, moreover, important technology drivers—the sources of demand that stimulate technological development—which change through time. Since World War II, for example, the automobile, aircraft, communications, consumer electronics, and defense industries have been important sources of demand for technology. More recently, telecommunications and manufacturing in general have become important drivers of microelectronics and computers. Thus, manufacturing and research and development are important because the rapid spread of technology permits countries to catch up to the leaders quickly. The fact that countries like Japan have closed the technology gap with the United States, therefore, makes competitiveness depend heavily on our ability to move ahead technologically.

The fourth area of competitiveness is also closely related to manufacturing—trade in services, especially in such areas as banking, transportation, insurance, and information systems. In fact, competition in the high value-added services is closely related to manufacturing success for the major industrial countries. The high value-added services, like high value-added manufacturing, require well-educated, well-trained human resources. Indeed, the natural process of development has been for countries to move first into elementary manufacturing from preindustrial agricultural and natural resource extraction industries and then to shift toward sophisticated manufacturing and ultimately into services. Competitiveness in the services depends on the size of the market and proximity to those manufacturing activities on which the services rely.

The size of the international service market also has been limited by trade restrictions. Trade in services is more restricted than in goods, both because the General Agreement on Tariffs and Trade does not cover services and because the critical importance of services like banking, telecommunications, and transportation to national power, sovereignty, and development makes all countries except those with clear competitive superiority reluctant to open these markets to unrestricted trade. Third World countries have resisted including services in the General Agreement because they fear their small domestic service industries could not compete with big multinational companies. For example, Third World countries have required their banks to make loans to domestic industries on better terms than those prevailing in the international market. Since services are vital to high-tech industries, Third World leaders are afraid that, in an open trading system, their disadvantages in the service sector would hinder their development of high-tech industries. Moreover, since free trade in services implies free foreign investments, Third World leaders are afraid that an agreement to liberalize the services trade in exchange for the developed countries' agreement to liberalize imports from the developing countries would gave the developed countries control of the sophisticated services that are increasingly the major sources of national sovereignty and power. The industrialized countries, by contrast, believe that trade restrictions on services deny them their comparative advantage at a time when the exigencies of international competition require that they shift resources into services out of those lower value-added manufacturing industries in which low-wage developing countries have the advantage.

Trade in services is especially important to the United States because of American firms' dominant position. In 1983, services accounted for about 18 percent of world trade and the United States had about one-fourth of that. Between 1970 and 1985, trade in services grew by about 11 percent a year, which was about the same growth rate as in the trade in goods, according to a Bank of England study.[14]

All four of these sources of competitiveness have certain common features. They all require sophisticated manufacturing, highly developed human resources, and coordinated national policies. The United States had clear, though diminishing, advantages in technology and services in 1986 but is prevented by trade barriers and inadequate U.S. economic policies from exercising its advantages in these areas to compensate for its disadvantages in labor-intensive industries that depend heavily on wage and price competition. The jury is still out on whether American companies can be competitive with their counterparts elsewhere, especially Japan, in complex, standardized manufacturing, where management systems are important. In many of these industries, authoritarian American management systems have not been competitive with more participatory, consensus-based Japanese management systems. As will be demonstrated later, economic institutions and organizations, not just the availability of human and physical resources and technology, are critical to economic performance.

Productivity

Of all the reasons for the loss of industrial competitiveness by U.S.-based enterprises, none is more important than their poor rate of productivity growth, the area that depends the most on democratic, participatory workplace decisions. Productivity—the ratio of outputs to inputs—is, along with labor and capital costs, an efficiency measure that determines unit cost of production. Productivity growth is thus one measure of the extent to which new and more efficient technologies are being used; and productivity is an important determinant of real wages and living standards, as well as of competitiveness in international markets. The decline in productivity growth experienced by all industrial countries in the sixties, but especially after the first oil price shock in 1973 and 1974, is one of our most serious economic problems. While the average level of productivity is probably still higher in the United States than in other countries, the rate of growth here was lower than in any other country between 1950 and 1980. The fastest rate of growth has been in Japan, whose productivity is about two-thirds to three-fourths of the American, but average levels are higher in Canada, France, and Germany. At present trends, these countries could overtake the United States by the end of the eighties, and the Japanese could overtake us by the end of the century. Indeed, these countries already have higher productivity in some important manufacturing industries. Productivity growth fell in all industrial countries after 1974 but rebounded everywhere except the United States. Other countries have had productivity growth rates four to six times those of the United States.

The rate of productivity growth—usually measured by output per hour of work—declined in the United States from 3.2 percent between 1948 and 1965 to 2.2 percent between 1965 and 1973, and has been less than 1 percent since 1981. Other measures use different types of input than labor (or attempt to measure output per unit of total factor input) but, while they have different levels of productivity, all show declines in productivity growth since the sixties (see table 3.2).

These declines are very important for industrial and national welfare. National welfare is affected because declining productivity makes it more difficult to maintain growth in real gross national product (inflation adjusted output relative to all factor inputs rather than per unit of factor input). If we could increase productivity we could get higher output from the same or lower amounts of capital or labor. Similarly, declining productivity growth affects international competitiveness through unit labor costs (which equal wage payments minus productivity gains, or plus losses; see table 3.3). A country like Japan, with relatively low levels of inflation and high productivity gains, had rising real wages (nominal wages adjusted for inflation) during the seventies, while the United States, with high rates of inflation and low productivity growth, experienced declining real wages. Indeed, during

TABLE 3.2

Output Per Hour, Capital Effects, and Multifactor Productivity in Manufacturing, 1950–1973 and 1973–1983
(Average annual percent change)

Period	Productivity				Inputs			
	Output per hour of all persons	Output per unit of capital	Multi-factor productivity[a]	Output[b]	Hours of all persons[c]	Capital services[d]	Combined units of labor and capital inputs[e]	Capital per hour of all persons
1950–1983	2.5	−0.2	1.7	3.1	0.5	3.3	1.3	2.7
1950–1973	2.8	.6	2.1	4.0	1.2	3.4	1.9	2.2
1973–1983	1.8	−2.1	0.8	0.9	−1.0	3.0	.0	4.0

SOURCE: U.S. Department of Labor, Bureau of Labor Statistics, *Trends in Manufacturing: A Chartbook* (April 1985), Bulletin 2219.

[a]Output per unit of combined labor and capital inputs.

[b]Gross domestic product originating in manufacturing, constant dollars.

[c]Paid hours of all employees, plus the hours of proprietors and unpaid family workers engaged in manufacturing.

[d]A measure of the flow of capital services used in manufacturing.

[e]Hours of all persons combined with capital input, using labor and capital shares of output as weights.

the seventies, the United States had lower real wage increases than any major industrial country. Just as declining productivity growth makes it more difficult to sustain overall economic growth, declining real wages make it difficult for families to maintain their real incomes. American families have been able to sustain their incomes mainly because of more women working; but this measure works only once; not many families have another wife to put into the work force.

As can be seen from table 3.3, manufacturing productivity gains were lower in the United States than in other major industrial countries both before and after 1973. However, the slowdown between 1973 and 1983 was pervasive, though it was greatest relatively for Germany and Japan, which had the highest rates of growth between 1950 and 1983.

Because of the rising value of the dollar after 1981, there is a big difference between wages and unit labor costs stated in dollars and in various national currencies. As can

TABLE 3.3

Manufacturing Productivity, United States and Other Major Industrial Countries, 1950–1983

| | Output per employee hour in manufacturing (average annual percent change) | | | Change, 1950–1973 to |
	1950–1983	1950–1973	1973–1983	1973–1983
United States	2.5	2.8	1.8	−1.0
Canada	3.5	4.3	1.8	−2.5
France	5.4	5.8	4.6	−1.2
Germany	5.6	6.5	3.7	−2.8
Japan	9.0	10.0	6.8	−3.2
United Kingdom	3.0	3.3	2.4	−0.9

Source: U.S. Department of Labor, Bureau of Labor Statistics, *Trends in Manufacturing: A Chartbook* (April 1985), Bulletin 2219.

be seen from table 3.4, the measurement of unit labor costs in dollars gave other countries important advantages. This table shows the combined influence of the rising value of the dollar and productivity differences on hourly pay (wages plus fringe benefits) differentials in manufacturing. In 1981, Germany had virtually closed the pay gap with the United States, and Sweden's level was 8 percent higher than America's. By 1984 the expensive dollar had increased the gap again, despite relatively low wage increases in the United States. For 1984, no country's hourly compensation levels were more than 75 percent of the U.S. average, and Japan's was only 56 percent. Compensation levels in Taiwan, Mexico, South Korea, and Brazil were less than 15 percent of the U.S. average. These rates made the United States uncompetitive in industries that could standardize other elements, such as technology and management.

Some analysts believe that the trend toward decline in productivity growth has been reversed since the 1981–1982 recession, which hit bottom in November 1982. This conclusion is highly questionable. American productivity growth at the peak of recovery from that recession remained below that of all other OECD countries, whose recovery lagged behind ours. The growth of productivity since November 1982 has been only about half as large as would be needed to restore the trend rate of productivity growth. As the following Bureau of Labor Statistics data show, productivity recovery from the recession was smaller than for any nine-month recovery period since 1954: in the nine months after the 1954 recession, the productivity rate changed by 2.6 percent; after the 1961 and 1970 recessions, by 4.4 percent; after the 1975 recession, by 3.5 percent; and after the 1982 recession, by only 2.4 percent. Despite the much lower increase in productivity, however, smaller wage increases during the 1982–1983 recovery caused unit labor costs to rise less than at

TABLE 3.4

Unit Labor Costs in Manufacturing, Measured in National Currencies and in U.S. Dollars, Selected Countries, 1973–1983
(*Average annual percent change*)

Country	National currency basis			U.S. dollar basis		
	1973–1983	1973–1980	1980–1983	1973–1983	1973–1980	1980–1983
United States	7.0	8.4	3.9	7.0	8.4	3.9
Canada	9.9	10.2	9.2	7.6	7.8	7.3
France	10.8	11.0	10.5	5.0	11.8	−9.3
Germany	4.4	5.2	2.6	4.8	11.0	−8.4
Japan	2.8	4.5	−1.1	4.1	7.2	−2.8
United Kingdom	14.5	18.5	5.9	9.2	17.6	−8.2

SOURCE: U.S. Department of Labor, Bureau of Labor Statistics, *Trends in Manufacturing: A Chartbook* (April 1985), Bulletin 2219.

any time since 1961. Nonfarm productivity fell by .2 percent in 1985, a very disturbing event because it was the first time a drop in productivity was not accompanied by at least one quarter of economic decline. The bad productivity performance continued into 1986. Productivity for nonfinancial corporations fell at an annual rate of 2.5 percent during the first quarter of 1986.

BLS data also indicates that lower productivity was associated with a relatively rapid rate of employment growth: after 1954, it was 2.5 percent; after 1961, 0.8 percent; after 1970, 3.0 percent; after 1975, 3.1 percent; and after 1982, 3.9 percent. Employment growth, in turn, was associated both with the depth of the 1981–1982 recession and with the relatively small growth in unit labor costs. As noted in chapter 1, there is a rough inverse relationship between changes in employment and changes in real wages (with the exception of Japan, which during the seventies had employment growth rates second only to the United States and Canada, but had the highest real wage growth of any major industrial country). The United States generally has had higher employment growth than most major European countries, at least in part because policy makers in the United States were less concerned about the quality of jobs and had lower income support programs.

Lester Thurow demonstrates that most of the productivity slowdown has been due to declining productivity by white-collar workers.[15] He notes, for example, that between 1978 and 1985 American business firms reduced their blue-collar payrolls by 1.9 million workers (from 31.9 to 30 million), or 6 percent, while real business gross national product was increasing by 18 percent. These changes represent a 24 percent increase in productivity, or over 3 percent a year. But these same firms added 10 million white-collar workers (from 48 to 58 million), an increase of 21 percent. Since output was up by only 18 percent, white-collar productivity actually fell, wiping out much of the blue-collar productivity gain.

What Causes Productivity Change?

Despite numerous studies using a variety of econometric and analytical techniques, there is little agreement on the weights to be attached to the various causes of slowdown in productivity growth.[16] Unfortunately, neither our data nor our techniques is strong enough to account for these changes. My own assessment follows.

The energy crisis undoubtedly played an important role in the slowdown, but the productivity slowdown started in the sixties, long before the first energy price shock of 1973–1974. However, something associated with the energy crisis appears to have reduced productivity growth. For one thing, the energy crisis promoted a substitution of labor and capital for energy, which reduced productivity as measured in terms of labor or capital. Moreover, the energy crisis caused some capital stock to become obsolete, which reduced the net capital available. The energy crisis also contributed to economic instability, which led to economic policy confusion and recession; productivity growth always declines during recessions and increases during recovery. Recessions and economic uncertainty also tend to reduce investments in human and physical capital.

There is no agreement over the impact of investment on productivity. There appears to be no clear relationship between changes in gross or net investment and changes in productivity growth; the years 1956 to 1960, for example, showed relatively low ratios of net investment to the GNP and yet relatively high productivity growth. What is involved, of course, is a complex set of influences, no one of which has an effect independent of the others through time. Investment could have had a strong influence but was counteracted by other forces, or the lags between investments and productivity growth were such as to defy measurements taken at any given time.

Some economists argue that the significant data are not aggregate investment, but ratios of capital to labor. International comparisons suggest a rough relationship between relatively high rates of growth in capital per employee and productivity growth (see table 3.5). Moreover, countries with higher rates of gross capital formation seem to have higher rates of productivity growth. As shown in table 3.2, however, the relationship between capital formation and productivity is not clear, and no consistent relationship can be measured between capital–labor ratios and productivity. From 1973 to 1983, capital per hour rose by 4 percent a year (from 2.2 percent annually between 1950 and 1973), while output per hour declined from 2.8 percent to 1.8 percent. Nor have recent Bureau of Labor Statistics studies established strong relationships between capital–labor ratios and productivity. Two conclusions can be made, though: the relationship clearly depends on the *quality* of the technology involved in the capital investment, not just aggregate capital expenditure; and there are time lags between expenditures and results that are difficult to determine.

It is not clear how much, if any, of the productivity

TABLE 3.5

Annual Average Compound Growth Rates of Capital per Employee

	1960–1973	1973–1980
France	4.8	4.5
Germany	6.2	4.7
Japan	10.6	5.8
Netherlands	5.9	3.4
United Kingdom	4.2	3.4
United States	2.1	1.0

SOURCE: United Nations, *Yearbook of National Account Statistics* (1972) vol. 3, table 2A; (1981) vol. 2, table 3. Copyright, United Nations (1982): Reproduced by permission.

growth differentials between the United States and other countries can be explained by differences in saving and investment in physical capital. My own view is that the importance of physical capital is greatly exaggerated. The United States has lower investment (and therefore savings) than most other countries except the United Kingdom, but this relationship has remained relatively constant and probably does not explain much of the differential in productivity between America and other countries.

The important point about investment, as noted in chapter 2, is its optimal level relative to other resources, not its absolute level. In this connection, the cost of capital in the United States has been high compared to that in other countries (table 3.6). Indeed, a DRI study concluded that the net after-tax cost of capital in Japan was 0.1 percent between 1973 and 1983 and 5.1 percent for the United States.[17] Moreover, compared to other major industrial countries, capital costs were rising faster relative to labor costs in the United States during the seventies and eighties. It therefore made sense for American companies to increase labor use relative to capital, which they did.

Technological innovation plays an important role in competitiveness and productivity improvement. As noted, the substantial—though diminishing—technologi-

TABLE 3.6

Average Weighted Cost of Capital to Industry, 1971–1981

	1971	1976	1981
United States	10.0 %	11.3 %	16.6 %
France	7.5	9.4	14.3
West Germany	6.9	6.6	9.5
Japan	7.3	8.9	9.2

SOURCE: U.S. Department of Commerce, *Historical Comparison of the Cost of Capital* (April 1983).

cal lead of U.S.-based firms is their main international competitive advantage. Moreover, as will be demonstrated in the next chapter, U.S. firms frequently lag behind their foreign competitors in process technology and in the introduction of the latest technology. These practices have more to do with management systems than with the availability of technology.

Research and development is assumed to improve technological innovation, but it is only part of a much larger process—the ability to convert ideas into new products and processes. Since the forces underlying innovations are not well understood, researchers focus on measurable research and development expenditures as a proxy for innovation. A number of studies using this approach have found research and development to have a significant impact on productivity.*

Total research and development expenditures (in constant 1972 dollars) peaked at $29.8 billion in 1968, remained essentially the same through 1976, and subsequently increased modestly. Spending in this area declined from about 3 percent of the GNP in 1964 to 2.26 percent in 1980 and 2.4 percent in 1981. While the United States still spends a larger proportion of its GNP on research and development than other major countries, the gaps have narrowed. Both Japan and Germany spend higher proportions of their national product on *civilian* research and development than does the United States.† And while the U.S. share of major technological innovations declined from 79 percent of the world total

---

*The most convincing evidence has referred to more detailed components of the economy, given the econometric difficulties of separating the effect of research and development from aggregate timetables. For example, Zvi Griliches and N. E. Terleckyj reported that research and development was significantly related to productivity growth in manufacturing, contributing about 0.3 percentage points. J. W. Kendrick estimated somewhat higher contributions (0.85 percentage points) for the 1948–1966 period.[18]

†In 1983 both the Germans and Japanese spent significantly higher proportions of their GNP for nondefense research and development than the United States: 2.47 percent, 2.57 percent, and 1.88 percent, respectively.

in 1953 to 37 percent in 1973, Japan's share rose from 16
to 23 percent and Germany's from 5 to 10 percent.

Human Capital

Despite the heavy emphasis in U.S. policy on physical
capital formation, the evidence is very strong that investments in human capital have been much more important
sources of growth in productivity and total output. There
is also evidence that human resource development programs are much more effective when workers' interests
are reflected in the process. On-the-job training and apprenticeship systems are important skill development
processes, and are most successful when conducted
jointly by labor and management. This principle is best
illustrated by looking at training in which the workers'
job security concerns are balanced against management's
interest in profitability. A profit-maximizing employer
has little interest in providing expensive training and education, because the employer pays for the training and its
employees or other employers derive the benefits. In order
to align the benefits and costs of training, the profit-maximizing employer tends to fragment training in order to
make it job-specific and recoup training costs as soon as
possible. Where the workers' interests are represented, by
contrast, training and education are likely to be more
systematic. This is true, for example, in companies that
provide job security and competitive wages. In this case,
workers and employers have an interest in broader training and education to upgrade workers' skills and allow
them to perform a wider range of jobs. As a result, workers become more adaptable to changing demand for the

enterprise's output and to varying job conditions within an enterprise. Since adaptability and skills are critical to competitiveness in the internationalized information world, joint labor–management training systems in which workers' interests are protected will perform better than those unilaterally developed and administered by management. An example of superior systems can be found in the apprenticeship programs in the construction industry, which have provided union contractors a strong productivity advantage over nonunion contractors; indeed, it is generally conceded that nonunion contractors would have great difficulty operating if they could not hire their most skilled workers from among those who have been trained in the joint apprenticeship programs.

Protecting the workers' interests also provides superior training and education in those American firms in which workers have job security and the Japanese "lifetime employment" programs (discussed in the next chapter) have been adopted. Both of these benefits help companies reap the rewards of their human resource development costs. Job security for workers is also important in strengthening management. Job security makes it difficult for managers to shift the costs of change to workers in the form of layoffs, and therefore forces managers to pay more attention to good management.

It should not be surprising that human resource development has been so important to competitiveness in an internationalized information world. All the keys to competitiveness in such a world—productivity, quality, flexibility, and innovation—depend on well-educated, well-trained people. What is not so well known, because of the dominance of financial and business concerns in economic development policy, is that human resource development has *always* been a major determinant of economic development.[19] People are the active agents of development; developed people are an almost unlimited asset; undeveloped people can be a serious liability. Trained, educated people will develop the skills, technology, and products at competitive prices. Human resource development permits us to use fewer resources to produce more and better outputs with limited physical resources. Anthony Patrick Carnevale, summarizing substantial economic evidence, makes the point well:

> Historically, human resources have been gradually replacing all others. In 1890, resources extracted from Mother Earth, including minerals, energy and food, accounted for 50 percent of GNP. In 1957, extracted resources accounted for only 13 percent of GNP. Over the same period, returns to human resources grew to account for more than four-fifths of the nation's total economic output.

Carnevale believes that the "historical dominance of the human factor in economic growth and productivity will persist and grow." Moreover:

> People, not machines, are the well-spring of productivity. Since 1929, growth in on-the-job know-how, the reallocation of labor through retraining, and increased labor quality through education, training, and health care consistently have accounted for more than three-quarters of productivity improvements and most of our growth in national income. By comparison, over the same period, machine capital has contributed a consistent and disappointing 20 percent or less.[20]

The PCIC, composed predominantly of business interests, concluded:

> Technology and human resources constitute the key distinctive strengths for U.S. industry in future international competition. They are vital to the ability of the U.S. to be competitive in high productivity industries and to raise

productivity in all industries. Because of this "public good" character, both areas are vulnerable to market failures, which cause individual firms to underinvest in them. Reflecting this, the U.S. government already has a substantial role in both areas. However, government has carried out its role with inadequate attention to the competitive consequences of its actions.[21]

Table 3.7 provides information on the quality of human resources in the United States, Germany, and Japan. This

TABLE 3.7A

Human Resource-Quality

	United States	West Germany	Japan
Productivity			
Manufacturing Output (per manufacturing worker in thousands of U.S. dollars, 1981)	31.5	24.9	23.7
OECD Rank	(2)	(9)	(11)
Productivity Growth (Average of annual percentage rates of change in real GDP per employee, 1977–1982)	−0.1	1.5	2.9
OECD Rank	(20)	(10)	(4)
Education			
Education Expenditures (Total as percent of GDP, 1981)	8.3	4.7	5.7
OECD Rank	(4)	(16)	(11)
Enrollment in Secondary Education (percent of relevant age groups, 1980)	97	n.a.*	91
OECD Rank	(1)	(5)	n.a.*
Enrollment in Postsecondary Education, 1979 (percent of twenty-to-twenty-four-year-olds)	55	26	30
OECD Rank	(1)	(8)	(4)

SOURCE: Organization for Economic Cooperation and Development (OECD), Labor Force Statistics, 1983; OECD Historical Statistics, 1983.

*n.a. = not available.

table shows that the United States ranks relatively high on school enrollments, though other evidence suggests that it ranks lower in educational attainment on technical subjects. Indeed, in international competition, American students usually score very low among industrialized countries in important science and math tests. Enrollments in secondary schools are high in Japan but somewhat lower than in America. Japanese postsecondary enrollments are relatively low, but the Japanese have well-developed on-the-job training programs. Japanese blue-collar workers who are regular employees in large manufacturing companies appear to be much better educated than their American counterparts, especially in

TABLE 3.7B

Human Resource Quality (cont'd.)

	United States	West Germany	Japan
Labor/Management Relations			
Industrial Unrest			
(Days lost per 1,000 workers)	813	6	31
OECD Rank	(15)	(3)	(4)
Absenteeism			
(Nonvacation days lost per worker per year)	3.5	7.7	1.6
OECD Rank	(4)	(14)	(1)
Employee Motivation Index*	61.0	65.3	85.3
OECD Rank	(9)	(6)	(1)
Managerial Talent Index*	70.5	68.6	82.1
OECD Rank	(3)	(5)	(1)
Employee Turnover Index*	59	71	90
OECD Rank	(21)	(10)	(1)

SOURCES: European Management Forum, from OECD Historical Statistics, 1983; International Labor Organization, *Bulletin of Labor Statistics*, 1983; *Japan Labor Bulletin,* November 1982.

*0 = low, 100 = high. These indexes are based on subjective assessments gathered from over 1,000 respondents to a survey conducted by the European Management Forum (EMF). Respondents included company chief executives, economic and financial experts, bankers, and the heads of foreign-owned subsidiaries of large multinational companies, as well as key personalities from the press, trade unions, and business associations.

technical subjects and mathematics.* The United States ranks relatively low on industrial unrest, employee motivation, and turnover. We rank slightly above Germany on the managerial talent index, but far behind Japan. Note, however, that Germany has fewer days lost due to strikes than Japan, though Japan is very low on this index among OECD countries.

Numerous reasons for the slowdown in productivity growth have been studied in much detail by the most sophisticated techniques available to economists. While the evidence is inconclusive, the factors usually studied include interindustry shifts; changes in the composition of the labor force; growth of capital per worker; savings and investment levels; regulations and taxes; technological innovation; the energy crisis of the seventies; economic conditions; and various behavioral factors, especially labor–management relations.

A careful analysis of all these studies permits some general, if controversial, conclusions. The first is that the most powerful tools available to economists do not permit unambiguous conclusions concerning these factors.[23] The forces affecting productivity are simply too complex for economists' measurement and analytical tools. Second, some factors have proved to be much less important than popularly assumed, including the changing composition of the work force, where the better education of women and young people roughly offset their lower experience levels. Similarly, government regulations have negative and positive effects on productivity, but the negatives have been greatly exaggerated and on balance have not been very important. Similarly, productivity has very little to do with how hard people work, but improvements

*The United States has more functional illiterates (at least 20 percent of the work force, depending on the definition), more high school dropouts, and a higher percentage of high school graduates with limited proficiency in mathematics; and it graduates fewer engineers per capita than most other industrialized countries.[22]

in the quality of human resources and the organization of work systems can have very positive effects. Finally, the shift to services does not appear to have been a very important factor in the productivity slowdown.

Whatever the reasons for the decline in the productivity growth rate, greater attention to human resources and worker participation in technology and other workplace decisions can accelerate that rate. More generally, better labor–management relations can be an important source of productivity improvement. Traditional economic analysis ignores important behavioral influences on productivity because it "typically neglects the human dimensions of production and the institutional contexts within which economic actors operate."[24]

Although productivity is conditioned by what happens in the general economy, a deeper understanding requires that we examine what goes on at the workplace. Behavioral elements are difficult to incorporate into mathematical models, but they are often critical factors in productivity growth. Productivity can be facilitated by general economic conditions, but it happens in the workplace. No understanding of the productivity problem can therefore be complete without considering these workplace relationships.

Chapter IV

The Role
of Management

MANAGEMENT organizes and directs production, so it is a major determinant of economic performance. Management has traditionally been authoritarian, but it has been challenged in all industrialized countries by worker organizations, first through collective bargaining and more recently through other forms of worker participation in management decisions and processes. Since it extends democracy to the workplace, collective bargaining is sometimes called industrial democracy. Social democracy, by contrast, refers to government's provision of minimum benefits such as social security, unemployment compensation, health care, and minimum wage regulations. Since World War II, new forms of worker participation have emerged in various countries to complement collective bargaining; these include various forms of worker involvement in workplace decisions; worker representation on corporate boards; and worker ownership—sometimes called economic democracy.

The Japanese companies' successful performance relative to their American and European competitors since the sixties has led many experts to conclude that other countries must either emulate or learn to compete with the highly participatory Japanese management systems. Many American companies have become convinced, and some are abandoning more authoritarian management practices in favor of processes that give workers a greater say in workplace decisions. Unlike their counterparts in Europe and Japan, however, American managers are more hostile to unions—despite the fact that they are weaker than in Japan or Europe—and are therefore attempting to develop a nonunion industrial relations model. This chapter and the following two will examine traditional management systems, collective bargaining models, and the newer forms of worker participation and ownership.

The American Management System

In order to be viable, any management system must be efficient in meeting public needs for goods and services and in achieving such economic objectives as stability, growth, and competitiveness. So it is not surprising that when the economy is not performing very well, the status and privileges of management as a class are challenged by the public. In order to maintain its position in a democratic society, management must convince the public that its role is legitimate in the sense that its privileges and rewards are given for valuable services rendered to the whole society. Traditionally, managers as a class owe their positions to the public's belief that existing managers can operate the economic system more effectively than other groups. In times of prosperity and relative success, this belief is rarely questioned; but during depressions and times of economic trouble, such as the 1930s, 1970s, and 1980s, managers are subjected to closer scrutiny and criticism.

Hard times expose weaknesses in business organizations as well as in management practices. One of the most influential studies of corporations was made during the Depression by Adolf Berle and Gardiner Means, who argued that "the separation of ownership from control [of large public corporations] produces a condition where the interests of owner and of ultimate manager may, and often do, diverge and where many of the checks which formerly operated to limit the use of power disappear."[1] Many critics have argued that American corporate managers are preoccupied with their personal welfare and that they are not checked by stockholders, who are too dispersed or interested mainly in stock prices or short-run dividends to pay much attention to corporate affairs. In this situation, managers are free to enlarge their own salaries and perquisites— which often bear little relation to corporate performance. This problem is considered by many to be aggravated by the growing percentage of stock held by institutional investors, who are mainly interested in quarterly reports and stock prices and have little or no interest in a corporation's long-run economic viability or competitiveness.* With globalization, criticism of business organizations will probably grow because, as noted in chapter 1, what is good for international corporate management will become more divorced from what is good for countries, workers, and communities.

In the eighties, growing criticism of American business

*For a recent critique see Mark Green and John F. Berry, *The Challenge of Hidden Profits* (New York: Morrow, 1985).

practices was heard from business schools and business leaders, as well as academics, politicians, and intellectuals. In an influential article published in 1980, for example, Robert Hayes and William Abernathy of the Harvard Business School attributed the "marked deterioration of competitive vigor" and the "growing unease about [the] overall economic well-being" of American business to "the failure of American managers to keep their companies technologically competitive over the long run." To a significant degree, these failures have been due to a preoccupation with short-run financial and marketing concerns while neglecting production. Abernathy and Hayes attribute managerial failure mainly to a reliance on "principles which prize analytical detachment and methodological elegance over insight, based on experience, into the subtleties and complexities of strategic decisions. As a result, maximum short-term financial returns have become the overriding criteria for many companies."[2]

This pursuit of short-term gain has caused managers to become less innovative and to ignore long-run technological viability. As a consequence, American managers are increasingly financial and legal experts with limited technical training and little "intimate hands-on knowledge of the companies' technologies, customers and suppliers." This problem is aggravated by the growing standardization of management practices at a very narrow and superficial level:

> What has developed in the business community . . . is a preoccupation with a false and shallow concept of the professional manager, a "pseudo-professional" really—an individual having no special expertise in any particular industry or technology who nevertheless can step into an unfamiliar company and run it successfully through strict application of financial controls, portfolio concepts, and a market-driven strategy.[3]

This orientation has also led managers to pursue such unproductive and debilitating activities as takeovers and mergers, which divert resources from more productive undertakings and shift managerial attention away from core technologies and markets: "the great bulk of this merger activity appears to have been absolutely wasted in terms of generating economic benefits for stockholders."

Others, including many business leaders themselves, have made similar charges. One of these is Seymour Melman, an industrial engineering professor at Columbia University, who questions whether American managers as a group are "interested in and capable of restoring competence in production" required for national industrial renewal. "A generation of managers has been trained by our business schools to make money, not goods. Gripped by a dogma called 'management science,' the schools have played an important institutional role in the erosion of the competence for production."[4]

Melman argues further that "until recently, American managers were the world's best organizers of industrial work," which was the basis of their claim to large personal incomes. American managers became a source of national pride and international envy during and after World War II. In fact, in 1969 the French journalist Servan-Schreiber in *The American Challenge* argued that U.S. management methods were so superior to European ones that the Americans were in the process of taking over the European economy. But according to Melman, the picture has changed:

Management's social contract with workers and the community has been broken as managers have turned to making money by means other than production. The result of this transformation in management's professional imperative is visible in the dissolution of production competence in once great industries. . . .

As managers' competence in making goods becomes increasingly rare, and ploys for making money dominate, industrial decay spreads. Top managers in central offices leave entire communities and regions economically stranded. Imported goods replace American goods. Jobs in producing occupations are severely reduced, hardly affected by the trickle of work in high tech industries.

It is Melman's judgment that increased worker involvement could help correct these management problems. "If there is to be a rebirth," he writes, "America must turn to those who have a direct stake in making goods—production workers and engineers—for an alternative to managerialism." Unfortunately, however, engineers and production workers "have had little voice in the governance of industry, of their own work."[5]

Many business leaders have also been critical of American management practice. One prominent example is the widely respected Reginald Jones, former chairman of General Electric, who believes too many corporate managers let their companies get "fat and sloppy" in the boom years of the fifties and sixties and thus failed to meet foreign competition in the seventies. There were many other reasons for their economic decline (world economic turmoil, government regulation), but according to Jones, "the evidence is that our foreign competitors are moving quickly to adopt the new technologies that will dominate the factories and offices of tomorrow." Jones concludes: "there is a legitimate complaint against the tyranny of Wall Street, with its myopic concentration on quarterly results. . . . There has been a fundamental change in the ownership of American industry—a great decline in the investor and an increase in the trader, who was also under great pressure for results."[6]

Jones's assessment was confirmed by a 1982 survey of top U.S. business executives, which concluded that "Management ineffectiveness is by far the greatest single cause of declining productivity in the United States."[7]

The Japanese Management System

As has been noted, many experts attribute Japan's economic success mainly to that country's consensus-based management practices.[8] What features of the Japanese management system are supposed to account for its superiority? The first is lifetime employment, in which regular workers are hired until age fifty-five. The lifetime employment system has the disadvantage of concealing unemployment during recession, but has the advantages of giving workers and employers long-term relationships; making employers more willing to provide better training; and causing workers to identify more with the company and to be more willing to be rotated into a variety of jobs. Lifetime employment contributes greatly to flexibility in labor use. Japanese companies are also likely to take a holistic approach to workers, being concerned about how they fit into the culture of the enterprise and providing for needs beyond paying wages. Lifetime employment causes Japanese management to view regular workers as fixed costs, so they seek to expand output and market share, especially during slack business periods. The American practice, by contrast, is to attempt to maximize short-term profits by holding prices up and laying off workers.

A second Japanese management practice is the seniority

and bonus compensation system. Japanese workers are paid more by education and by seniority or age than by the specific job they do. In fact, regular Japanese workers view their work as careers rather than jobs. American wage systems are likely to compensate the job, while Japanese systems compensate the worker. A large part of the Japanese worker's wage is likely to be in the form of a semiannual bonus that is typically as much as a third of the workers' annual income. This practice creates a much more flexible wage system—it is much easier not to pay a bonus, for reasons everybody understands, than to try to cut wages during economic downturns. The bonus wage system is also partially responsible for the much higher rate of personal savings in Japan. Moreover, the spread between the salaries of top managers and workers is likely to be much smaller than in the United States, which inspires greater unity between workers and managers.

Enterprise unionism is another unique feature of the Japanese system. The main structure of collective bargaining is the enterprise, a reflection of strong company identification and lifetime employment.

Enterprise unionism, "lifetime protection," and the bonus compensation system combine to reinforce the competitiveness of an enterprise. The American practice has been to try to take labor out of competition by requiring uniform wages in all companies within an industry. In the American system, output and employment are the adjusting mechanisms, whereas in the Japanese system employment and output are maintained and labor compensation and prices absorb the shocks. Moreover, the Japanese unions and companies negotiate overall wage increases during annual spring wage offensives, while American wages are negotiated at different times of the year, typically in three-year contracts with periodic cost-of-living adjustments. The American system encourages "whipsawing" (playing one union or company against another) and "leapfrogging" (in which rival unions attempt to obtain successively higher wages). The Japanese system gears wages much more to conditions in the economy and in the firm and is less likely to accelerate inflationary pressures.

The Japanese place heavy emphasis on communication and consensus management. This focus is hard for Westerners to understand or to articulate because it is an amalgam of control from the top and consensus-building to ensure that the workers thoroughly understand the decision. The Japanese have a strong sense of group consciousness that has deep cultural and historical roots. Cooperation has been necessary for survival in Japan. Group consciousness is deeply embedded in Confucian thought. American thought emphasizes individual satisfaction, whereas the Japanese see individual satisfaction as deriving from the group. The consensus decision-making process is necessary because responsibilities are assigned to the group and not to individuals, so some mechanism is required to ensure that individuals understand their responsibilities.

The American system is to stress hierarchical decision-making processes, fragmentation of work, and individual responsibility, which is similarly embedded in Western religion and Anglo-American law and custom. The American system attempts to control quality and work performance through management supervision, detailed work standards and specifications, and individual wage payment systems based on the job. In the Japanese system, group responsibility, coupled with strong identification with the company, generalized training, and heavy emphasis on quality control through preventing defects by means of good engineering and worker participation systems give Japanese companies a decided advantage. Indeed, this employment system is cited as a major reason for the Japanese "victory" in developing the 64K RAM chip.*

Are These Contrasts Valid?

The contrasts often made between Japanese and American management systems do have some basis in reality, but both are clearly based on stereotypes and myths that mask considerable diversity. One myth is that the Japanese system is deeply rooted in Japanese culture and cannot be transferred to other places. The system is compatible with Japanese culture, but many aspects of it—especially lifetime employment, harmonious labor–management relations, and enterprise unionism—were developed during the fifties after a period of considerable labor–management conflict in the immediate postwar period. At the same time, Japanese public officials, in close cooperation with business and labor leaders, developed an export-driven industrial policy. Quality production at low cost was emphasized in order to overcome Japan's economic problems and the early (pre-1960s) image of "made in Japan" as a mark of inferiority.

The Japanese management system is not unique to Japan, because there is considerable borrowing between management systems in different countries. In fact, in

*(The 64K RAM chip is a single integrated circuit with a 64,000-word capacity for random access memory.) Because of high turnover in the United States, according to a *Fortune* article, "the training and retraining of workers put a strain on Silicon Valley companies that the Japanese, with their traditional job stability avoided. Because of the workers' greater continuity . . . and possibly their greater dedication—the Japanese companies offered higher quality chips. The quality of U.S. chips has improved greatly in recent years but is still lagging behind the Japanese."[9] As a result of this victory, the Japanese have repeatedly been able to reduce prices, "[depriving] U.S. manufacturers of the early profits they had expected . . . profits they need to finance new products. . . . The Japanese have gained a long-term advantage in the memory market." By 1985, the Japanese controlled most of the world market for 64K and 256K chips.

order to improve their system in the postwar period, the Japanese called on foreign experts like W. Edwards Deming from the United States, whose ideas were widely accepted in Japan. Unlike most management specialists of his day, Deming conceived of an enterprise as an organic system with closely related components.* Management was responsible for this system: as he said, workers worked *in* the system and managers worked *on* it. Since there was great variation between and within systems, Deming taught that productive systems had organic lives of their own, derived from the resources and abilities of managers and workers at any given time and subject to continuous improvement through joint effort.

Contrary to typical American management's stress on responsiveness to stockholder interests, Deming emphasized the importance of giving priority to workers' concerns. He understood that a company that does not give priority to its workers is not likely to do much either for its customers or for its stockholders, and stressed the need for preventive quality control, productivity, incentive systems, and worker participation. Thus, many of the ideas behind the so-called "Japanese management system" were developed among American management experts but not widely accepted by American managers. However, some American companies, like International Business Machines (IBM) and Hewlett-Packard, have used programs such as job security, bonus incentive systems, and worker participation.

It also is a myth that the Japanese "miracle" is due to the management system. Indeed, it is curious how many single-factor explanations there are for the so-called Japanese miracle. The evidence shows the management system to be part of and closely related to larger systems, all of which combine to explain Japanese economic perform-

---

*I am indebted to Myron Tribus of M.I.T.'s Center for Advanced Engineering Study for several unpublished papers about Deming and his work. The following account is taken from those papers.

ance. It would be difficult if not impossible to single out any one part of a system or subsystem as *the* explanation. Because Japanese businesses are much better organized than ours, the concept of "systems within coordinated systems" is more obvious there than here.

There are other facets of the Japanese system that must be taken into account. For one thing, Japan has a great deal of national homogeneity and cohesion because of its history and the absolute necessity to be competitive in international markets. Japanese managers pay much more attention to the national interest in their corporate strategies and are far more likely than their American counterparts to have a close working relationship with the government as well as with their unions. The virtual absence of the adversarial relationships that characterize American labor–management and public–private relationships facilitates consensus-building, worker participation, and much better government regulatory and economic policy. Japanese health, safety, and environmental regulations, for example, are as stringent as those of the United States and cost as much relative to the GNP, but they are more effective because they are based on consensus cooperation and not litigation. The homogeneity of the Japanese population allows them to spend much less energy building harmony than we do in the United States.

Another factor to consider is that Japanese workers in large export-oriented companies are apparently better educated and trained than their American counterparts.*

---

*Over 90 percent of Japanese high-school-age youths graduate from high school, and 40 percent of these go to college. As noted, regular Japanese workers undergo extensive training on the job, including math and technical subjects. Japanese high school students typically take six years of science and math, one year of calculus, and six years of English; and the Japanese educate more engineers than we do, although their population is only about half as large as ours. In the United States in the early eighties, half of all high school graduates took no eleventh- or twelfth-grade math or science. Only 16 percent took one year of chemistry, 9 percent one year of physics, and 7 percent one year of calculus. At the same time, 25 million Americans could not read or write and 72 million Americans—including 47 percent of black seventeen-year-olds and 56 percent of all Hispanics—were functionally illiterate.

In fact, B. Bruce-Briggs of the Hudson Institute believes the quality of the Japanese work force to be the key to Japanese productivity and economic success:

> Labor, not the art of Japanese management, is the key to Japan's ascendancy. . . . Japanese labor discipline was not created by skillful corporate management. . . .
>
> Of course, "discipline" and "hierarchy" are Western terms; the Japanese talk of "expected behavior" and "harmonious relations." Once we understand that the Japanese do what their superiors expect of them, everything falls into place. . . .
>
> A disciplined labor force makes lifetime employment practical. Japanese workers come in the door properly trained by the family, by the school system, by the entire society.[10]

As will be demonstrated in chapter 8, we should also bear in mind that the Japanese management system has worked within the framework of a relatively well-coordinated, comprehensive, export-driven industrial policy based on close public–private cooperation. That policy was made possible by a permissive international market, especially during the Korean War and the later fifties and sixties. The ingredients of that policy included the maintenance of low interest rates; a credit system that reduced risks to the enterprise and made it possible for companies to have relatively high debt–equity ratios, which relieved management of the need to rely on stock markets and facilitated long-range decisions; high savings and investment ratios; a trade policy that encouraged exports and limited competitive imports until Japanese industry was ready to compete; production sharing, whereby low-wage work was sent to the Third World while high-wage work was kept in Japan; and heavy emphasis on technology.

Emphasis on lifetime employment in Japan has created the myth that Japanese workers have greater job security

TABLE 4.1

American Versus Japanese Job Security

| Age Group | Percent with same company for twenty or more years | | |
| | U.S. | Japan | |
		all	all male
25–39	1	7	11
40–44	7	22	31
45–49	17	23	32
50–54	25	17	24
55–59	30	13	18
60–64	33	9	13
65+	35	11	14

SOURCES: For the U.S. data, Robert E. Hall, "The Importance of Lifetime Jobs in the U.S. Economy," *American Economic Review* (September 1982); for the Japanese data, Kogi Taira, "Economic Growth, Labor Productivity and Employment Adjustment in Japan," paper presented at the annual meeting of the Industrial Relations Research Association, 1982.

than Americans. Although Japanese workers in large companies probably have greater *continuity* of employment because of the lower levels of unemployment and greater economic stability, Japanese workers do not have greater job security across the board. In fact, only a relatively small 15 to 20 percent of the workforce has true lifetime employment. As table 4.1 shows, many American workers actually have greater job tenure than the Japanese. Job security is greater in Japan for relatively young workers, especially males, but greater for older American workers than for older Japanese workers.*

This unexpected fact raises another important qualifica-

*This conclusion was confirmed by a recent study, which concluded that "Japanese male workers . . . have longer employment tenure than American workers. Also, Japanese workers have steeper earnings profiles that peak in about the same year after entering the current firm as American workers. In particular, growth rates in earnings attributable to tenure are far greater in Japan than in the United States."[11] Note, however, that this study was for males only, whereas other comparisons are for males and females.

tion about the Japanese management system: it permits job security for between 15 and 20 percent of all workers, concentrated in roughly the third of the economy heavily devoted to manufacturing. This system conceals inefficiencies in the rest of the economy and is made possible by less secure "shock absorbers," many of which would not be either legal or feasible in the United States. These shock absorbers include a subcontracting system in which the workers have lower wages and much less security (what the *Economist* in 1981 termed "little more than sweat shops"); a secondary labor force made up of older workers, women, minorities, and the less educated; production sharing; and the bonus system, which provides wage flexibility.

An analysis of Western Electric and five Japanese electronics manufacturers by Andrew Weiss found that absenteeism was lower at Western Electric than at its Japanese counterparts; Japanese workers did not appear to work harder, but average earnings rose faster in Japanese companies (4 percent in Japan, 1.6 percent at Western Electric). Weiss concluded that the main advantages the Japanese companies enjoyed were more engineers per worker, very selective hiring practices, steep wage profiles (low wages to new employees and high wages to experienced workers), an effective incentive system that permits big lifetime differences in pay for workers with the same experience and education, and a unique capital structure:

> The principal stockholders of Japanese companies are normally other companies. Individuals hold less than 10% of the stock in 97% of the companies listed on the first section of the Tokyo Stock Exchange, which includes the 1,005 largest publicly-traded companies in Japan. Suppliers and customers are apt to be more interested in having the company in which they own stock produce a high level of output at a low price

than in maximizing its operating profits by producing a lower output at a higher price.[12]

It is predictable that U.S.-based companies will continue to lose their competitiveness unless they give greater emphasis to workers, manufacturing, and market shares and unless there is a substantial revision of U.S. economic policy.

These contrasts were supported by a joint study of international business executives in 1985, conducted by Booz, Allen and Hamilton and Japan's leading business daily, the *Japanese Economic Journal.* This survey of over 300 senior executives, about equally divided between the United States, Western Europe, and Japan, confirmed the experts' general consensus that American companies had clear, but diminishing, advantages over their European and Japanese counterparts. The American advantages included general corporate capabilities, the qualities and depths of technological resources available in America, and the virtual absence of business, social, or labor restraints on American companies. Both U.S. and Japanese managers ranked the United States first in basic technology, commercialization of new products, organizational flexibility, and the management of information. Most respondents ranked the Japanese first in four key areas: application of technology, manufacturing technology, productivity, and quality control. Surprisingly, the United States and Japan tied on "long-term strategic outlook." European companies were rated third (and usually a distant third) in all categories. The views of European executives resembled those of their American counterparts more than those of the Japanese, but they generally considered themselves to be in third place behind the United States and Japan in their ability to compete.

The executives in this survey generally believed that the Japanese had acquired the substantial advantages in the fundamentals of production required to establish long-run superiority over both the United States and Europe. Moreover, the survey confirmed the attitudinal and motivational disadvantages of American companies discussed earlier. When asked what was the single overriding objective they wished to achieve for their companies, 51 percent of American chief executives listed "create shareholder value" and only 18 percent cited the desire to make their companies industry or market leaders. By contrast, 41 percent of the Japanese respondents listed "industry or market leader" and only 18 percent cited "creating shareholder value." The Europeans also gave priority to maximizing shareholder value, but assigned this objective much lower priority than their American counterparts. The Europeans are more concerned about business survival than either their Japanese or their American counterparts. Japanese aggressiveness is suggested by the fact that in every category in which they see themselves trailing the United States in 1985, they see themselves gaining substantial ground by the year 2000.[13]

What We Can Learn

Certain generalized conclusions can be drawn from this survey of management practices. First of all, many of the criticisms leveled against American management practices are justified. Management too often takes a short view and ignores long-run viability. The neglect of technology, the authoritarian management system that ignores workers' ideas and drives a wedge between workers and managers, the preoccupation with takeovers and mergers, and ignoring the need to compete in international markets are special problems. However, to some degree the problems are largely systemic and reflect the fact that the American and world economies are in considerable ferment, requiring adjustments in public and private management systems. As Peter Drucker has observed: "The greatest danger in turbulent times like ours is not the turbulence, but that you act rationally in terms of yesterday."[14]

Another inference that can be drawn is that while much can be learned from studying the industrial relations systems and management practices of other countries, little can be copied because of conditions unique to each country. Moreover, there is a danger of stereotyping and perpetuating myths, as has been done with the Japanese and American management systems.

The Japanese experience also indicates the importance of job security as a way to strengthen flexibility in labor utilization and long-term commitment to the enterprise. It is clearly better, in terms of maintaining real output, to have a system that adjusts to change with compensation and price flexibility rather than by reducing output and employment. Well-managed American companies have learned that job security improves productivity.* An IBM executive explains this connection as follows:

Our people, by using their minds as well as their hands, have cut two-thirds off the hours that go into manufacturing our product. The cost of the product went down 45 percent during a ten-year period when wages vastly increased. That achievement would have been impossible without productive and committed employees. And much of their commitment stems from the security they know is theirs through our practice of full employment.[15]

*American companies with variants of "lifetime" employment include IBM, Hewlett-Packard, Eli Lilly, Digital Equipment Corporation, and Delta Airlines.

There appears to be growing recognition among American employers that layoffs are an inefficient way to control costs in an ongoing enterprise. Layoffs are costly because of severance pay, unemployment compensation, and other costs; layoffs could also cause the best employees to take other jobs; and job insecurity leads to employment rigidities from narrowly defined seniority lines and rigid job descriptions with prohibitions on work outside a job classification. Instead, job security improves training, long-range human resource planning, flexibility in employee utilization, and continuity of interpersonal relationships. These long-term relationships can lead to improved productivity. In the absence of job guarantees, employers can substitute layoffs for improved management. IBM's policy is possible because of an " 'ongoing commitment to creative, dynamic planning.' Each operating unit in the corporation submits a strategic plan that gives broad statistical projections for a five-year period and precise numbers for the next two years."[16]

Of course, while a full employment strategy improves productivity, it also requires shock absorbers like those developed by the Japanese to buffer the enterprise from changes in demand and other external shocks. Within the firm, flexibility can be achieved through education, comprehensive training, and more flexible compensation systems. A compensation system based on company performance (perhaps measured by value added to a product by the company) would have productivity as well as overall economic advantages.[17]

The last conclusion to be drawn is that the Japanese–American management comparison also demonstrates the importance of fair and effective compensation systems for managers as well as for the rank and file. This is a problem for many American managers, whose compensation systems are widely regarded as unfair. American compensation practices focus attention on the fact that stockholders

actually have very little to do with the management policies in many large corporations. Compensation systems
geared to short-run profits tend to reinforce the short time
horizons that have put many American companies at a
competitive disadvantage. It would be much better policy
to have executive bonuses and other incentives geared to
the company's performance over a long period or after
executives retire in order to force managers to adopt
longer, more strategic planning horizons. Executives in
companies that have not performed very well over a period of years—as was the case with the American automobile industry in 1983—and which depend heavily on support from workers and the government, are very
shortsighted to pay themselves exorbitant salaries and
bonuses.

These salaries are particularly questionable in light of
those paid Japanese executives, who earn a fifth or less as
much for what is often better performance. Salaries at this
level also underscore the extent to which American corporate executives are free to set their own incomes. Clar-
ence Randall, the late chief executive of Inland Steel, explains: "True, his board of directors must give pro forma
approval of his [the chief executive's] compensation
recommendations, but it almost never challenges them. In
actual fact, therefore, he himself decides what compensation he shall receive." As a consequence, researchers have
found "absolutely no relationship between stockholder
return and executive pay."[18] Perhaps greater worker representation on boards of directors would create at least a
few objections to this "legalized embezzlement" in large
American companies.

Companies should adopt Drucker's suggestion that
"the maximum compensation of all executives [should
be] a multiple of the lowest paid regular employee." He
suggested fifteen to one for small businesses and twenty-
five to one for large ones, which Green and Tenneriello

calculated to be $433,000 a year. They add: "If this puny amount shocks business executives, let us recommend a modification: any compensation packages that exceed the established ratio would have to obtain super-majority stockholder approval of, say, 70 percent. Executives would think twice before seeking the publicized approval of $1 million and $2 million remuneration."[19]

The main point to be made about the Japanese and American management systems, despite the myths about them, is that while the Japanese system is not the principal reason for Japan's economic performance, it is an important part of the wider system that has made Japan the most competitive major industrial country. It is unlikely that the Japanese management system could survive if it were embedded in an economic policy apparatus that was as uncertain, erratic, and uncoordinated as that of the United States. It is significant that even American multinationals have maintained their international market shares much better than have their American-based operations alone.[20] Besides the advantages it derives from Japanese economic policy, the Japanese management system owes its competitiveness to its heavy emphasis on its workers, quality, market shares, and long-run strategic manufacturing orientation.

Chapter V

The Role of Collective Bargaining

UNTIL AFTER World War II, collective bargaining was virtually the only form of worker participation in Europe or America but was not very well developed in Japan before the postwar era. The main approach of unions in all industrial market-economy countries (IMECs) was to use the workers' organized economic and political power to remove labor groups from a competitive position. Competition was considered to be bad for workers because individually their bargaining power was much less than that of their employers. Moreover, competitive markets often forced companies to depress wages and working conditions, weakening the workers' ability to support their families and therefore damaging a society's important human resources. Collective bargaining also promoted efficiency by forcing managers to adopt more productive systems rather than try to become competitive at the expense of the worker.

The IMECs therefore all developed the concept of industrial democracy—or collective bargaining—as a logical extension of political democracy. Social democracy—the welfare state—was a companion process whereby the government took labor out of competition by regulation. Today, democratic principles are increasingly being extended in the form of workplace participation, in addition to (or sometimes instead of) collective bargaining. Some European theorists even believe it is time to move to the fourth stage of democratic evolution—worker ownership or "economic democracy." To determine whether these forms of participation are viable, their economic costs and their relevance to political, economic, and social realities must be considered. Efficiency is important, because democratic societies are not likely to support any institution for very long if it costs too much in lost output and productivity. Of course, democratic institutions that also increase efficiency are likely to be especially durable.

Industrial Relations Systems

As they emerged in the immediate postwar period, the industrial relations systems of the United States and other IMECs were closely related to and reinforced by Keynesian demand management economic policies. It was believed that depressions resulted from the inability to sell all of the output that could be produced at full employment. The price system was held to be sufficiently imperfect, or was supposed to result in such unrealistically low wages and interest rates, that fluctuations in demand, supply, and prices would not automatically clear markets and sustain full employment, as had been postulated by the prevailing pre-Keynesian laissez-faire economic orthodoxy of the 1920s and 1930s. Keynesians believed that in order to achieve full employment, governments might have to stimulate demand—directly, by running budget deficits, or indirectly, by maintaining low interest rates to stimulate investment—and adopt social and industrial relations policies to maintain purchasing power. Thus, it was thought that collective bargaining, by sustaining wages, helped maintain high levels of income and employment.

By the end of World War II there consequently emerged in most IMEC countries implicit or explicit social contracts that business interests should accept unions and that labor movements should accept industrial market economies, at least temporarily. However, the labor movement in America was alone in explicitly embracing the capitalist system. Major American companies were especially willing to recognize unions and collective bargaining as necessary social institutions when, because of their own sales problems, they realized the economic system's need to maintain purchasing power. They also felt the need for capitalists and managers to establish ideological legitimacy in the face of anticapitalist threats from more radical European labor movements.

The American System: Uniformity and Regulating Competition

In addition to the characteristics it shares with other IMECs, the American industrial relations system has several unique features. The most important one is the legal right of workers to vote in government-supervised elections to determine whether they want to be represented by unions. This right has had a strong influence on the American industrial relations system, creating competition between union and nonunion employers and between unions and employers for the workers' allegiance. There can be no doubt that nonunion employers treat their workers better than they would if there were no threat of union organization. Similarly, the unions' need to appeal to workers in representation elections has made them more responsive to those workers' interests. For example, the need to organize black workers and women was a major factor in overcoming racial and sexual discrimination by unions.[1] Decentralization and competition between union and nonunion sectors has promoted greater wage flexibility than exists in European industrial relations systems, which are more centralized, make it more difficult for employers to discharge workers, and do more to sustain the incomes of those who cannot work.

Other major differences between the American and European labor movements include the relative weakness of the American unions in terms of the proportion of the work force organized, the absence of a labor party in the United States, the much greater hostility to unions by American employers, and the more decentralized U.S. bargaining system. Greater business hostility to unions in the United States is both a cause and an effect of union weakness. The greater political and economic power of European and Japanese unions makes them more of a threat to hostile employers. In addition, there seems to be greater acceptance abroad of the idea that free labor movements are essential to free and democratic societies. It is inconceivable, for example, that a major European business organization would form a Council for a Union-free Environment—as the U.S. National Association of Manufacturers did in 1977.

After the war, collective bargaining and the implied social contract were institutionalized until the sixties. In addition to their general role in legitimizing the system, unions performed a number of specific functions for employers. Perhaps the most important was to help regulate competition. There was a strong inverse correlation between the degree of competition and collective bargaining coverage. Very few highly competitive industries were ever well organized. The exception was coal mining, which in the thirties was considered by most coal operators to be a "sick" industry crippled by "excessive competition." By taking labor out of competition, collective bargaining reduced market competition for the product as well. The well-organized, nonoligopolistic industries were the regulated industries in transportation and communications, which also had very limited competition. Indeed, a basic objective of collective bargaining unions had always been to reduce market competition for labor. In addition to regulating competition, unions performed such personnel functions as training, job referral, improved grievance and information systems, and contractual guarantees of labor costs. From the unions' perspective, the overriding goal of collective bargaining was to establish worker protections through contracts that contained detailed work rules, wage rates based on the common rule of equal pay for workers in similar jobs, and pattern bargaining over wage increases.

The predominant wage patterns have traditionally been set by major companies and followed by others—union as well as nonunion. Wage patterns within major industries were fairly uniform regardless of the firms' financial conditions, though nonwage benefits were more diverse. In the immediate postwar period, the American and other IMEC industrial relations systems were relatively stable because high rates of growth in productivity and total output made rising real wages possible.

Economically, the American system relied less on flexible prices (which were blamed for the Depression) and more on demand management, legal enactment, and stable or even rigid work rules established by collective bargaining. The IMECs all relied heavily on markets to allocate goods, services, and resources, even though the industrial relations system, oligopolistic pricing, and product and labor market regulations caused prices to be less downwardly flexible than they had been before the Depression. After World War II the system was further stabilized by the Bretton Woods international institutions, which fixed exchange rates and established rules for the international trading and financial systems.

The Japanese System: Cooperation for Productivity

The Japanese industrial relations system enjoys a unique position in economic performance. In the immediate postwar period, trade unions were encouraged by the Allied occupation forces as part of a democratization policy. Particularly important for the character of the postwar labor movement was the fact that the Communist Party, which was considered an important counterforce to the military–industrial elites, was legalized, and Communists and other left-wing groups assumed leadership positions in the labor movement. Before the war most Japanese workers had very limited experience with trade unions. The most expedient response to the occupation government's orders to form trade unions, therefore, was for labor organizations to be formed at the enterprise level by Communists and other left-wing leaders who had superior knowledge of and interest in labor organizations.

The Communist-led unions adopted class-struggle strategies, leading to frequent political strikes. These leaders even planned a general strike for February 1, 1947, which moderate union leaders believe was designed to establish a Communist regime in Japan. Even though General MacArthur prevented this strike, left-wing union leaders conducted numerous strikes over the next ten years. These strikes even bankrupted one company,

Amagasaki Steel. While management offered very limited opposition to the radical union leaders, there emerged a more moderate union leadership with a stronger interest in labor–management cooperation and productivity. These leaders believed it would be impossible to protect real wages and employment through confrontation and conflict. The productivity concept was developed by the Japan Productivity Center (JPC), a group combining representatives of labor, management, and government established in 1955. The organization was created because the Japanese recognized the importance of improving productivity. As one of the leading union leaders put it, "The first thing the newly-built JPC did was to send mixed teams of labor and management to Europe and the U.S.A. . . . to study the superior technologies, management methods, and highly efficient production of Europe and the U.S.A., especially those in the U.S.A."[2]

But there remained strong resistance from Japanese managers to discussing productivity with unions, since productivity was considered to be a "management prerogative." Similarly, the militant left-wing trade unionists also opposed labor–management cooperation and the substitution of productivity improvement plans for class conflict. The dominant and left-wing Sohyo (General Council of Trade Unions of Japan) argued:

> The productivity movement of Japan is meant to realize the military and political objectives of the [United States–Japanese] Mutual Security Act.
>
> JPC is an institution whereby capitalists study in the name of productivity improvement the means to intensify [the] workload and to suppress wages.
>
> The movement means exploitation and dismissals.[3]

Sohyo continued to oppose the productivity movement, but, after intensive debate between 1955 and 1965, the rival Zenro (All-Japan Trade Union Congress, which subsequently became Domei, the Japanese Confederation of Labor) adopted a productivity improvement policy. This policy, according to one of its initiators, was the "biggest factor" in eliminating Marxist influence from the labor movement.

Ten years after the establishment of the JPC, Japanese labor–management relations became more cooperative, trade unions became more economic institutions than political, and managers changed their opposition and supported participatory processes based on prior labor–management consultation and use of the latest technology to improve productivity.

The term "productivity" took on a special meaning among Japanese trade unionists. It was not the same as "efficiency," which could result from using labor more intensively or from the introduction of technology to displace workers. More moderate union leaders considered it very important for Japanese industries to promote "international competitiveness to make it possible to develop industry, protect employment and improve living standards." After "heated discussion" between "experts and representatives of labor and management" lasting several months, three principles to improve productivity were formulated:

(1) Employment must be protected. Any redundancy which results from improved efficiency must be protected within an enterprise through measures such as reassignment so that no dismissals will take place.

(2) Consultation in advance. Any concrete measures to improve productivity must take place through mutual cooperation of management and labor and must be studied and discussed in advance by both.

(3) Fair distribution of productivity improvements. Any fruits achieved must be distributed fairly between workers, enterprises, and consumers.[4]

According to Ichiro Shioji, former president of the Confederation of Japanese Automobile Worker's Unions and a key architect of the productivity policy, "it can be said that productivity is something that is embodied in the bridge that is placed between 'efficiency' and 'fairness': The frame of the bridge is the question of labor and management consultation."[5]

Shioji believes the productivity concept overcomes the greatest weakness of socialist and capitalist systems—inefficiency and inadequate attention to fairness, respectively. The principle of fairness at the national level involves such factors as better wages and working conditions, enhanced social security, stricter environmental controls, and more evenly distributed wealth. In the international context, fairness refers to "international fair labor standards. The preconditions for promoting . . . free trade . . . must be that trade is conducted on the basis of fair competitive conditions."[6]

Shioji believes, further, that "how labor and management are related has a decisive influence over the degree of . . . productivity improvement." Productivity improvements require a sense of "community in the company and the workplace" where workers spend an important part of their lives; the worker "wishes to make friends in his workplace and tries to cherish human relations." Community "means that there is something within the company that makes workers feel a sense of purpose in life. These in many cases make workers . . . have attachment [to] their company and affection [for] their product." With respect to the layoff system in the United States, he declares that "the layoff system and productivity cannot get along with each other." Shioji believes the main cause of cooperative labor–management relations in Japan to be trust; however:

Mere talk can never produce trust. What is needed are achievements. And what is required of the people concerned is sincerity. Nothing can be born out of insincere human relationships and of mutual distrust of labor management relationships . . . the relationship of trust between labor and management is the most important factor for the improvement of productivity.[7]

Collective Bargaining and Efficiency

One of the most controversial aspects of collective bargaining is whether it promotes economic efficiency. Most people in the IMEC countries support unions and collective bargaining as necessary to provide worker participation at the workplace and in free and democratic political and governmental processes. But there is also a popular belief that since unions interfere with economic efficiency, their power should be carefully controlled to prevent their economic costs from rising too high relative to the political benefits that accrue. Despite these popular beliefs there is considerable evidence that while unions have both positive and negative effects on productivity, productivity is higher in union than in nonunion firms. It is not clear why this is true. The reasons undoubtedly vary from industry to industry, but in general collective bargaining seems to permit more effective labor management. The fact that a successful industrial relations system can improve productivity has long been recognized, but America's poor productivity performance relative to some of our competitors, especially Germany and Japan (which have stronger unions and better-developed systems for worker participation), has inspired a revived interest in this subject.[8]

An important cause of greater efficiency through good industrial relations is undoubtedly improved information exchange. The processes of negotiation and contract administration are good ways for management to obtain valuable information that may only be available at greater cost in other enterprises. Workers can express their preferences directly regarding wages and other conditions of work. Likewise, management can convey its priorities for improvements in technology and the organization of production in an orderly fashion, making workers and union leaders participants in proposed changes. Rules can be changed gradually to accommodate changed technological and market conditions without eliciting employee resistance. Finally, grievance machinery can provide a framework for systematic channeling of the disputes and tensions involved in day-to-day labor–management relations. Depending on the way grievance machinery operates, it can provide substantial information to management regarding workers' preferences and production operations.*

The participatory process improves communications between all parties in a production system, which facilitates the adaptability of different parts of the system to the whole. Within any organization there are various processes that might produce the optimal output for that organization, but each organization has to develop the best processes, including work rules and reward and penalty systems, for its particular needs. Different organizations confronting the same economic realities and decision options will make different choices and achieve different results. Where the work processes require cooperation and discretion—which is increasingly the case in an information society—participation and information sharing can improve quality and productivity. The result can be an interchange between workers and managers

---

*Again, the industrial relations literature provides substantial case-study evidence on the impact of increased labor–management cooperation on productivity.[9]

that narrows the differences between perceptions of the same facts and increases the commitment to achieve commonly derived objectives.

The reluctance of some analysts to accept the conclusion that unions and collective bargaining improve productivity stems partly from the assumption that unions impede technological progress. However, a 1979 study for the National Science Foundation concluded:

> The most common response that this country's labor unions make to the introduction of new technology is willing acceptance. The next most common initial response is opposition. That is followed by adjustment, encouragement, and finally competition. However, while opposition ranks second on a short-term basis, that response is very often a temporary one and is usually followed by a move to adjustment or willing acceptance. Thus, in the long run, it is willing acceptance followed by adjustment that constitutes the most common union reaction to technological innovation.[10]

Similarly, R. B. Freeman and J. C. Medoff conclude that "the limited evidence does *not* indicate that unionism is associated with a lower elasticity of substitution between labor and capital and thus with whatever technological change is embodied in new capital."[11]

The Hazards of Collective Bargaining

The fact that productivity has been higher in union than in nonunion workplaces does not mean that unions cannot restrict productivity or that productivity could not be further improved in unionized enterprises. Most studies detect positive and negative effects but find that the positive effects usually outweigh the negative. Especially important negative effects include the preservation of outmoded work rules that prevent flexible work assignments. These rules have become fixed mainly as a result of job insecurity and the adversarial relationship between labor and management, and because rules, once established, are difficult to change. Examples of restrictive work rules include limits on subcontracting and output; prohibiting managers and supervisors from doing work assigned to union members; requiring more workers than necessary to do the work, or to form standby crews; and limiting the type of work that can be done by particular workers (jurisdictional conflicts). Moreover, some research suggests that although productivity might be higher with unions, the increased cost of union labor offsets the higher productivity. An estimate for 1957 put the loss as a result of union work rules and other activities at 0.4 percent of the GNP,[12] and a 1950s study found that building trade unions' restrictive practices raise home prices by 2.5 to 7 percent.[13]

Complaints about union effects on productivity have been particularly important in the construction industry, in which the measured productivity slowdown has been greater than in any other industry, according to the American Productivity Center (APC) in Houston. From 1965 to 1973 construction productivity dropped at an annual rate of 0.9 percent and the decline accelerated to an annual rate of 3 percent between 1973 and 1979. It was −1.3 percent for 1980–1982, according to the APC.[14]

Criticism of union work rules has come from industrial relations experts as well as from business groups. For example, D. Quinn Mills, a professor of business administration at Harvard, argues that "The existence of a multitude of rules, many of which attempt to 'stretch the work' to maintain jobs in ways reminiscent of depression-era tactics, constrains productivity and raises costs." Moreover, "Study after study of U.S. managers has shown that managers fear the imposition of restrictive work practices far more than the higher wages and benefits which unionization may bring." Once established, these rules are very difficult to change: "Sometimes a company can pay a high price and 'buy the rules out,' or a union can persuade some workers to give up favored positions for the good of the membership as a group. But often, change cannot be accomplished without a bitter struggle between management and labor." Mills also believes that the rule-making process generates attitudes that cause labor–management relations to become excessively adversarial and legalistic "rather than to attempt to work out problems. . . . An organization which depends upon adherence to a myriad of rules will always be vulnerable to competition from other organizations which operate in a more consensual and cooperative fashion, even when the latter have fewer resources."[15]

An example of the impact of both a good labor–management relations system and a bad one can be found in the American coal industry.[16] In the fifties and early sixties, the unionized sector of this industry, under an effective industrial relations system, enjoyed average productivity advantages 25 to 30 percent higher than comparable nonunion mines. As labor relations in the union sector deteriorated in the late sixties and seventies, however, this relationship was reversed, and by 1975 union mines operated at about a 20 to 25 percent productivity disadvantage. Improvements were reported following the 111-day strike in 1977 and 1978 and the establishment of the president's tripartite Commission on the Coal Industry and an industry labor–management committee, but this experience remains to be thoroughly evaluated.

Several studies have used econometric techniques to provide more general and objective analyses of the unions' productivity effects. These econometric studies use controls for capital and labor inputs, scale of operations, other relevant determinants of productivity, and union status, in order to capture the independent net impact of unions. Charles Brown and James Medoff found that productivity in organized manufacturing establishments was 20 to 25 percent higher than in comparable unorganized establishments, mainly because of reductions in turnover and better morale, motivation, and training.[17]

Several industry-wide studies have produced similar results. Kim Clark found a positive union productivity advantage of about 6 to 8 percent in the cement industry, due mainly to more efficient management induced by unionization.[18] John Frantz found a positive union productivity effect of 10 to 15 percent in the wooden household furniture industry, due primarily to improved management, good worker–management communication, and better worker motivation.[19] Similarly, Steven Allen found output per employee to be substantially higher in unionized construction projects.[20]

Industrial relations and labor specialists have gone beyond the approach used by most economists to measure the impact of worker attitudes and behavior on productivity. At General Motors, Harry Katz, Thomas Kochan, and Kenneth Gobeille found a strong association between high grievance rates and low productivity and weaker (but significant) associations between productivity, quit rates, and unauthorized strikes.[21] J. R. Norsworthy and Craig Zabala constructed a different model that deepens our understanding of the relations between worker behavior and productivity and helps account for the slowdown in productivity growth since the sixties in ways that could not be explained by the econometric studies cited in chapter 3. They examined the relation between worker attitudes and productivity in the U.S. automobile industry from 1959 to 1976. They estimated an index of the effects of worker behavior on total factor productivity (based on all costs except imputed overhead), labor productivity, and the cost of production. This model improves on that of Katz and others by using total factor

productivity (TFP), not just labor productivity. Norsworthy and Zabala found a negative relation between
their index of worker behavior and both labor and TFP,
and a positive correlation between worker behavior and
unit cost of production. Thus, negative worker attitudes
reduce productivity and increase costs. Moreover, they
show that:

> For the period 1959–76, the effects of worker behavior on
> productivity and the cost of production are increasingly neg-
> ative: our index of worker behavior shows a 29 percent in-
> crease over the period as a whole, and even higher, more
> negative values in some years. . . . We estimate that, other
> things equal, a 10 percent improvement in worker behavior
> would have improved the total unit cost of production in the
> industry by about 5 percent in 1976, which would corre-
> spond to a total factor productivity of the same amount.
> . . . our study offers strong evidence that the benefits of
> improving worker behavior can be enormous.[22]

Additional evidence with respect to the impact of industrial relations on productivity is produced by Freeman
and Medoff, who conclude that "productivity is generally
higher in unionized establishments than in otherwise
comparable establishments that are nonunion, but that
the relationship is far from immutable and has notable
exceptions."[23] The main ways unions increase productivity, according to these writers, are to induce managers to
manage more rationally, and to reduce quit rates by improving personnel practices and by causing wages to be
higher; they hold that union workers earned about 30
percent more than comparable nonunion workers in 1980.
Unions have both beneficial and undesirable consequences for society, but the empirical evidence demonstrates that the beneficial effects predominate.

In general, therefore, it is reasonable to assume that the

shock effects of collective bargaining would give unionized workplaces a productivity advantage. The evidence
is also strong that unionized workplaces have lower turnover. It could be argued that unions might prevent mechanization by restrictive rules, but, as noted earlier, there
is no evidence to support this contention. In addition,
Freeman and Medoff's evidence that profits are lower in
nonunion firms has caused some to speculate that in the
long run investment might be lower, offsetting the tendency of unionized employers to substitute physical capital for labor. There is no credible evidence to support this
hypothesis, however. Thus, while Freeman and Medoff's
conclusion is convincing, there is enough doubt to make
it a controversial one.

It seems much more credible to argue that good industrial relations can improve productivity and poor industrial relations can damage it. Good industrial relations
imply the existence of a union that is democratically controlled and represents the consensus interests of all its
members, of management that accepts the union's legitimacy, and of worker job security. Additionally, the union
must perceive a positive relationship between the workers' interests and improved productivity and profitability,
and management must perceive a strong relationship between profitability, productivity, and worker participation in decision making. Under these circumstances, management shares information with workers and unions and
has mutual trust and understanding with the unions. A
common interest develops in improving productivity.

Unfortunately, the evidence suggests that industrial
relations in the United States can not be characterized as
conducive to productivity improvements as they should
be, especially in the sense of achieving employee motivation and commitment and labor–management cooperation. The American industrial relations system has been
notoriously adversarial and legalistic. There are indica-

tions that American managers and workers have had very limited commitment to productivity and efficiency. This is not because of an absence of commitment to the work ethic, as some observers argue. Research by Yankelovich suggests that while work *behavior* may well have deteriorated, a deterioration in the traditional work ethic is not responsible.[24] In fact, based on their own surveys and those of others, the Public Agenda Foundation concluded that the work ethic enjoys broad support among American workers, with a majority of those interviewed agreeing that it was important to "do the best job I can regardless of pay." An astonishing 73 percent of the employees surveyed thought there was little connection between their pay and the quality of the work performance. Despite this belief, less than one-quarter of the work force thought they were working at their full potential. Three-fourths of the employees attributed reduced performances to management's inability to motivate the work force. Twenty percent thought their distance from the final product was a factor in poor performance. Finally, a U.S. Chamber of Commerce survey (cited by Public Agenda) found that only 9 percent of employees believed they would benefit directly from improved productivity in their companies; another survey found that 93 percent of Japanese workers thought they would benefit from improved productivity. These findings suggest that the perceived decline in work behavior is not attributable to a decline in the work ethic but to management and industrial relations systems that fail to reinforce it.

Two more factors that can influence productivity are the size of the union wage advantage and the degree of competition between union and nonunion workers. Indeed, where unions have direct control over productivity, as in the construction and clothing industries, they have developed productivity improvement programs as a way to sustain higher union wages in competition with nonunion employers. Similarly, union productivity differentials appear to be largest where unionized employers face the strongest nonunion competition and both unions and managers have strong incentives to improve productivity, as in the Southwest.[25] Moreover, a 1965 study by Mandelstamm identified competition from contractors in Detroit as the main source of greater efficiency in heavily unionized Ann Arbor than in nearby less unionized Bay City, Michigan. Similar evidence has been found in other industries.[26]

There is a natural tendency for managers to doubt the notion that unions and collective bargaining improve productivity. The conclusion that unions and collective bargaining increase productivity likewise seems to some to be inconsistent with their resistance to unions. This resistance can be accounted for, however: employers are motivated mainly by profits, not productivity. There is no necessary relationship between productivity and profits; lower wages could more than offset the productivity disadvantages of nonunion firms. Finally, some things that increase productivity (like better and more expensive training, capital investment, and research) reduce short-run profits, even though they might increase productivity. The latter point is very important because, as discussed in the last chapter, too many American companies are motivated mainly by short-run profit maximizing, which can interfere with long-run productivity and competitiveness.

American Industrial Relations: A Double-edged Sword

The traditional American industrial relations system has had further economic consequences beyond affecting productivity. Together with the Keynesian economic policies to which it was closely related and the expanding international economy facilitated by the Bretton Woods institutions, it contributed to a long period of relatively high growth in productivity and total output. Collective bargaining permitted most union members to participate more in both workplace and societal decisions and outcomes and therefore to achieve middle-class incomes.

At the same time, these traditional systems in the United States and Europe contained inflationary biases, because they gave inadequate attention to flexibility and efficiency. The decentralized American system was conducive to "whipsawing" (raising wages by playing one employer off against another) and "leapfrogging" (union leaders escalating wages in competition with each other). Long-term contracts with cost-of-living adjustments and annual improvement factors tended to cause temporary factors to increase the wage base and push compensation upward. The Keynesian-inspired safety nets of unemployment compensation and income maintenance programs for those who were unemployed or not expected to work reduced the impact of unemployment on wages, as did the growth of families with multiple wage earners. Finally, the full employment policies pursued by governments created less incentive for employers to resist wage increases or for unions to hold wages down, because wage and price increases were likely to be offset by government monetary and fiscal policies.

As noted in chapter 2, the American system was not as flexible in adjusting to change as the Japanese system but was more flexible than most European systems. The factors that made the United States more elastic than Europe included the right to vote in representation elections for or against unions; a more decentralized bargaining system; lower levels of income support for those not working; lower degrees of unionization and the competition between union and nonunion companies; the American economy's greater openness to immigration and imports;

the greater internal displacement of labor from American agriculture, which created pools of underemployed workers; and the greater ease with which American employers could close plants and lay off workers.

Japan is superior to either America or Europe in this regard because of its highly interrelated consensus-based economic policies that have emphasized the upgrading (in terms of both productivity and quality) of the Japanese industry mix; an enterprise management system stressing labor–management cooperation, participation, and consensus; mechanisms within enterprises to absorb shocks in demand, including the bonus compensation system, production sharing (whereby low-wage work is done in Third World countries), subcontracting, and use of temporary workers; and one of the world's most effective positive adjustment programs to shift resources from noncompetitive to more competitive industries. The Japanese industrial relations system gains flexibility by stressing continuing education of an already well-educated work force (because education and training make individuals more flexible), the concentration of collective bargaining at the enterprise instead of the industry or sectoral levels, and the annual adjustment of wages through a spring wage offensive that minimizes whipsawing and leapfrogging; the heavy reliance on consensus mechanisms at every level rather than the detailed regulations that characterize the American and European systems; and the bonus wage payment system, which prevents wage increases based on temporary factors from becoming imbedded in the wage base, thereby avoiding the American practice of ratcheting up wages. Finally, lifetime employment contributes to flexibility in job assignments and training, causes workers to be less concerned about protecting particular jobs, and makes companies more willing to finance long-term education and training for their employees.

Transforming the System

The trends discussed in the introduction and chapter 1 have transformed the traditional American industrial relations system. Especially important has been the emergence of a more integrated world economy. There were many simultaneous trends affecting the relations among the actors in the industrial relations system. The decline in productivity growth after the mid-sixties made it much harder to sustain the increase in output and real wages. Stagflation upset the economic policy framework that had sustained the industrial relations system. Technological changes (especially the information revolution) made scale less important (and adaptability to change more possible and more important) to an enterprise's viability and competitiveness; they also shifted employment out of heavily unionized industries, companies, and places into smaller firms, rural areas, white-collar work, services, and the Sunbelt, where unions are weaker. The increased participation as permanent, integral parts of the work force by women—who are generally not as unionized as men—put pressure on work rules and compensation systems oriented to male heads of households and based on the assumption that women were temporary, peripheral labor market participants. Finally, between 1950 and 1984 the proportion of the work force in the information occupations had increased from less than 20 percent to about 60 percent.

The American system as it was established in the thirties, forties, and fifties was partly justified as a stabilizing system that took wages out of competition; but internationalization made it harder for unions to insulate labor from competition. Stagflation, declining real wages, and the slow growth of real incomes made people more price-conscious and led to deregulation of economic activity, especially airlines and trucking, where unions were strong. The Keynesian system assumes a closed national economy—or at least works best under those conditions. It also does not permit wage decreases, which makes competitiveness for European and American industries difficult at the international level.

Most of the inflation of the seventies originated in external commodity and exchange rate shocks outside American product and labor markets, but the industrial relations system did not have the wage and price flexibility to achieve the real wage and income reductions required to bring about equilibrium in foreign transactions in the face of declining productivity growth and much higher prices for imported energy and commodities. Real wage cuts had to be attained indirectly through inflation, which was followed inevitably by rising unemployment. The American management and industrial relations systems accelerated inflationary pressures and forced the external shocks to be absorbed by employment and real output and not by prices and wages. The old system must be transformed into one that can address the requirements of international competition.

Declining Union Strength

Inevitably, these powerful economic, technological, and demographic trends have weakened unions in their dealings with employers, and many American companies have found their positions weakened by the emergence of more efficient and competitive systems in other countries. Union membership in the nonagricultural work force declined from about 30 percent in 1970 to 24.7 percent in 1980 (see table 5.1) and to less than 20 percent in 1985. Unions lost 2.6 million members between 1980 and 1985. According to union membership experts Leo Troy and

TABLE 5.1

U.S. Labor Organization Membership, 1970–1980
(in thousands)

Year	Membership	Total labor force* Number	Percent members	Nonagricultural establishments Number	Percent members
1970	21,248	85,903	24.7	70,880	30.0
1971	21,327	86,929	24.5	71,214	29.9
1972	21,657	88,991	24.3	73,675	29.4
1973	22,276	91,040	24.5	76,790	29.0
1974	22,809	93,240	24.5	78,265	29.1
1975	22,361	94,793	23.6	77,364	28.9
1976	22,662	96,917	23.4	80,048	28.3
1977	22,456	99,534	22.6	82,423	27.2
1978	22,757	102,537	22.2	86,697	26.2
1979	22,579	104,996	21.5	89,886	25.1
1980	22,366	106,821	20.9	90,657	24.7

Source: Courtney D. Gifford, ed., *Directory of U.S. Labor Organizations: 1982–83 Edition* (Washington, D.C.: Bureau of National Affairs, 1982), p. 1. The data were gathered by the U.S. Department of Labor and represent a revised report of earlier released data.

*Totals exclude Canadian members and members of single-firm labor organizations.

Neil Shaflin, union membership dropped to 19.8 million in 1984, a 16 percent decline from a peak of 23.7 million in 1975. This slump, coupled with the growing labor force, left unions with 19 percent of nonfarm employment and 16 percent of the civilian labor force, down from 33 percent and 25 percent, respectively, at the 1953 peak.[27]

Although basic trends have tended to weaken unions' relative strength, such findings can easily mislead. Economic and industrial relations systems have not ordinarily changed rapidly or dramatically except in response to cataclysmic events like major wars, depressions, or other very serious economic catastrophes. Moreover, the percentage of the nonagricultural work force organized is an imperfect indicator of union strength because it includes

managers and professional people, categories not actively
recruited by unions. The proportion of eligible workers
who actually join unions fell from about 45 percent in the
sixties to about 28 percent in 1984.[28] Unions and employee associations account for perhaps 35 percent of
nonfarm wages (because unions are in high-wage occupations and collective bargaining covers nonunion workers
as well as union members) and actively influence the remainder since nonunion employers usually follow union
wage patterns in order to retain key workers and to avoid
unionization.

The main reason for the unions' declining membership
since the sixties has been their failure to keep pace with
a very rapidly growing work force, which grew at about
1.3 million a year in the sixties and 2.1 million a year in
the seventies. At the same time, union membership was
standing still; the unions' losses from declining employment in the basic unionized industries have not been
offset by union gains in the rapidly growing areas, which
have mainly remained nonunion. During the seventies,
when manufacturing and construction accounted for 50
percent of AFL-CIO membership, 90 percent of all job
growth was in the services, which will account for three-
fourths of the labor force by 1990. The manufacturing
sector, by contrast, lost 2.3 million jobs between 1980 and
1985, probably 90 percent of them for good. The service
industries were only about 10 percent organized in 1984
and accounted for only 20 percent of the AFL-CIO's
membership.

One of the most important challenges to unions during
the sixties was the emergence of a nonunion alternative
to collective bargaining. Before that time, union industrial
relations practices tended to control wages and working
conditions for blue-collar workers in the nonunion sector.
Thomas Kochan, Robert McKersie, and Harry Katz conclude that "somewhere in the 1960s the leadership and

innovative position shifted from union to nonunion employment systems."[29] This shift occurred as unions continued to stress comparable wages and real wage advances despite such adverse economic conditions as rapid inflation, international competition, reduced union organizing success, impaired growth of productivity and total output, and the declining competitiveness of American industry. These developments widened the union–nonunion wage gap: the unions' relative wage advantage increased from between 10 and 15 percent during the fifties and sixties to between 20 and 25 percent during the late seventies.[30]

The reasons for the nonunion sector's increase are fairly clear. Most of the post-1960 economic and demographic trends weakened the unions' traditional geographic, firm size, and occupational bases and made the main elements of the traditional collective bargaining system less effective. Even during the fifties and early sixties, American employers had remained hostile to unions and collective bargaining, but most of them stifled their overt opposition until the later sixties. The risks of opposing increasingly stronger unions backed by favorable public opinion and government officials was too great and might have elicited even stronger union actions and more restrictive regulations. As union power weakened in the later sixties and seventies, though, there emerged a group of human resource professionals who helped antiunion employers develop alternatives to collective bargaining.

In industries with strong unions, nonunion models matched union wages and fringe benefits. In nonunion industries the new models called for paying higher than prevailing wages, but those wages were still "lower than in the union rates found in more highly unionized markets." The nonunion model also stressed "greater flexibility in job design and work organization, more extensive communication and participation in task-related decisions, and other behavioral science strategies designed to increase the commitment, loyalty, and job satisfaction of employees. As a result, employees have fewer incentives to unionize."[31]

These union avoidance strategies were relatively successful. The data "show significant declines in union membership between 1977 and 1983 in firms that (1) assigned a high priority to union avoidance as a labor relations strategy, (2) opened new plants, (3) introduced workplace innovation in nonunion facilities, and (4) lacked the presence of a dominant union representing employees anywhere in the firm."[32]

Growing Employer Opposition

Despite some temporary accommodations in the forties and fifties, the prevailing preference of most American employers has always been to operate nonunion. As a 1979 study by the Conference Board, a management organization, put it, "It is no secret that management would prefer to operate without a union. Indeed, in many ways, all aspects of supervision—of personnel relations—might be subsumed under 'union avoidance.' "[33] Employer opposition to unions appears to have intensified during the seventies, when almost all employers actively resisted union organizing, usually with the help of consultants who have become expert at union avoidance. More companies have recently been willing to take the risk of a strike because high levels of unemployment during the eighties has made it relatively easy to recruit strikebreakers.

The reasons for this increased employer opposition are not clear, but various hypotheses may be advanced. First, the unions' declining economic and political power reduced the risks of openly opposing them. In the fifties and sixties, it looked as if unions would continue to gain polit-

TABLE 5.2

Approval of Labor Unions
(by percent)

	Approve	Disapprove	No opinion
1985	58	27	15
1981	55	35	10
1979	55	33	12
1978	59	31	10
1973	59	26	15
1967	66	23	11
1965	70	19	11
1963	67	23	10
1961	63	22	15
1959	68	19	13
1957	76	14	10
1953	75	18	7
1949	62	22	16
1947	64	25	11
1941	61	30	9
1939	68	24	8
1936	72	20	8

SOURCE: Gallup Poll, May 19, 1985 (reprinted by permission).

ical power, as was reflected in their high standing in public opinion polls. As can be seen from table 5.2, unions had an approval rate of 76 percent in 1957 and 70 percent in 1965. During the sixties, it would have been unthinkable for Pan Am, Phelps Dodge, or Greyhound to have attempted to break a strike, as they did in the eighties; it would have been equally unthinkable for the National Association of Manufacturers to form a Council for a Union-free Environment, as it did in 1977.

A second cause appears to have been that internationalization, declining productivity growth, the widening union–nonunion wage differentials, deregulation, intensified competition, and rising unemployment all put a much higher premium on controlling labor costs. In this environment, multinationals gained considerable power, and the human resource management function became more important within corporate structures. Employers considered the informal social compact of the thirties to be no longer operable because unions could no longer protect companies from low wage competition. At the same time there was growing worker discontent, reflected in a rising incidence of strikes and labor unrest. Public concern was also mounting about inflation—which was blamed on unions. For this and other reasons, unions' approval rating fell from 70 percent in 1965 to 59 percent in 1979.

The weak penalties for violating the National Labor Relations Act and the development of experts who could show employers how to avoid collective bargaining legally, together with the fact that less public disapproval attached to union hostility, encouraged greater legal and illegal employer resistance.

Finally, antiunion forces have been strengthened in the eighties by a sympathetic president, who has adopted stronger antiunion positions than any of his modern predecessors. He has advertised his hostility to unions by his appointments to key labor agencies and by breaking the Professional Air Traffic Controllers' strike in 1981 and eliminating that union (which, ironically, was one of the very few unions to support his candidacy for president).

Declining Public Support

Public opinion is one of the most important determinants of union strength in the United States. For whatever reason, during the seventies unions lost some of their reputation as institutions representing the concerns of all workers and acquired the image of being mainly concerned about their own members' narrow interests (see table 5.2). Moreover, the declining viability of Keynesian economic policies removed part of the intellectual support for unions as institutions that helped strengthen the economy. The new economic problems were perceived to be productivity, innovation, efficiency, and flexibility, and unions were seen as forces for inefficiency, backwardness, and rigidity. This changing image undoubtedly derived from well-publicized strikes and wage increases as unions sought through collective bargaining to maintain real wages in a period of rising inflation. While the basic causes of inflation originated outside labor markets, rapidly rising nominal wages (which nevertheless lagged behind inflation) created the appearance of wage-push inflation.

Similarly, the decline in productivity growth and rising unemployment created tensions between unions and their former allies in the civil rights movement. Conflict over the Vietnam War (which the AFL-CIO supported) and antiwar elements in the Democratic Party further split the former labor-liberal coalition, as did social issues, over which many unionists took much more conservative positions than liberal Democrats. The widely publicized cases of union resistance to accepting black members was particularly damaging to the labor movement's image among liberal Democrats and blacks. In addition, in the minds of many former supporters, the unions' image was tarnished by widely publicized examples of corruption and undemocratic practices in a few unions, notably the Teamsters. Unfortunately for the unions, the public does not always distinguish between "good" and "bad" unions, and the publicity always tends to exaggerate the magnitude of the negatives. It is worth noting, however, that the unions had lost sufficient moral power that they had inadequate residual defenses against bad publicity.

The declining public image was also a reaction to the perception that unions were becoming too powerful, politically and economically. The public image of powerful organizations seems to vary with the perception of

whether that power is being used for narrow selfish purposes or to promote the public interest. Powerful organizations that promote the public interest are acceptable;
powerful organizations that merely promote their own
interests are not. Unfortunately for the unions, during the
seventies they became known as powerful special interests. During the eighties, by contrast, a declining incidence of strikes and perceptions of union weaknesses undoubtedly account for the modest increases in public
approval.*

A Look on the Bright Side

Despite the negative trends, the prospect for unions has
its positive side. The American labor movement has a
very solid base of about 20 million members (the largest
in the free world; the Japanese labor movement is second
with 12.5 million members, 29.1 percent of the work
force); it is therefore not likely to disappear. This base is
the largest it has had during any generally adverse period
in its history. A large base is important because it provides

*A poll reported by the AFL-CIO in 1985 confirmed these negative public
attitudes about unions. It found that most nonunion workers did not believe
unions could increase their fringe benefits (53 percent) or job security (74
percent). Most nonunion respondents also believed unions were not very democratic: 65 percent agreed with the statement that unions force workers to go
along with decisions they don't like; 63 percent agreed that union leaders decide
on strikes regardless of their members' wishes; and 50 percent of all respondents
(union and nonunion) thought that unions no longer represented their members' interests. Third, it revealed that most respondents also thought that unions reduced economic efficiency: 54 percent thought unions increased the risk
of companies going out of business, while 57 percent thought they stifled work
initiative. There was considerable variation in union approval among different
groups. As might be expected, approval was greatest among union families,
blacks, unskilled blue-collar workers, Democrats outside the South, eighteen-
to twenty-nine-year-olds, families with incomes under $25,000 a year, and high
school graduates. However, Republicans were the only group of which less than
50 percent of respondents approved of unions; the next lowest approval rate
came from the South with 51 percent. Republicans, college graduates, South-
erners, and high-income groups (annual income $25,000 and over) had the
highest relative disapproval rates.

a foundation from which union membership can accelerate rapidly when the right combination of conditions occurs. Unions in the United States have never grown steadily. Certain events—such as wars and recoveries following long depressions—make conditions ripe for membership explosion. Usually during such periods, unions have been stimulated by intense organizing, sometimes, as in 1937, because of interunion rivalry.

The general public approval of unions by a ratio of more than two to one (58 percent versus 27 percent) is encouraging. The unions' long slide in public approval appears to have come to a halt by 1985. Moreover, union members and their families still strongly approve of unions; about three-fourths of union respondents to the AFL-CIO poll believed unions improve wages and fringe benefits, and 80 percent felt that unions were needed to address the legitimate complaints of workers. These data and the fluctuations in union approval rates suggest a strong undercurrent of public belief that unions are necessary organizations in democratic societies to represent workers' interests.

There are indications that workers will organize when the conditions are right. For example, public-sector unions, which are relatively insulated from competitive market forces, gained 1 million members between 1971 and 1983, while private-sector unions lost 200,000 members. A major difference between public and private sector unionism is the fact that public employers increased their support for collective bargaining during the 1960s and 1970s when private employers were becoming more hostile to unions.

Another encouraging fact is that some well-organized areas have reversed their long-run economic decline during the eighties and will probably grow in the future. This is true of the New England and Midwestern states, which have important competitiveness advantages over most of the Sunbelt states. In fact, the use of percentage growth figures always exaggerated the growth of the Sunbelt— the ten slowest-growing states will still have higher absolute growth by the year 2000 than the ten fastest growing states. Moreover, many of the types of industry found in the Sunbelt are noncompetitive with Third World countries.

The competitive advantages of the New England and Midwestern states are due to their higher per capita incomes, which make them attractive to market-oriented activities; their concentrations of basic industries (like automobiles) which are automating, changing their structures, and becoming more competitive; the presence of more highly skilled and educated workers; the emergence of political leadership—especially governors—who have adopted industrial policies based on consensus building between labor, business, academic, and public groups; and the emergence of more cooperative relations between unions and employers in highly unionized industries. Massachusetts is an example of such changes. That state had one of the nation's highest unemployment rates in the 1974–1975 recession, but one of the lowest in 1982–1983. During the eighties, most Sunbelt states in the Southeast, whose development strategies had stressed anti-unionism and low wages, had higher unemployment rates than Midwestern states, where unemployment was declining and both wages and union strength were greater. As noted earlier, in the internationalized information era, well-trained, educated workers and effective public policies and economic institutions are major assets. In these matters, the New England and Midwestern states have long-run advantages over the Sunbelt states. The Southern states are making vigorous efforts to make their education systems world class, but they lag behind the Frost Belt states on most measures of educational quality.

This optimism must be qualified, however, by noting that unions as institutions are doing much better in other countries, which suggests that the American unions' problems are not duplicated to the same extent in other countries. Indeed, in neighboring Canada, where union membership represented about the same proportion of the work force in the sixties (30 percent), the proportion of the Canadian work force organized had increased from 30 to 39 percent by 1984, while the proportion of U.S. workers had declined to less than 20 percent. These data suggest that it is not just unions as institutions that have had trouble, but that U.S. policies and conditions were uniquely hostile to unions. In particular, Canadian public policy has been much more supportive of unions and collective bargaining.[34]

But it is promising to find evidence that the labor movement is attempting to change not only its public image, but its practices as well, in order to adapt to the new economic and political climate. Unions are slowly merging to form stronger organizations; there have been fifty mergers of national unions since that of the AFL and the CIO in 1955, with ten of them between 1981 and 1984. They are also developing new organizing strategies to compensate for their greater difficulty in winning traditional strikes. They are engaged in "investment bargaining" in the transportation industry to trade concessions for greater worker control. Another tactic is to use the labor movement's substantial financial power to induce corporations' creditors, directors, consumers, and bankers to pressure targeted companies to recognize the unions. Such a corporate campaign helped the Amalgamated Clothing and Textile Workers' successful campaign against J. P. Stevens, which had become a symbol of strong employer opposition to unions by whatever means.

In several successful campaigns in the eighties, organizers used innovative tactics because they felt that traditional strikes would have been useless, in view of the availability of strikebreakers and management's ability to shift jobs, especially computer work, to other locations. For instance, boycotts and community support were used by Service Employees Local 925 to organize Equitable Life Assurance Society at Syracuse, where most of the employees were women. At Yale, Federal University Employees Local 34 worked hard to keep the rank and file involved and stressed issues other than wages, especially workers' participation in workplace decisions, a very popular issue among employees. The Yale organizers also conducted a corporate campaign, taking their case to the members of the university's governing body. Lastly, they used strike and nonstrike approaches; they struck for some weeks and then went back when the university was less vulnerable to the strike, but threatened to strike again when it was more vulnerable. The renewed strike threat finally pressured the university to negotiate a settlement.

A number of American unions are learning from their experiences and complementing collective bargaining with various forms of worker participation and ownership to gain worker control of enterprise decisions and to strengthen the competitiveness of unionized employers, or both. Finally, some unions have streamlined their internal structures to make them more efficient and have launched a number of organizing campaigns, which in 1985 seemed to be producing higher success rates than in the seventies and early eighties.

Are Unions Obsolete?

The unions' problems have prompted some futurists and management experts to argue that unions are either obsolete or irrelevant. For example, management guru Peter

Drucker raises the question of whether unions have lost "The true strength of the labor movement . . . its claim to be the political conscience of a modern secular society." He contends that the unions' claim to be more than an interest group justified unusual privileges, which cannot be maintained any longer:

> The union may no longer be able to maintain the unique position it has reached in this century in all developed non-communist countries. To use traditional terms the union has become an "estate of the realm" with substantial immunities —from taxes, from antitrust, from damage suits, for instance —and with legal privileges not too dissimilar from those enjoyed in earlier times by the army in Prussia or by the church in pre-revolutionary France. The union is considered legitimate as no other non-governmental institution is. And in accepting and protecting the union's right to strike we have given one group in society a right of civil disobedience.[35]

Drucker suggests, in addition, that unions could be destroyed by demographics, especially the conflict between young workers and retirees. This generational conflict will, in his opinion, manifest itself as tension between unions and the trustees of pension funds. This is an important conflict because these funds

> now own up to 50% of our large businesses, [making the] employees . . . the "real" owners and their pension funds the main source of capital for productive investment. Conversely, the stake in the retirement funds is increasingly the largest single asset of the American family, once the head of the household is 45 years or older.

> "Power follows property" is one of the oldest and most thoroughly tested laws of politics. Employees—or "public trustees" . . . will predictably be brought into the supervision and management of pension funds. . . .

The result will be what any union fears the most and fights the hardest: an organ of the employees that expresses the identity of interest between enterprise and workers, is independent of the union and bypasses it, and, inevitably, will oppose the union as an "outsider." This is, in effect, what has happened in Japan. There "lifetime employment," by restricting labor mobility and therefore reducing the threat of strikes, has made the union impotent in the private sector and little more than an organ of management.

The only alternative is codetermination, "But if the union representatives in management and ownership act responsibly—that is, in the interest of the enterprise—they soon will be tagged as company stooges and of having 'sold out to the management.' . . . to become again a dynamic, effective, legitimate organ, the labor union will have to transform itself directly."[36]

Other critics, especially management consultants, also consider unions to be obsolete. According to one such critic, American unions have fallen so out of step with economic and social change that "within a generation they will have lost most of their influence in the national workplace."[37]

Similarly, labor economist Audrey Freedman of the Conference Board argues that the outlook for unions is very bleak. "They will not disappear, but they are fading into the background of American public life." She believes the unions are led by "administrators, caretakers and bureaucrats [who] . . . seem unable to transform themselves. . . . During its evolution from group to organization to institution, the union movement developed a paralyzing orthodoxy that prevented growth." She thinks American unions "missed at least two major opportunities to broaden their appeal and renew their sense of purpose." The first was failing to espouse the increasingly popular cause in equal opportunity employment, "campaigning on behalf of blacks and women for access. When government pressed employers to open jobs to the formerly excluded, unions were often found protecting the already entrenched." The other was "the growing public concern about environmental exposure to disease-causing elements." Instead of "creating a countervailing power . . . to protect public health, [the unions] . . . passed up the opportunity," ceding the issue to government regulators.[38]

Are unions really as inflexible and entrenched as these critics imply? There is no question that unions, like other major institutions in a democratic society, are responsive mainly to their members, and sometimes their members' interests clash with the interests of outsiders. After all, unlike corporations, unions are democratic organizations, and leaders must respond to their members' interests or get voted out. There is no question either that many craft unions excluded blacks and women from membership and otherwise discriminated against them. On the other hand, some unions, especially the Packinghouse Workers, the UAW, the State, County and Municipal Employees, the needle trade unions, the International Union of Electrical Workers, and the AFL-CIO were in the forefront of the civil rights struggle. Indeed, civil rights leaders concede that Title VII of the Civil Rights Act would not have been passed without the support of the AFL-CIO. That is why civil rights leaders, like the Reverend Martin Luther King, Jr., were outspoken union supporters.[39]

It must also be conceded that the unions were the main force for the passage of occupational safety and health legislation, as well as the implementation and protection of occupational safety and health programs. Some observers believe legislation to protect workers weakens unions by doing things unions formerly did. But unions everywhere properly stress the logical division of labor between "legal enactment" and collective bargaining. Collective bargaining can protect employees where workers have enough power to organize and get contracts. But legal enactment takes the protected actions out of competition for all workers. American labor laws are not self-enforcing, so unions have an important role in helping government agencies monitor compliance. Employers and those who speak for them are more likely than union representatives to consider protective labor legislation to be inimical to collective bargaining.

There are several other flaws in the argument that unions have become irrelevant. The most important is that workers need organizations they control to represent their interests just as much, if not more, in a global information world as they did at the beginning of industrialization. It is doubtful that there can be effective long-run participation without some independent worker-controlled organization or process. The ability of workers to decide for themselves whether they want to bargain collectively is therefore an important protector of nonunion as well as union workers' rights. In the absence of unions, individual workers would have limited ability to protect their rights in political or work matters.

There is no question that unions are in trouble, that their membership has failed to keep pace with the growth of the work force, and that their operating principles have not adjusted rapidly to the requirements of the global information economy. However, the argument that they are obsolete or irrelevant is premature. It is highly doubtful that worker participation in decision making or profit sharing will eliminate the need for unions or turn them into weak "company unions," as Drucker alleges to have happened in Japan. This is a serious misreading of the Japanese situation. The fact that unions tend to cooperate with Japanese enterprise management is due more to the union leaders' and members' belief that it is in their interest to cooperate than to their inability to fight. Cooperative relationships were established in Japan after the parties realized that the disruptive conflicts of the fifties were self-defeating. The comparative rarity of union strikes is not a sign of weakness; indeed, strong unions do not have to strike, especially in a consensus society like Japan where all parties realize how much damage the workers could cause with strikes and on-the-job protest actions. In fact, Japan's strike record during the seventies was about the same as that of Germany, and it would be hard to argue that the German labor movement is weak. Similarly, the so-called lifetime employment system in Japan was established because of demands from unions for greater job security. For whatever reason, Japanese managers are more responsive to their workers' interests, involve them more in decision making, and keep less distance between managers' and employees' salaries than has been normal in the United States. Similarly, Japanese workers have enjoyed higher real wage growth and less unemployment under their bargaining arrangements than American workers since the sixties, when Japan emerged as a formidable international competitor. Finally, the Japanese unions represent much larger proportions of their work force—about 30 percent—than the American unions.

While American unions have lost their image as a *cause*, they have not just supported activities for their members. No other major private institution has as consistently supported measures that were good for all workers (and, indeed, the great majority of people) as the labor movement. Unfortunately for the unions, they have acquired the image of a narrow interest group and have not devised public relations strategies to overcome that image. In part, however, these problems are due to the fact that unions' operating procedures, like those of corporations, tend to lag behind the requirements of the emerging economy.

Every enterprise will have adversarial as well as cooperative relations. Cooperation is most effective where the power of the adversaries is not greatly unbalanced. In the absence of countervailing force, management will naturally assert its own interests to the detriment of the interests of workers and even of stockholders, and the long-run viability of the enterprise itself. In every form of worker participation unions can perform such valuable functions as helping workers to be well trained in order to participate more effectively in the affairs of the enterprise and providing critical technical assistance for that participation, whether it be employee stock ownership plans, quality control circles, or worker buyouts.

Drucker's analysis has several factual deficiencies. It requires considerable bias to argue that unions have more privileges and immunities than U.S.-based multinational corporations—which have had the absolute right, in the absence of contract, to fire workers, close plants, and shift capital anywhere in the world. Moreover, corporations are given privileges, such as limited liability for their debts, formerly reserved only to governments. Some items in Drucker's list of special union privileges are not that at all: employers as well as unions are exempt from antitrust laws in *labor* markets. Indeed, there have been numerous suits against unions for violation of antitrust laws in product markets. Employers are as free to lock out workers as workers are to strike. Strike and picketing conduct are more circumscribed by law than the corporation's right to shift capital to low-wage areas or overseas or to shift work between plants and companies during strikes. And strong unions are prohibited by law from helping weaker ones through secondary boycotts, but antiunion corporations boycott unionized construction companies, apparently with legal impunity. As several union leaders, including AFL-CIO President Lane Kirkland, have suggested, repeal of all laws regulating collective bargaining would probably strengthen unions more than it would corporations.[40]

It is very doubtful that workers could gain control of pension funds without the political support of unions. Drucker is conceptually correct; pension funds are technically deferred wages and therefore should belong to the workers and be managed at least jointly by their freely chosen trustees. The reality is that except in the multiemployer pension cases, where control is joint, employers are more likely than workers to be in control. This accounts for the ability of so many companies to divert pension funds to company treasuries during the early eighties, when lower than prevailing interest assumptions caused these funds to be "overfunded."

Although the positive answers are uncertain, we can pose the questions that will be critically important to the American labor movement's future. Will more aggressive and overt antiunion campaigns result in a backlash that will help the unions? Will the unions be able to change their structures and policies fast enough to appeal to the rapidly growing number of service, professional, and technical workers? Will they be able to reestablish their former public image as institutions representing all workers, not just their members? Can they revive the public view that they are democratic, grassroots organizations responsive to their members' interests and at the same time retain sufficient organization, unity, and leadership control to respond quickly and imaginatively to threats and opportunities? Can they establish reputations for productivity, adaptability, efficiency, and promotion of human resource development, justice, full employment, and competitiveness? Will unions be able to heal their political wounds with liberals, minorities, and women in order to help develop a new progressive political alliance? Will the labor movements of the world develop enough countervailing power to counteract multinational and transnational corporations, and enough moral, political, and economic power to be recognized as speaking for workers on an equal footing with business and financial institutions in the formulation of national and international policies? Finally, will public policies change to strengthen the penalties for violating the NLRA and otherwise streamline the NLRB's procedures to make the workers' de jure right to decide for themselves whether or not they want to bargain collectively a de facto right as well?

It is impossible to know how these questions will be answered and what the future of the American unions will be, but those who predict their demise might note the prediction of the president of the American Economic Association, who declared in 1932: "American trade unionism is slowly being influenced by changes which destroy the basis on which it is erected. It is probable that changes in the law have adversely affected unionism. . . . I see no reason to believe that American trade unionism will . . . become in the next decade a more potent social influence."[41] Later in that decade, American union membership growth exploded, doubling in one year (1937) and emerging from World War II as a much more important institution.

My conclusion is that unions are integral and necessary institutions in a democratic market economy. A union-free environment would jeopardize a free enterprise system. Unions will survive because this principle is well established in the democracies. Whether they merely survive or prosper depends heavily on the extent to which unions' institutions and policies succeed in adapting to the conditions of a global information world. These conditions include being able to protect and promote workers' political and economic interests in the workplace and in society at large. At the workplace level, greater attention must be paid to worker security and participation in management decisions, as well as rules governing wages, hours, and working conditions, and the development of human resources. American unions have done a good job of improving productivity, and they also have been more flexible than their European counterparts. Whether they and American managers are able to compete with the Japanese and more participatory European systems depends heavily on how well unions are able to overcome their power and image problems relative to multinationals and how well they adjust to noncollective bargaining forms of worker participation.

Chapter VI

The New Thrust: Worker Participation and Ownership

COLLECTIVE BARGAINING may be the form of worker participation most common to the United States, but other forms of worker participation are becoming well entrenched here, as well as in Europe and Japan. These newer forms became more popular after World War II and include participation in workplace decisions, representation on company boards of directors, and ownership. Such arrangements have been prompted by diverse economic and political developments, as well as by a greater desire for participation among workers themselves. The desire for participation is natural, especially with better-educated work forces, but in Europe and the United States there seems to be a pervasive belief that the economic problems—especially increasing insecurity, rising unemployment, and declining real wage growth—confronting the advanced industrial democracies will not be solved by traditional public policies and management processes. Workers therefore want greater direct control over their own affairs. The fact that some countries (especially Germany, Sweden, and Japan) with more advanced forms of worker participation have higher levels of productivity growth or lower unemployment than the United States has stimulated greater interest in worker participation at home.

One of the difficulties in analyzing the impact of worker participation processes is their bewildering multiplicity and the complexity of the terms used to describe them: asset sharing, autonomous work groups, codetermination, comanagement, company democracy, democracy at work, economic democracy, financial participation, ergonomics, industrial democracy, job redesign, job enrichment, parity, participation, quality of working life (QWL), self-management, shop floor democracy, sociotechnical systems, work reorganization (reform restructure), worker control, worker management, and work councils.[1]

Worker Participation in the United States

Around the world, unions display a variety of attitudes to participatory systems other than collective bargaining. Much depends on the nature of the processes and the structure and objectives of the unions. In places where Communism is strong, such as France and Italy, worker participation is opposed as class collaboration. In Scandinavia the unions are strong, so they have felt secure with participatory processes. German unions, likewise, have favored them and have normally controlled the works councils set up by law to require worker participation in certain matters. Moreover, workers in Germany have stronger representation on corporate boards than in any other IMEC country, though such codetermination has been an active political issue in other European countries. Indeed, the European Economic Community (EEC) is developing worker participation standards for all member countries.*

By contrast, American participatory processes (other than collective bargaining) have most often been initiated by management, are apolitical, and are based mainly on a desire to strengthen organizational effectiveness by improving QWL. In the United States, unions have traditionally been suspicious of QWL programs, which have often been used to defeat unions.[2] In addition, the greater business hostility to unions in the United States has fueled union suspicions and made them more reluctant to encourage cooperative activities. American unions have also been more comfortable with adversarial relationships such as collective bargaining and are wary of management efforts to work directly with employees in ways that exclude unions.

Yet American unions are becoming more flexible on the participation question. United Automobile Workers officers believe, for example, that in order to protect the workers' interests as the automobile industry changes its management system to become more competitive internationally, unions have to be involved in the key decisions that affect workers—including participation on boards of directors and in other programs. The UAW has therefore established cooperative programs with American auto-

---

*The EEC member countries are Belgium, France, Italy, Luxembourg, the Netherlands, and West Germany; the organization is designed to promote economic unity of interest among its members.

mobile companies. Several unions have demanded greater participation, including representation on boards of directors, in exchange for concessions made by union members to strengthen the competitive position of their companies. This has happened at Chrysler and American Motors, and at Pan American, Western, Republic, and Eastern airlines, among others.

The attitude of unions that are cautiously embracing worker participation systems was expressed by Glenn Watts, former president of the Communications Workers of America, who observed that a participatory movement was emerging in the communications industry. Unlike the "gimmicky" QWL programs designed to thwart unions or merely to increase productivity for management's benefit, this more serious effort involved a long-term change in management style based on a philosophy of trust and respect for employees. According to Watts, this positive QWL effort is emerging in many of our largest companies because it makes good business sense:

> In a rapidly changing economy with increasing pressure from international competition, authoritarian management is a liability; it produces organizations which are slow to adapt to change and full of conflict. That is why many of our most successful companies are searching for ways to involve their employees in decisionmaking.[3]

The CWA's experience with QWL has strengthened collective bargaining, according to Watts, because it reduced grievances, thereby freeing union representatives for other activities. Furthermore, it offers "the Labor Movement the opportunity to deal with many issues which have been beyond the reach of traditional collective bargaining." The CWA's program with AT&T provides some useful guidelines for labor–management cooperation, and includes five key points. First, it is a joint program; the union is involved as an *equal* partner from planning through implementation and evaluation. Second, it is voluntary. Third, worker participation is separate from collective bargaining, though obviously successes in both areas are mutually beneficial. Fourth, no one can be laid off or downgraded as a result of ideas that come from the participatory process. Lastly, the goals of the process include both human satisfaction and economic efficiency.[4] The CWA uses these principles as a checklist to determine whether a company is serious about worker participation.

Not surprisingly, Rex Reed, former vice-president of labor relations for AT&T, has similar views:

> It is absolutely essential for our survival that we make some basic changes in our relations between workers and employers. American workers just won't accept regimentation any more. We are going to have to give workers a piece of the action and stop treating them like children, or, even worse, like machines with nothing to contribute to their jobs but their bodies.[5]

That worker participation does not interfere with collective bargaining is suggested by the fact that efforts by AT&T to extract concessions from the CWA led to a twenty-two-day strike in 1983. The contract settling that strike included a number of provisions to strengthen worker participation and labor–management cooperation, including provisions for training, retraining, and education to permit workers to select entirely new career paths. These programs are "to be generic in nature, different from current company training programs which are job specific." During the first year of the new contract, joint labor–management training advisory boards "that recommend training delivery systems—colleges, technical institutes, and home study programs—available to be used in these programs"[6] were set up at AT&T in each of the new Bell companies following the divestiture on January 1, 1984.

The QWL program in the 1980 AT&T contract was extended in the 1983 agreement to all of the divested Bell operating companies "to provide greater employee participation in the working environment, so jobs can be made more satisfying with a corollary result of improved organizational performance and service quality." The 1983 settlement also provided for common interest forums to provide "a framework for early communication and discussion on matters such as planning of new technologies, and innovations to improve competitiveness. . . . Also, we are hopeful these forums will lead to an improved understanding of the company–union environment as a means to minimize or avoid unnecessary disputes and dampen the level of labor–management confrontation." An Occupational Job Evaluation Committee was created to improve "understanding and communication of the way jobs are measured and compensated. . . . CWA is a strong advocate for comparable worth—equal pay for work of the same value—and an Occupational Job Evaluation Plan should help us to fight discrimination against women in the way jobs are classified and compensated." Watts concludes: "The telecommunication industry is moving into the deregulated, competitive environment, an environment with many new participants. That means there will be some losers as well as winners. I believe those companies which practice worker participation will come out the winners in the competition. They will be the innovators."[7]

The CWA is also restructuring itself to accommodate the rapid technological changes affecting the communications industry and the breakup of AT&T. The CWA's Committee on the Future, chaired by Watts, adopted proposals to deal with a wide range of issues facing that organization. Watts disputes the claim by some futurists that unions had been rendered obsolete or irrelevant by the changes associated with the internationalized information world; in his view, "Workers caught up in these massive disruptions need unions more than ever."[8] The Committee on the Future's proposals recognize the inevitable displacement of workers by technological change, plant closure, and international trade, and envision a highly flexible work force, constantly being retrained to meet the requirements of the global information economy. Moreover, benefits are likely to be more portable, following workers from job to job, and the new concept will emphasize employment security instead of job security. The committee also recommends that the CWA cautiously explore possible new approaches to avoid conflict with employers and "to seek greater participation in management decisions."

Tom Murrin, president of Westinghouse's Energy and Advanced Technology Group, is also a strong supporter of worker participation. He has had considerable experience in Japan and believes worker participation to be the main reason for the Japanese advantage over American companies in key industries. The Japanese have demonstrated that "quality and productivity go hand-in-hand. Simply stated, improved productivity and improved profitability are inevitable by-products of improved quality." Murrin believes that some aspects of the Japanese system are applicable to the United States, as demonstrated by certain American businesses' successful experiments:

> Businesses in the United States were faltering, and Japanese businessmen entered with the key ingredients—leadership, capital, and attitude and turned them around. For example, Quasar, Sanyo, Sony, Honda and others have had remarkable performances under Japanese management and American

workers. . . . In Japanese-managed American plants, we find a highly-motivated work force; stringent and clear engineering design requirements that emphasize quality; extensive training programs; participative management; emphasis on teamwork—and management insistence on high quality.

In much of U.S. industry, management treats its workers the same as they did at the turn of the century. Virtually all planning is done by engineers in isolation from the manufacturing supervisors and work force—and, as a result, quality and production have suffered. But the American work force is not the same today as it was in the early part of the century. Today's workers are more knowledgeable—and are better able to participate in the management and training processes.[9]

Westinghouse and other American corporations have established participation processes that have generally achieved quantifiable productivity increases. Westinghouse established an overall corporate goal for productivity improvement, based on expected annual constant dollar value added per employee of 6-plus percent per year; the corporation's Public Systems Company achieved a productivity increase of over 7 percent a year for three years and in 1982 was striving for 10 percent.[10] Douglas Danforth, vice-chairman and chief operating officer of Westinghouse, expressed an attitude that is quite different from the traditional authoritarian view of many American managers: "the people actually doing a job are the ones in the best possible position to determine how that job can be done better. Their ideas are presented so well that management readily accepts the recommendations. But, most important, the ideas belong to the employees, so the implementation proceeds smoothly."[11]

After surveying the reasons for declining U.S. productivity and international competitiveness in some basic American industries, William H. Batten, chairman of the

New York Stock Exchange, concluded that "worker participation programs are essential for a climate in the workplace that will allow the United States to continue to outproduce all other nations of the world." Similarly, a General Motors labor relations official declared, "I don't believe our authoritarian corporations can continue to coexist with democratic institutions in a democratic society, and the reverse is true too. . . . In this country we must democratize our corporations." But this official warned against what Glenn Watts called "gimmicky" approaches: "pretending to give workers a role in decision-making, pretending to involve them, but, in reality, doing it all for cosmetic purposes; we have to be honest with each other or it will inevitably fail."[12]

Although support for the concept is growing, there is no agreement among American unions or managers about the desirability of worker participation. As noted earlier, while Watts accepts participation within the plant, he has serious reservations about serving on corporate boards since he believes it would be difficult for him to "decide to close a plant, even if it made economic sense, because of the effect it would have on workers." Despite his support for cooperation, Watts approached this matter with considerable caution. Like most American labor leaders, he was skeptical of the good faith of employers:

> You can't ask unions to walk hand-in-hand into the unknown land of worker participation while going full-speed ahead with union-busting anti-labor programs. There has to be greater acceptance of unions in this country. I want very much to cooperate in consensus-building and problem-solving, but management can't expect cooperation when the hand it puts around my shoulder also has a knife in it.[13]

By contrast, Douglas Fraser, former president of the UAW, believes the presence of a worker on the board could prevent the closing of a plant, and he was able to do so as a consequence of his membership on Chrysler's board. Even where closures are necessary, worker board members get advance notice and might force the company to provide more relocation help for laid-off workers. Fraser advocates board membership for workers because he believes they must be represented wherever the decisions are being made.

The traditional union view about worker participation was expressed by Tom Donahue, secretary-treasurer of the AFL-CIO. Donahue thought management was not, and should not be, a union concern:

> We do not seek to be a partner in management, to be, most likely, the junior partner in success and the senior partner in failure. We do not want to blur in any way the distinction between the respective roles of labor and management in the plant. We guard our independence fiercely—independent of government, independent of any political party, and independent of management.[14]*

Noting that Americans have developed "the world's most elaborate, extensive, and complex" system of collective agreements, Donahue stressed the American system of bargaining among equals. Subsequently, the AFL-CIO has stressed the primacy of collective bargaining as the basic form of American participation.

Other union representatives, especially from the United Electrical Workers and the Machinists, actively oppose any form of union–management cooperation other than collective bargaining. In their view, expressed in an article

---

*However, in 1980, Donahue called for a "marriage of convenience" with management "in the search for solutions to economic problems, management problems that . . . have created this productivity problem and the quality of work life problem for all of us. We insist, however, that this marriage of convenience ought to be one of those so-called 'new marriages,' in which neither partner is the exclusive head of the household."[15]

by a Machinist and a UEW representative, labor–management cooperation has not worked in the past and is not
likely to work in the future because:

> Our economic system is based on management control of the
> work force and the work place. It is the nature of manage-
> ment to push workers for more service or production at less
> cost. Just as naturally, workers want to preserve a reasonable
> pace of work and improve living standards. The push and
> pull of this inherent conflict transcend any form of owner-
> ship or degree of worker participation in management. . . .
>
> In the long run, both workers and management are better
> served by a healthy, tempered, adversarial relationship in
> which each is conscious of and bargaining hard for their
> separate interests. . . .
>
> . . . labor–management cooperation cannot revive a labor
> movement sapped of its bargaining strength and organizing
> vigor. What unions need is a return to the basic principles
> that animated the early struggles of the American labor
> movement and the building of the CIO: class solidarity, in-
> dustrial unionism, aggressive organizing, grass-roots coali-
> tions, hard bargaining, tough striking, political independence
> and independence from management influence.
>
> In contrast, the turn to employee ownership and participa-
> tion in management represents a turn toward company un-
> ionism.[16]

Similar positions are expressed by Barbara Reisman and
Lance Compa of the UEW, who contend that the best
course for labor and management is "a well-tempered
adversarial relationship. The two sides have fundamen-
tally different interests: healthy conflict is organic to the
system." Moreover, "rather than cheerleading proposals
for labor–management cooperation, union leaders should
push for economic advances and shop-floor autonomy."
They warn: "In union shops, leaders with a reputation for
endorsing concession bargaining and labor–management

cooperation will eventually face rebellion from their members."[17] But in other unions, like the UAW, the Steelworkers, and the CWA, union leaders report that labor–management cooperation is so popular with the rank and file that reluctant leaders have been forced by their members to move from adversarial to more cooperative stances.

Another influential view of worker participation, by a building trades union leader, was expressed by John T. Joyce, president of the International Union of Bricklayers and Allied Craftsmen. In 1978 Joyce's union formed a cooperative organization, the International Masonry Institute, with the Mason Contractors Association of America. Joyce explained to an international meeting on worker participation that collective bargaining was a form of codetermination that had produced important results for American workers, but it is limited because it "does not cover enough U.S. workers . . . management retains entire control over such strategic entrepreneurial decisions as product research and development, pricing, investment in plant and equipment . . . collective bargaining . . . is an adversary system in which in the final analysis disagreements are settled on the basis of economic power." He added:

> The climate of U.S. labor–management relations is worse than it was ten or twenty years ago . . . the labor law reform "battle" of 1977–78 is perhaps the single episode which most clearly symbolizes the growing polarization. The issue raised by the reform effort was "just how difficult should it be for workers to organize?" Management's harsh, doctrinaire and almost universal answer was that self organization should be as difficult as possible.

> This led one highly respected senior official of the AFL-CIO's Industrial Union Department to observe what many feel, "For a number of years now I have believed there can be an accommodation and cooperative attitude between labor and

management. But I don't believe that any more, the labor law reform effort has showed me beyond a shadow of a doubt that we are enemies."[18]

Joyce believes improvements in collective bargaining require not only labor law reform but the right of labor and management "to bargain to an impasse on any subject of mutual interest that is not clearly contrary to public interest . . . with collective bargaining as its core, worker participation can be extended on one side to the question of how to improve the quality of work life and on the other side to the strategic questions that determine whether a given plant, firm, or industry will stay in business and at what level of activity." Workers have a stake in these strategic decisions, according to Joyce, because they affect jobs, industries, and communities in which workers have invested their lives:

> In this pragmatic sense codetermination is not alien to the U.S., nor does labor in the U.S. oppose it. We are, to be sure, skeptical of the new psychotechnicians of industry who seek to increase "worker satisfaction" without giving workers the means to treat with their employers on an equal footing. Without the hard muscle of collective bargaining and union representation, quality of work life projects are inherently manipulative and participation in policy making forums at best an opportunity to exchange views and information.[19]

Joyce identifies three participative processes: first, QWL or participation at the job site or shop floor; second, strategic decisions at the board level; and third, the adversarial process of negotiation.

> All three must be an integral part of the same process. When you move from "wages" and "working conditions" into other parts of the co-determination spectrum—into such matters as production, marketing and sales, financial management and so on—you move from an adversarial . . . [to] other approaches . . . [which] become more suitable because,

in one sense, you are not then talking about how to divide profits and benefits, but how to create them.

Codetermination thus defined will take many forms in different industries and countries. "There is, however, one constant: Genuine, meaningful worker participation must have collective bargaining at its core."[20]

The United Automobile Workers

The UAW has pursued worker participation in the automobile industry, which has been subjected to intense international competition, especially from Japan. The UAW had been in the forefront of aggressively improving wages and working conditions for its members, but made wage concessions in the early eighties in order to help the industry adjust to the more competitive environment. The UAW also sought to strengthen cooperative arrangements with the automobile industry and to gain a greater voice in management affairs, including representation on boards of directors.

Worker participation at Chrysler was strengthened by labor–management cooperation to gain support for the $1.5 billion federal loan guarantee program to save their company from bankruptcy in the late seventies. The UAW gained a seat on the Chrysler board and established a joint Product Quality Improvement Program (PQIP) which operates outside the collective bargaining system. Launched in 1980, the PQIP is a voluntary process of joint problem solving to improve quality. It has labor–management mechanisms in the plant as well as at the international level. Local PQIP committees provide communication and training on quality issues for the plant; launch "quality action teams" to tackle specific problems; stimulate individual worker participation to make quality improvements; and see to it that the efforts of individuals and teams are recognized.

The PQIP has produced numerous measurable improvements in Chrysler plants. In one plant sixteen teams eliminated over $1 million in scrap. In another case a team recommended a change in the product itself to solve a shop problem. And in numerous cases teams have improved "first time capability" by doing the job right the first time and achieving levels of acceptable quality of 85 to 99 percent. UAW vice-president Marc Stepp reported:

> Other benefits are less tangible—those being the enthusiasm and dedication with which UAW-Chrysler workers approach their jobs. . . . We have rekindled pride in workmanship in a mass production system which is impersonal.
>
> We are not confined to the arena of confronting each other over our differences—although we still do that and will continue to do so.
>
> But I think it is safe to say that we have found a decent way to "see the woods for the trees" by reaching for a common ground from which we all benefit.
>
> We could not have saved Chrysler by simply making wage concessions alone—our joint efforts on quality have been positive steps to strengthen this corporation, save jobs, and help get thousands of people back to work.[21]

In 1982, Chrysler and the UAW agreed to a joint National Pilot Projects Council to address the major challenges the company faces by developing one or two model projects to guarantee "Lifeline Job Security" to 80 percent of each facility's work force. These model projects include "experimental concepts in training, changing work practices, altered wage and benefit systems, modified classification structure and employee participation programs."[22] The Council also jointly examines innovative developments in other industries, commissions studies, and develops information through site visits.

In 1982, the UAW and Chrysler also established a Roundtable "to provide an opportunity for discussion of certain business developments that are of material interest and significance to the union, the corporation, and . . . employees." The Roundtable is a new structure that seeks to "improve communication and the exchange of information . . . determine approaches for improving operational competitiveness; identify and record new approaches for improving product quality; and discuss the corporation's general operations and certain other business developments on a broad, corporate-wide basis."[23]

The Ford Motor Company, General Motors, and Chrysler all emphasize better relations with the UAW in order to restore the dramatic loss of their competitiveness following the oil price shocks of the 1970s. These shocks exposed serious weaknesses in the companies' management systems and strategies. As a consequence, American auto companies' world market share declined from 27.9 percent in 1970 to 19 percent in 1982. Therefore all of the American companies developed strategies to improve quality, increase productivity, and reduce costs. In general, they made progress on all of these objectives during the 1980s. Chrysler, with a federal loan guarantee, reduced its size, lowered its break-even point, and became significantly more competitive by dramatic improvements in quality and productivity and by cost reductions. General Motors, by contrast, sought to maintain market share in the larger car market through reorganization, automation, importation of small cars and parts (mainly from Asia), and by simultaneously attempting to develop a competitive small American car through its Saturn project.

Even though all of the Big Three companies worked at better relations with the UAW, a number of factors hindered their success. Chrysler's relations with the UAW were strained because, until 1985, the concessions required by the 1979 Chrysler loan guarantee agreement caused that company's wages to fall below those of Ford and GM. When Chrysler became very profitable during the 1980s, its workers naturally demanded wage parity with Ford and GM and, after a 1985 strike, the UAW achieved this objective. Closer relations between General Motors and the UAW were jeopordized both by the company's demands for wage restraints and the high priority GM gives to outsourcing and foreign imports in order to sustain its competitive position.

Ford gave lower priority than GM did to a foreign strategy partly because it was less vertically integrated (and therefore had less need to import parts from foreign producers) and partly because of the importance Ford assigned to its close cooperation with the UAW. As Ford officials sought to transform the company during the early 1980s, they discovered the tight links between productivity, quality, competitiveness, and worker involvement. This new strategy was reflected in the 1979 Employee Involvement (EI) program and in Ford's 1982 and 1984 collective bargaining agreements. According to company officials, these contracts codified a new standard of behavior for Ford management, which emphasized the mutual interests (rather than *rights*) of labor and management.[24]

By the end of 1986, virtually all of Ford's U.S. facilities had implemented the EI process. By that time, Ford had over 175 full-time union and company EI facilitators and almost 1,200 Ford employees had attended workshops to learn how to make the system work and 9,000 managers and supervisors had been trained in the new participatory management style. In addition, 3,000 Ford-represented workers had participated in the UAW–Ford Employee Development and Training Program (EDTP). EDTP, with a budget of $30 to $40 million per year, makes it possible for active and laid-off Ford employees to seek education and training opportunities.

UAW and Ford officials agree that the EI processes have improved collective bargaining, though they also stress that these mechanisms are not intended to be substitutes for the more adversarial bargaining arrangements. In addition, because of worker sensitivity to the issue, union and company officials are careful to emphasize that EI's primary objective is not to increase productivity. For whatever reason, the Ford Motor Company's fortunes improved dramatically by 1986 when, for the first time since 1924, its earnings exceeded those of General Motors (GM has been twice the size of Ford for most of the postwar period). A common assessment by Ford management is that 85 percent of the company's remarkable turnaround in 1985-86 was due to EI and better management.

After two years of operation and an extensive education program to get workers involved, the results of EI were described as follows: "The support of both management and the union has resulted in improved shop-floor relations between employees and supervisors, fewer absences, fewer grievances, and increased job morale and performance. . . . Overall, EI seems to increase both product quality and employee satisfaction."[25] By 1986, the Ford program had produced impressive company-wide results. Production costs and absenteeism had been reduced, quality was up 52 percent, and job satisfaction ratings had risen from between 20 and 30 percent before the program to 75 percent in 1985. In addition, workers' bonuses averaged $2,100 in 1984 and $1,200 in 1985.

The 1982 Ford–UAW agreement strengthened labor–management cooperation by introducing five innovative programs. First, it established a profit sharing plan. Second, it created a job protection provision that included six months' advance notice of plant closing and counseling and placement assistance for displaced workers, including the right to apply for jobs in other Ford facilities. There was also developed an income security program that guarantees minimum income and insurance coverage until age sixty-two or retirement, if earlier, for employees with fifteen or more years of seniority and a "redundancy program" to strengthen the supplementary unemployment benefit (SUB) funding. Fourth, a new, joint, independent "National UAW-Ford Development and Training Center" was founded to provide training, retraining, and developmental opportunities for active and displaced employees. Finally, it established Mutual Growth Forums at the local and national levels "as a new adjunct to the collective bargaining process, but not a replacement for it . . . [to] provide a new framework to promote sound management–union relations through better communication, systematic fact-finding, and advance discussion of certain business developments that are of material interest to the union, the employees, and the Company."[26]

General Motors

The emerging collective bargaining relationship between GM and the UAW is considered by many industrial relations specialists to be "a major shift in labor relations, and . . . is likely to exert a substantial influence on agreements in other industries."[27] The traditional wage-setting relationship established in the auto industry in 1948 was based on formula wage determinations consisting of an annual improvement factor, which was set at 3 percent a year after the mid-sixties, and a cost-of-living adjustment geared to the consumer price index. This system was applied to all companies in the auto industry, regardless of their individual financial conditions, and resulted in an 81 percent real wage increase in the industry between 1945 and 1983. These formulas, together with multiple-year agreements, brought industrial relations stability to the auto industry at a time of expanding sales; but there remained considerable underlying labor discontent because of shop floor problems. Indeed, the system already was showing signs of trouble in the sixties and seventies when young, well-educated workers were becoming increasingly dissatisfied with authoritarian management discipline and fragmented work processes. Productivity and quality therefore deteriorated, giving foreign competitors important quality and price advantages.

In 1982, when GM incurred its first losses since the twenties and Chrysler, Ford, and American Motors were in serious trouble, the UAW made its first concession to GM. It had become clear to the UAW that job security for its members required alterations in the traditional labor–management relations system. UAW leaders became convinced that they would have to gain security for their members by greater attention to labor–management cooperation, flexibility, and increased productivity. For their part, GM and other major American auto companies recognized that their economic viability required the UAW's cooperation. This posture was strikingly different from that of management in other American industries, who were becoming more overtly antiunion at this time. Like most American employers, the automobile companies would probably have preferred to operate in a union free environment, but the UAW was too well organized and entrenched in the industry to permit its elimination without high costs to the companies.

The threat faced by the UAW was that a failure to make the industry competitive would either cause a loss of jobs to foreign imports or induce American firms to accelerate the shift of more of their operations overseas. At the same time, the UAW was encouraging highly competitive foreign companies to open plants in the United States as a means of maintaining employment for its members. During this period of declining employment in the American auto industry (from a peak of 1,018,800 in 1978 to 638,400 in February 1982) and falling UAW membership (which declined from 1.5 million in 1978 to 1.2 million in 1985), the UAW gave much higher priority to job security and the competitiveness of unionized employers than to its traditional preoccupation with improving wages and fringe benefits.

In its 1982 agreement with GM, therefore, the union took the unusual step of abandoning a wage system based entirely on contractual wage increases for one that included wages and bonuses based on company profits and productivity. The bonus compensation system, together with base wages, creates a direct trade-off between wages and employment. As in Japan, the bonus system gives management greater price flexibility, making it possible to preserve output and employment instead of the traditional approach of wage and price rigidity at the expense of output and employment. Another UAW–GM agreement in 1984 provided for a relatively small 2.25 percent wage increase, despite company profits of $4.9 billion. But that agreement strengthened the workers' job security through a $1 billion fund to pay and retrain workers whose jobs were lost because of technological changes or increased acquisitions from abroad. The job security and retraining programs are jointly planned and operated by the UAW and GM management. In exchange for its help in making GM more competitive, the UAW was given written assurances by management concerning future production in the United States, including investment commitments to keep the company competitive. The UAW reached similar agreements with Ford and Chrysler.

The 1982 UAW–GM contract set up numerous labor–management cooperation committees, including a New Business Venture Development Group to develop nontraditional business areas. Union representation in this group not only makes it possible to shape the company's future, but also sharpens the union members' business skills. In this new partnership arrangement, "the concept of earning pay increases has largely replaced that of pay increases as a matter of entitlement."[28] The bonus system also gives workers a direct stake in the company's profitability. In addition to changes in the wage payment system, GM and the UAW cooperated in the establishment of automated manufacturing systems and greater worker participation processes.

The boldest UAW–GM agreement was in the 1985 pact covering the supermodern Saturn plant to be located in Spring Hill, Tennessee. The highly automated Saturn plant is designed to supersede Japanese and other auto-making systems. Although its original projected size was cut in half by 1987, this facility is expected to be about twice as productive as traditional auto plants. The facility is projected to reduce the labor time needed to produce a car from 130 to 60 hours (some estimates were even as low as 30 to 40 hours) in order to reduce the $1,500 to $2,000 cost differential between U.S. and Japanese autos.

This new system will be a dramatic break with the one that has dominated auto production in the U.S. throughout this century. The Saturn agreement is all the more noteworthy because it involves an effort by a unionized plant to be more than competitive with a nonunion Nissan plant also located in Tennessee.* The UAW welcomes the competition with Nissan and expects that its Saturn local could form the basis for organizing the Nissan plant.

The Saturn industrial relations system will build on innovations already established in the industry. All workers will be salaried; 80 percent will have "lifetime" employment, except for severe economic conditions or "unforeseen or catastrophic events, and union representatives must concur in that judgment," according to a UAW news release of July 26, 1985. There will be a high degree of flexibility in work assignments, and worker participation will be encouraged. Work will be done in teams of six to fifteen workers who are substantially self-managed. The teams will make decisions on such matters as job assignments, schedules, inspection, maintenance, absenteeism,

---

*Two other Japanese companies, Toyota in Fremont, California, and Mazda at Flat Rock, Michigan, operate with UAW agreements. Honda in Marysville, Ohio, operated nonunion in 1985. Toyota has also announced that it will build a new plant in Kentucky by 1988.

and health and safety. Workers at each station will have the ability to stop the flow of the work if they need more time to ensure quality. Each team will elect a counselor to represent the union in the work unit, with responsibilities similar to those of shop stewards in conventional plants. Workers are also to be represented on plant committees. Unlike the traditional, highly fragmented work system, there will be very few job classifications: one for production workers and three to five for skilled workers.

The Saturn agreement provides for recruitment primarily from the UAW's 400,000 active and laid-off GM members. The union and management will jointly develop the recruitment, selection, and orientation procedures. In fact, the agreement provides for full partnership by the union from the work unit on the shop floor to the Strategic Advisory Committee overseeing long-run strategic planning. But the new contract has not eliminated a complete grievance procedure, including binding arbitration. Although consensus is emphasized and desired, the agreement provides that either party may block a proposed decision. This agreement is, in addition, based on the "living document" concept developed by the UAW in the fifties; problems will be solved through ongoing negotiations, and workers retain the right to strike at any time.

Starting rates for UAW–GM members who join Saturn will be $13.45 per hour for production workers and $15.49 per hour for skilled trades. The incentive wage system will pay workers a salary equal to 80 percent of the industry's average direct wages plus a bonus based on productivity and profits. Provision is made for a full range of fringe benefits.

The Saturn agreement actually represents more of a change for GM's management than for the UAW, which as early as the fifties had proposed a flexible compensation system and annual bonus-based salaries for its members. UAW President Walter Reuther proposed such a system to General Motors in 1955. He thought a guaranteed annual wage plus a bonus would provide greater wage and price flexibility and protect his members from the chronic risk of layoffs due to fluctuations in demand and model changes. GM rejected Reuther's proposal "on grounds that it would put labor and management on the same level, undermine corporate authority and ultimately interfere with production and hold profits down."[29] In fact, GM's chairman told Reuther that the guaranteed annual wage and bonus proposal was a threat to the capitalist system.

While the Saturn agreement builds on experiences at GM and other companies, it is not at all clear to what extent this model will become an industry-wide pattern. Chrysler and Ford have developed some of the same industrial relations features, especially changes in the compensation system, flexibility in job classifications, and greater worker involvement. During the 1985 negotiations with the UAW, Chrysler expressed an interest in a Saturn-type agreement, and GM sought to make the Saturn agreement an industry precedent, but the UAW demurred. The preliminary Saturn agreement proposal by management had called for the knowledge, technology, and experience gained through this project to be spread throughout GM, but the union insisted that this clause be removed. GM then sent the union a letter stipulating that Saturn was intended to preserve small car production in the United States and would not serve as a precedent at GM or other companies.[30]

In 1986, Chrysler and Mitsubishi, in cooperation with the UAW, were planning a joint venture, Diamond-Star Motors, Inc., which would have features similar to the Saturn agreement. Diamond-Star expects to begin production in 1988 or 1989. The main uncertainty was whether a National Right to Work Legal Defense Fund (NRTWLDF) challenge to the Saturn prehire agreement would be upheld by the National Labor Relations Board and the courts. As a practical matter, the NLRB's decision is not likely to make much difference, because both Saturn and Diamond-Star are likely to hire workers favorable to the UAW, as will Toyota when they open their new plant in Kentucky, projected for 1988. A similar agreement has been readied at the new Mazda plant in Flat Rock, Michigan. In general, if management wants to deal with a union, it usually can find legal ways to do so, despite harassing actions like those from the NRTWLDF —and GM considers its agreement with the UAW to be crucial to its success. These charges that the Saturn agreement violated the National Labor Relations Act (discussed later) were dismissed by the NLRB in 1986.

General Motors and Toyota

Another example of the union's willingness to make concessions to companies in exchange for job security was the 1985 agreement between the UAW and New United Motor Manufacturing, Inc. (NUMMI), the Fremont, California joint venture by GM and Toyota to manufacture the Chevrolet Nova subcompact. This, the UAW's first formal contract with a Japanese auto maker, was part of that union's effort to encourage Japanese companies both to locate in the United States and to contract with the union. The Toyota-GM NUMMI contract gave local management a freer hand in internal policy making and covered all of the plant's 1,200 skilled trade and production workers. Most UAW agreements had separate contracts for each group; but the NUMMI contract formalized a 1983 letter of intent between the UAW and management permitting fewer classifications and greater internal flexibility in exchange for union recognition and the company's agreement to hire most workers from among employees who had worked at GM's Fremont plant before it was closed. NUMMI also agreed to pay wages comparable to those paid in other U.S. auto plants.

Some experts criticized the Fremont deal because of its probable impact on U.S. competitiveness. In this view, the GM-Toyota joint venture is not a triumph of cooperation but a failure to answer the challenge of the Japanese auto industry: "There is little doubt that the joint venture benefits [Toyota and GM]. However, the cars will be assembled in Fremont, but most of the advanced-technology, high value parts of the factory and the cars—robots, engines, transaxles— will be imported from Japan, allowing the company to avoid some of the impact of import quotas." It is not clear to these critics that the Fremont deal will result in a net increase in U.S. employment. In addition, the U.S. will lose control of the manufacturing process. "The plant will be organized by Japanese thought and controlled by Japanese designs," according to Stephen Cohen of the University of California. "What will be left to Americans are the kinds of jobs that eventually will move to Mexico or other low-wage nations."[31] There were, nevertheless, some immediate improvements at NUMMI: absenteeism was less than 2 percent in 1986, compared with 20 percent when the GM plant closed in 1982. Before it closed, the Fremont plant had one of GM's worst labor relations records, wildcat strikes were frequent, and over a thousand grievances were pending. During the first year and a half, NUMMI had almost no grievances, several thousand workers had been recalled, and quality was high.

The Impact of Quality of Worklife Programs

A 1984 study by Thomas Kochan, Harry Katz, and Nancy Mower provides some quantitative information concerning the impact of QWL programs on workers and on union membership. This survey of 900 union members in five locals from plants with QWL programs found that while workers were very interested in having a say in the way the work gets done (even more than were interested in pay scales), it was not clear that QWL involvement actually improved employees' influence over workplace issues: "only in the case in which the union was involved as a joint partner in the work team/autonomous work group processes were these differences consistently large and significant."[32]

The most direct effect of greater worker participation was "movement away from the detailed job control unionism characteristic of U.S. collective bargaining." This movement requires different roles for unions, managers, and workers. The union must relinquish detailed job control, "one of its traditional bases of power and security in return for greater information and perhaps influence over a wide array of issues that traditionally have been reserved to management." For workers, "this new arrangement means exposure to a wider variety of tasks and more advanced training, and therefore, wider opportunities for skill acquisition and enhancement. On the other hand, it also implies greater responsibility for decisions that would otherwise have been left to a supervisor or low-level manager." For managers, greater worker participation "implies a trade of some of its traditional prerogatives and a redesign of the role of the first line supervisor in return for greater flexibility in human resource management and a reduction in the detailed rules governing job definition."[33]

Finally, the experiences of Ford, GM, and other companies suggest that a really effective worker participation system will have a much greater impact on management than many managers seem to realize. The process, once started, acquires a life of its own. As Jackson Grayson, president of the American Productivity Center, has put it, effective QWL programs will dramatically transform labor–management relations and cause workers to become much more involved in decisions affecting such matters as job security; union involvement; how to organize production; compensation systems; management decisions and control; hiring practices; whether to have supervisors and, if so, how many; information sharing; training and re-training; labor–management equality; and management compensation and perquisites.[34]

Guidelines for Worker Participation

A detailed analysis in 1983 by the Economic Policy Council of the United Nations Association derived the following principles for successful worker participation. First, it is imperative to involve employees (and in the case of a union, the union's leadership as well as its rank and file) in worker participation activities from the outset. Instead of trying to make workers accept programs that are developed by management and then implemented from the top down, companies should endeavor to in-volve employees at all levels from the initial development stage and throughout implementation. Only when em-ployees begin to regard these activities as the result of mutual effort and see them as tailored to their specific needs will they be genuinely responsive.

Second, efforts to involve employees in problem solving and decision making related to their work and work envi-ronment must be regarded as a continuous process rather than as a short-lived program. Unless employees perceive worker participation as a basic reorientation of existing adversarial worker–management relations, unless they are convinced that their voices will be heard—indeed sought out and taken seriously—they are likely to regard these procedures as gimmicks concocted by management to ma-nipulate the work force.

Third, worker participation programs must not be de-signed solely to increase productivity; rather, higher pro-ductivity should be regarded as one of the *results* of this effort. They must be geared to improving the overall qual-ity of working conditions. By enriching the professional lives of the work force through training and education, by helping workers to solve problems that affect their job performance, and by improving the relations between management and labor, an environment can be created that will benefit the work force, the company, and the consumers.

Fourth, managers must move from an authoritarian to a more participative style of management. The effort to cultivate a management style based on the active involvement of employees must go beyond a simple open-door policy to the solicitation of workers' opinions and insights. Improved communication and actively encouraged employee input in decision making and problem resolution are integral to this process. Furthermore, managers must begin to move beyond emphasis on short-run goals to a longer-term perspective. And corporate policy makers should develop incentives for managers to take a long perspective and avoid excessive compensation for managers regardless of company performance.

Fifth, proper training and education programs are essential to the success of worker participation. Not only must employees be trained to participate effectively in the quality-control circles and problem-solving teams, but they must also be involved in education programs that expand their professional skills and capabilities. Furthermore, this training should be extended to managers as well as to hourly employees. By giving its employees easy access to means of continually upgrading their skills and by encouraging their employees to make use of these facilities, many companies have found that they can greatly improve the skills of their work force, thereby increasing their value to the organization. The importance of ongoing education cannot be overemphasized.

Sixth, worker participation must be voluntary. Unless workers enter these activities voluntarily and with a positive attitude, worker participation schemes will only engender resentment and suspicion.

Seventh, worker participation programs should be supported by a corporate climate that helps workers fulfill personal needs. It is only logical that employees who lead balanced personal lives will perform better at work than those employees who face serious difficulties in their private lives.

Eighth, no one should be laid off or downgraded as a result of ideas that come from the participation process.

Finally, worker participation is separate from, and should not interfere with, collective bargaining. In fact, worker participation is most effective where there is collective bargaining.

Ownership

Labor experts have long believed that worker ownership, or economic democracy, would improve productivity and broaden the distribution of economic power and income. In recent years some labor leaders, especially in Europe, have advocated economic democracy or worker ownership and control as a way to ensure both a more equitable distribution of income and the reinvestment of corporate earnings in order to improve economic viability and job security. Indeed, because of the dim prospects for really effective international labor movements to check the powers of management in multinational companies, some labor leaders see economic democracy as the only practical way to force such corporations to give greater attention to national, worker, and community concerns. These leaders believe worker control is necessary to guarantee the economic viability of enterprises in their countries and to avoid closure of profitable plants just because higher returns can be earned in other countries or activities. Swedish and Danish labor leaders have advocated economic democracy to transfer ownership and control gradually to workers. One such plan was a major issue in the 1976 Swedish elections, when this issue helped defeat the Social Democrats, and again in 1982 and 1985, when it helped them win.* In the United States, worker ownership has been regarded as a way to strengthen democratic institutions, gradually redistribute profits to workers, and make workers more committed to the affairs of their enterprises. Proponents generally believe that increased productivity and improved quality require maximum employee commitment.

Some supporters of employee stock ownership plans (ESOPs) to give workers greater ownership are particularly concerned about the grossly unequal distribution of corporate wealth, which, they fear, is likely to become even worse in the future. About 1 percent of the population of the United States owns over half of corporate stock and the 200 largest corporations increased their share of corporate assets from 48 percent in 1950 to 61 percent in 1974.[35] The Congressional Joint Economic Committee reported in 1976 that only 0.5 percent of the population owned 50 percent of the market value of corporate stock and 72 percent was owned by 6 percent of the population. In addition, the tendency of some large corporations to close down profitable companies has stimulated interest in worker ownership to provide continuing jobs and economic bases for communities and workers. It is reasoned that worker-owners could halt corporate flight to low-wage countries and areas because they would be motivated not by short-run profit maximizing but by the desire to strengthen an enterprise for long-run and secure employment opportunities. In other words, a worker-controlled firm interested in making profits and preserving, or even maximizing, employment could compete successfully with pro-

---

*For a discussion of the original version of this plan see Rudolf Meidner, *Employee Investment Funds* (London: Allen and Unwin, 1978).

fit-maximizing firms, especially if the latter had less internal cohesion and gave less attention to the development and use of technology and to productivity improvements. Perhaps because of these beliefs, there is surprisingly widespread support for worker ownership in the United States, as suggested by the relatively easy passage of legislation to encourage stock ownership plans through offering favorable tax treatment. Under federal tax laws, principal devoted to, as well as interest derived from, ESOPs are tax deductible, and banks and other financial institutions are exempt from income taxes for half of the interest earned on loans to ESOPs. This results in ESOP loan rates at 80–90 percent of the prime rate.

Senator Russell Long, a very strong supporter of ESOPs, outlined the basic case for wider ownership of corporate stock. He was particularly worried that "in this, the world's most avowed capitalistic nation, we have only a scanty sprinkling of capitalists." He cited a National Bureau of Economic Research study, which found that the most important wealth for a majority of American families "is now their entitlement under our pay-as-you-go social security system. Thus, for the majority of Americans, their most significant asset is an assurance that their children will be taxed on their behalf." Senator Long cited numerous studies that have found companies with substantial employee ownership to be much more profitable and productive than comparable conventionally owned firms. Moreover, in May 1983,

the American Business Conference published a 2-year study designed to show how and why mid-sized growth companies have outpaced the nation in sales, profits, jobs, and exports. In the high-growth companies studied, employees own over 30 percent of the company stock—a surprisingly high proportion for companies averaging over $200 million in annual sales volume.[36]

Additionally, Senator Long feared the grave political and social consequences of increasing inequality, which he felt could be halted with a more equitable distribution of ownership. The long-term objective of ESOPs was "to create income-generating mechanisms to supplement the income earned through employment. The goal is to link a growing number of American households to economic growth—as well as the capital income—represented by newly-created capital."[37] Despite their tax advantages, however, probably only a few hundred of the over 7,000 ESOPs in the country have a majority of employee owners. However, several well-publicized cases have caused worker-controlled ESOPs to play a much larger role in the eighties than in the seventies. An examination of some of these experiences provides greater insight into the uses and limitations of ESOPs in the United States.

Weirton Steel

One of the most important, and so far the most successful, of these efforts was the sale of the Weirton Steel Company, a subsidiary of National Steel, to its employees in 1984. This company had over 7,000 employees (down from 13,000) and sales over $1 billion a year. Nine months after the employee takeover the company's earnings were rising, and 1,200 workers had been recalled.[38] Weirton was a relatively modern steel company, though it was in a declining market because its main product—tinplate for cans—was losing out to aluminum. Although Weirton had a book value of $322 million, National Steel sold it to the workers for $193.9 million, including $74.7 million in cash and a 20 percent wage cut. National Steel had an earnings-on-equity requirement of 20 percent, and Weirton had been earning only about 4 to 5 percent. It was estimated, however, that the favorable price to the workers could produce earnings of 12 to 15 percent. An important problem for Weirton was the fact that—apparently to prevent an outside union from taking over bargaining rights from the company's local independent union—management had granted wages and benefits above the industry average in an industry that had higher than average wages. It was estimated that average wages of $27 an hour in 1984 were $3 an hour above the industry average and $13 an hour above the Japanese.

Weirton proved to be one of the most profitable steel companies in the United States during 1984 and 1985. Productivity increased 15 percent the first year, labor costs declined 32 percent, and earnings on sales were 10.1 percent, more than double the industry average of 4.5 percent. In 1985, the company's net worth exceeded the $100 million required before the workers could receive a dividend, so that profit-sharing payments of $20,345,000 were made that year. These represented one-third of net profits; workers are to receive one-half of profits when net worth reaches $250 million. Net profits were $61 million in 1985 and $60 million in 1984. The company had also invested $136 million in modernization. The employees acquired Weirton through an ESOP trust that borrowed money to buy Weirton stock. As the company repays the trust to pay the debt, the stock will be distributed to the workers.

At Weirton, the workers originally elected only three of twelve directors. The rest were chosen by the lenders and Lazard Freres, the investment banker that engineered the deal. The workers will gain all of the seats after four years, when they will also vote on whether to allow workers to sell their stock to the public.

By selling out to the employees, National Steel was able to shed assets that did not meet its high earnings expectations and, if the company remains profitable for five years, avoid sizable pension liabilities. Moreover, since National was Weirton's principal customer, it had some ability to ensure that its former subsidiary remained profitable.[39]

The Transportation Industry

ESOPs have also been used to deal with some of the problems the transportation industry has suffered as a result of the intensified competitive environment caused by high energy prices and deregulation in the late seventies and eighties. Adjusting to these changes was a major problem for old companies, whose cost structures were based on regulations and who had many high costs built in because of their age.

The established companies in deregulated transportation industries responded to the new, more competitive environment in a variety of ways. Some, like the Greyhound Bus Company, opted for contests to weaken unions. Others, like Continental Airlines, opted to use Chapter XI of the bankruptcy laws to break existing labor agreements. The highest unemployment since the Great Depression made it easy for Continental and Greyhound to recruit strikebreakers. Continental slashed wages and benefits by 50 percent, eliminated seniority and sick leave provisions, increased working hours, and instituted many new work rules.

Pan American used a different approach. In the summer of 1981 Pan Am was experiencing serious financial problems for the second time in less than a decade. Union and management representatives, with the aid of a lawyer skilled in ESOPs, worked out a plan whereby the company gave the ESOP 11 million shares of stock (13 percent), an employee representative on Pan Am's board, quality-control circles to guarantee worker input, a joint labor–management board to administer the ESOP, monthly briefings by top management for union leaders on financial and operational plans and procedures, and an extensive information program to explain the ESOP to the workers. In 1983, "after years of red ink," Pan Am was operating in the black. Both management and union representatives gave the ESOP high marks for the turnaround.[40] Unfortunately, however, labor–management relations were seriously damaged in 1985 when management reneged on a promised wage increase and demanded more union concessions, which it got after a strike. Union members were embittered to such an extent that some experts think poor labor relations threaten Pan Am's survival.[41]

Another effort to use worker participation to help save an airline was the December 1983 agreement between Eastern and three unions representing its 37,500 employees.* In exchange for wage concessions of $367 million (representing wage cuts of 18 to 22 percent) and work rule changes to improve productivity, the employees were given 25 percent of Eastern's stock and four members on the company's eighteen-member board of directors. In addition, labor leaders were to have complete access to Eastern's financial information and were to help formulate the company's business, financial, and equipment purchase plans—with appeal of management decisions to the board of directors in the event of disagreements.

Unfortunately, the 1983 agreement did not end Eastern's troubles, despite an initial surge of optimism and labor–management cooperation. This cooperative spirit was washed away by the summer of 1985, when the airline's financial recovery began to falter. In the ensuing negotiations, Eastern's management again asked for wage concessions. ALPA agreed to a 20 percent wage cut and a two-tier wage system, which paid beginning pilots substantially less than those already on board. However, the IAM refused to make concessions unless Eastern's chairman, Frank Borman, resigned. The airline's board of directors rejected the IAM's demand and in February 1986 accepted an offer to sell Eastern to Texas Air Corporation, which already controlled New York Air and the merged

---

*Memberships in these unions was distributed as follows: the International Association of Machinists (IAM), 13,500; the Transport Workers Union (TWU), representing flight attendants, 6,000; and the Air Line Pilots Association (ALPA), 4,000.

Continental and Texas International. Eastern's management apparently assumed that its threat to sell to Texas Air, which was controlled by union buster Frank Lorenzo, would cause the IAM to cave in; but they miscalculated. The end of Eastern's independence was dictated by its inability to compete with low-cost discount airlines without additional wage concessions, which the IAM's leaders could not sell to their members.

Investment Bargaining

Although economic conditions have put unions in a weak position for achieving gains by traditional means, these same conditions have strengthened some unions' power to achieve greater ownership and participation for their members through investment bargaining—trading concessions for greater job security or ownership. Investment bargaining is possible when unions are deeply entrenched and cannot be dislodged or decertified by management. In such situations, concessions and labor peace can be major determinants of company success, giving unions considerable power to gain stock and positions on boards as well as to determine the outcome of outside takeover attempts.

In 1985 the IAM, the ALPA, and the TWU successfully blocked a takeover of TWA by Texas Air Corporation's chairman, Frank Lorenzo, after he had had the deal "virtually sewed up." Lorenzo was responsible for Continental's renouncing its union contract and slashing wages by 50 percent. Lorenzo wanted to consolidate TWA with Texas Air's subsidiaries Continental and New York Air. In the end, the unions helped financier Carl Icahn take control of TWA. The union's bargaining chip was wage concessions worth about $200 million a year, which they exchanged for up to 20 percent of TWA's common stock and up to 20 percent of profits for three years; $300 million of a special class of preferred stock; a portion of any profits on the sale of stock by Icahn; and certain protections against asset and stock sales. The final agreement giving Icahn control of TWA was the result of tough negotiations in which the unions were helped by outside experts. The key to the unions' success was the unity between IAM and ALPA, a unity many observers thought unlikely. But this alliance was "rooted neither in trust nor an affinity, but in a mutual, cold-eyed calculation of material self interest."[42] In these negotiations, the union's power was based on the fact that wage and working condition concessions were required to attract or retain outside capital. Moreover, the almost certain labor unrest that would have resulted from a hostile takeover by an antiunion employer would have been costly to TWA.

Unions probably also hold the key to other contests for control of transportation companies, including Conrail, created by the federal government out of the ruins of several northeastern railroads. Conrail became profitable under government ownership, but in 1985 the Reagan administration proposed to sell it to Norfolk and Southern. However, the unions' bargaining power was enhanced by the fact that Congress has to approve the sale and several other interests wanted to buy the company, including Conrail's present managers. All of the potential buyers had offered sizable concessions to the unions in exchange for their support.*

Such negotiations could provide a new role for unions in takeover and company reorganization efforts. If unions get involved early, they become active investors or even deal makers, using their considerable financial and political leverage to protect their members' interests; if they wait until negotiations are completed, they become passive players attempting to avoid drastic wage and benefit cuts and layoffs.

---

*By the end of 1986 the Conrail case had not been resolved, but it was fairly clear that the administration's plan to sell to Norfolk and Southern was unlikely to be approved by Congress.

Thus, by 1986, ESOPs have become well-established institutions. There are currently over 7,000 ESOPs in the country, though only 800 to 1,200 of these have a majority employee ownership. An even smaller number are actually controlled by employees, though the stage has been set for greater future employee control.

Examples show, moreover, that workers and unions sometimes have had negative experiences with ESOPs. The first buyout using an ESOP was at the South Bend Lathe Company in Indiana, completed in 1975 over the opposition of the Steelworkers. At South Bend Lathe, workers were given nonvoting stock and little say in the company's management. The company has remained profitable, but labor relations have not been good, partly because the workers were not given voting stock. In 1979 the United Food and Commercial Workers (UFCW) completed the first employee buyout of a failing company —Rath Packing Company in Waterloo, Iowa—where the workers traded wage concessions for 51 percent of the stock and a majority of the seats on the board of directors. Unfortunately, Rath finally closed in 1985 after much turmoil, during which the company was forced into bankruptcy and was picketed by its employee-owners.

The first UAW endorsement of an ESOP was in 1979, in connection with the plan to save Chrysler. In exchange for wage concessions and a federal loan guarantee of $1.5 billion, Chrysler employees got $162.5 million worth of stock and a seat on the board of directors. Although no further contribution was made to the ESOP, the plan eventually came to own 12 percent of the company. As a result of Chrysler's recovery the stock quadrupled in value, offsetting the workers' concessions.

In 1981, a UAW local bought Hyatt Clark industries for $53 million. Employees named three board members, including two union representatives; but employees will not be able to vote their stock until the ESOP loans are repaid in 1991. Moreover, this company's only customer was GM, which caused considerable uncertainty for Hyatt Clark's future when GM canceled its contract in 1985.

In 1982, UFCW locals in Philadelphia initiated a plan to buy and reopen several closed A&P supermarkets as employee-owned enterprises. This purchase was financed by a unique fund created by the local union and A&P.

In 1983 and 1984, stock-for-wage concession plans were negotiated at a number of airlines, including Eastern, Western, PSA, and Republic. These negotiations gave workers 15 to 33 percent of the stock, voting rights, representation on boards, and a variety of participation plans. Several trucking firms initiated similar plans, but these were usually last ditch efforts to save failing companies and were generally unsuccessful.

Also in 1984, a number of major companies used ESOPs to carry out leveraged buyouts, sometimes as a defense against takeovers. In these buyouts workers received 20 to 100 percent of the stock. Companies using this strategy included Dan River Mills, Blue Bell, and Raymond. Other local union buyouts that year included Atlas Chain (Pennsylvania) and Seymour Specialty Wire (Connecticut). These companies were democratically structured and the ESOPs were financed largely from private sources. In one of the first efforts by a union to use an ESOP to start an employee-owned company from scratch, a local of the International Union of Operating Engineers organized a union construction company in Pompano Beach, Florida. The union successfully defended the use of pension funds for this purpose in suits carried all the way to the Supreme Court.

The Steelworkers announced in 1984 that it would actively pursue opportunities for employee ownership and participation in management decisions. This made the Steelworkers the first major union to pursue such a strategy actively, though other unions—the UAW, the CWA, and the National Maritime Union—have endorsed the concept. In 1985, the Steelworkers accepted ESOP stock plans and profit sharing in exchange for wage concessions at Bethlehem Steel, Wheeling-Pittsburgh, and Kaiser Aluminum and were engaged in buyouts at other companies. The workers also gained one seat on Kaiser's board.

While union attitudes about worker ownership have become more positive since the seventies, as they have with other forms of noncollective bargaining worker participation, the ESOP movement in the United States originated mainly with managers and owners who did not extend voting rights to workers. A survey of 299 manager-initiated ESOPs established in 1975 and 1976 found that trustees were chosen by the workers in only 3 percent of the cases, and only 21 percent of the companies gave workers full voting rights. In fact, the managers said that they initiated the ESOPs for three reasons: to improve productivity, 51 percent; to finance company growth, 35 percent; and to avoid unions, 8 percent.[43] Since the mid-seventies, however, unions have demonstrated that properly structured ESOPs can be used to protect workers' jobs and to extend their participation in management decisions.

Although profit maximization is not necessarily their main objective, the National Center for Employee Ownership claims that studies show ESOP companies to be 50 percent more profitable than non-ESOP companies.[44] Evaluations also show that the ESOPs have significantly greater productivity than similar non-ESOP firms.[45] A survey of ninety-eight firms with employee ownership, sixty-eight of which were ESOPs, found a positive relationship between employee ownership and both profits and productivity and concluded that employee-owned companies appear to be "more profitable than comparable conventionally owned companies."[46] Similarly, a study by the National Center for Employee Ownership "strongly indicated" that "employee-owned companies grow at a much faster rate than all companies in their economic sector. Overall, employee-owned companies averaged an employment growth rate 2.78 times higher than that of comparable conventional firms."[47]

At least up to now, however, the positive results of worker-owned enterprises are more a consequence of tax advantages and changes in worker attitudes than of worker participation in company management, which tends to remain largely with professional managers even when workers serve on boards of directors.[48] In the typical ESOP, stock ownership is heavily skewed toward management. Indeed, trustees ordinarily hold title to the stock, and the trust tends to be a means of perpetuating control by current managers.

For most workers, ESOPs are retirement benefit plans. This is an important consideration, but if the ESOPs are *substitutes* for regular, more diversified pension fund investments, workers will probably be worse off. Indeed, a major concern for critics of ESOPs is that conglomerates or failing companies will attempt to use them to avoid pension liabilities. This was a major concern in the sale of Weirton Steel to its employees. While competent outside consultants apparently made sure that the workers' interests were protected, older workers who would have had early retirement rights opposed the Weirton buyout.[49]

Thus, ESOPs have a variety of uses. They can help prevent plant closings or unwanted outside takeovers, preserve local control, or enable owners to transfer their businesses to their employees for whatever reasons. Their tax advantages can make ESOPs an attractive option for employees and owners alike. But transfer of ownership through ESOPs can be very complicated (especially in large companies like Weirton), requiring independent professional help to guarantee that the employees' interests are protected in a way that will attract adequate capital for the company's ongoing needs.

There is considerable skepticism about the desirability of employee ownership because large companies up for sale are ordinarily in trouble, which makes it questionable that workers should assume this liability. Not all plants sold to workers are in trouble, though—sometimes the previous owners need the cash or a parent company can conclude that the subsidiary business no longer fits into its plans. With proper safeguards, ESOPs can be a good alternative for workers.

Those interested in ESOPs can learn from the failures as well as from their successes. On the basis of the experiences through early 1986, the Industrial Union Department of the AFL-CIO formulated a number of preliminary ESOP guidelines for its members. (1) Because of the legal, financial, and organizational issues involved, feasibility studies should be conducted at an early date to provide workers with a better understanding of the condition of the firm and industry and the options available to them. (2) Pension funds should be protected. ESOP benefits, unlike pensions, are not guaranteed by an agency of the federal government. Substituting an ESOP for a pension plan is risky because it depends on the health and survival of a single company, while the pension is protected by diversified assets. (3) If an ESOP is to have a chance for success, before it is set up mechanisms should be established to provide employee participation in decisions and information exchanges.

Some considerations are important once the ESOP is complete. (4) ESOP members must be able to vote their stock. One approach suggests that voting rights should be on a one person–one vote basis and that any other approach will lessen the opportunity for participation by all segments of the work force. (5) Whether or not workers can vote their stock, they should be represented on the company's board of trustees. (6) Stock should be allocated on an equitable basis. Stock can be allocated in various ways, including by salary, tenure, and hours worked. This aspect of ESOP design is very important. Over time, the allocation will determine which groups within the company will be in a position to consolidate owner control. (7) What will happen to the stock that is eventually distributed to employees should be worked out in advance. (8) Workers should have a complete and fully vested interest in stock within a reasonable period of time. (9) There should be an equitable evaluation of the stock that goes into an ESOP. In one recent case, a company was planning to sell 60 percent of its stock to a few managers and financiers for $3.30 a share and the rest to the employees for $44 a share. The union stopped this transaction by complaining to pension administrators at the Department of Labor.

There are two suggestions to help keep the ESOP stable over time. (10) It might be useful for unions to press for a broad definition of the employees eligible to participate in the ESOP, in order to dilute the possibilities that management will attempt to create and control a separate ESOP for nonunion employees. (11) In order to stabilize the group of employees eligible for the ESOP, personnel cutbacks should be undertaken as close to the outset of the ESOP undertaking as possible.[50]

A financial expert with experience in the use of ESOPs to support employee buyouts emphasizes a different set of guidelines to ensure proper management rather than just to protect the workers' interests: strong day-to-day management and an independent board to separate management from ownership, avoidance of unrealistic expectations, retaining traditional management–worker roles, and assuring adequate cash flow in the terms of the buyout for the ongoing business. At the same time, this expert warned that the seller might have objectives not in the employees' best interest, including such goals as avoiding pension liability; reconstituting the lost operation "as a low-cost captive supplier via the wage reduction"; setting a precedent to break union contractors in order to divide bargaining units; posturing to negotiate lower wages with no intention to sell; or saddling employees with obsolete plant and equipment.[51]

Cooperatives

Another form of employee ownership that has gained a toehold in the United States is the cooperative, based on the "one member, one vote" principle. Worker cooperatives therefore are more democratically controlled than corporations. A common arrangement is for the worker-member to own one voting share, but any number of nonvoting shares. Only employees can be members, though employees do not necessarily become members. Members usually make a financial contribution when they join and share in the company's profits. The cooperative has some tax advantages over corporations because the cooperative cannot be taxed for net earnings distributed to members.

According to the Industrial Cooperative Association of Somerville, Massachusetts, there were about 200 worker cooperatives in 1984, most with fewer than fifty employees. As with ESOPs, some cooperatives were set up to preserve jobs when companies were failing. However, the cooperative, which has achieved considerable success in Mondragon, Spain,* is more democratic than the ESOP because of the one member–one vote principle. In the Mondragon-type cooperative, each member buys a share and has full voting rights after a probationary period. Part of the profits of this type of cooperative are placed in individual capital accounts. After a defined number of years or when the worker leaves, the accumulated value of this account is paid to him or her. These individual capital accounts avoid a traditional problem with cooper-

---

*In Mondragon, the first co-op was started in 1956, but by 1984 there were 100 cooperatives with about 20,000 members.[52]

atives—the requirement that new members buy out the shares of retiring members—which could be very costly to young workers if the company has been successful and would threaten the cooperative's democratic character.

Massachusetts and Maine had passed enabling legislation for these cooperatives by 1984, and similar legislation had been proposed in New York and Connecticut. While these laws are not necessary for worker cooperatives, they create a kind of legitimacy that could give them a boost.

Pension Funds

Pension funds are another potential source of worker control. Pension funds are natural vehicles because they constitute the largest amount of external equity capital in the United States—over $1.3 trillion in 1986 and growing. Control of these funds can be a means of giving workers greater economic power because they represent deferred wages and are often used for purposes that unions and pension analysts consider contrary to the workers' best interests.

In 1976 Peter Drucker characterized American workers' ownership of industry through pension funds as "pension fund 'socialism' ":

> Through their pension funds, employees . . . own today . . . more than one-third of the equity capital of American business. Within 10 years the pension funds will . . . own at least 50 percent of the equity capital.
>
> But what is even more important . . . the large employee pension funds—those of the 1,000 to 1,300 largest companies plus the 35 industry-wide union managed funds . . . own a controlling interest in practically every single one of the "command positions" in the economy. These include the 1,000 largest industrial corporations . . . and the 50 largest companies in each of the "non-industrial groups."[53]

The trouble with Drucker's argument is that, while the workers own the pension funds (or should), single employer plans are rarely jointly controlled by employees. Indeed, during the eighties, when interest rates were about double the actuarial assumptions used in paying single employer plans, many company trustees changed the interest assumptions required to pay benefits and diverted hundreds of millions of dollars to the companies, thus weakening pension protection for the beneficiaries. Multiemployer plans are jointly controlled by unions and cannot be abused in this way.

In 1980 the AFL-CIO adopted an official position that sought to gain greater employee participation in the management of pension funds. After emphasizing that the "primary purpose of pension funds is, with prudent investment, to secure retirement benefits to workers," the AFL-CIO's position paper outlined four major objectives: to increase employment through reindustrialization; to advance social purposes such as worker housing and health centers; to improve the ability of workers to exercise their rights as shareholders in a coordinated fashion; and to exclude from union pension investment portfolios companies whose policies are hostile to worker rights. Most experts believe that in the immediate future the main objective of most American unions will be the joint control of pension-fund management. Unions regard this as a way to protect pension funds and to make sure that they are used to promote the unions' jobs and organizing objectives.

As of 1986, however, most American unions do not seek to use pension funds to control companies. These ideas are more common in European countries, where unions represent a larger percentage of the labor force, single mandatory pension systems cover all workers, workers have more political unity in labor parties, and unions are more unified in a single federation for bargaining purposes. These kinds of unified activities are largely absent in the United States, mainly because the American labor movement is less united and represents a smaller proportion of the labor force. Also, one single pension fund does not cover all workers, as is the case in some other countries; there are literally thousands of such plans, each of which, as one pension fund expert put it, is "governed by trustees whose main concern is not economic power, or corporate control (which most would regard as an academic exercise anyway), but the welfare of the plans' own members. It is possible, of course, that in time, efforts may be made to pool the economic power represented by such pension funds, particularly collectively bargained funds, but such efforts are not in the cards at the moment."[54]

On November 16, 1981, AFL-CIO President Lane Kirkland told the *New York Times* that he thought control of pension funds was a far more effective tool for unions than participation on boards of directors. Kirkland did not reject the idea of labor directorships, but thought most boards had very limited power: "I think most companies are management-controlled," he said. "The woods are full of professional board-of-director sitters. . . . There's been a growth in their theoretical liability that has not been matched by any enhancement of their real role in the corporation—which I think is the worst of all worlds."[55]

There are a number of reasons for the unions' negative attitudes about employee ownership. First of all, union leaders know that many efforts to establish worker-owned companies have failed in the past. Many of these efforts were initiated by local unions in order to save their members' jobs, sometimes at the expense of international union standards and policies. Internationals were especially afraid that competition among their locals would make it possible for companies to whipsaw down wages and working conditions.* Under those circumstances, companies use concessions extracted from weak locals in

---

*This has been a serious problem in the past and apparently was happening between some UAW locals in 1983.[56]

bargaining with others. Indeed, the prevention of whip-sawing was one of the reasons for the development of national unions and pattern bargaining in the first place. In the nineteenth century, employee-owned companies often reduced labor standards in order to compete. In the seventies and eighties international unions were also concerned about the preservation of pension funds, as was the case at the South Bend Lathe Company, where the Steelworkers' international officers opposed an exchange of the local's pension fund for company stock. This conflict was sufficiently serious to lead to a narrowly unsuccessful effort by local members to decertify the union.[57]

There is also considerable inertia in union policies, caused partly by a preference for tried-and-true, traditional approaches. But by 1984 international union leaders appear to have become more receptive to worker participation and ownership. Indeed, there appears to have been a significant shift in union attitudes between 1977 and 1980, and this trend has probably continued.*

The Future of Worker Participation in America

Experts disagree on the future of worker participation. One management expert described what was happening in Europe as "the third industrial revolution."[59] In 1981, *Fortune* termed the U.S. experience a potential "cultural

---

*The impression that international union leaders are softening their opposition to or even cautiously embracing worker ownership is confirmed by surveys of international union presidents or research directors in 1977 and 1980: "Regarding the general evaluation of employee ownership, 75 percent of the respondents in the 1977 survey took a position classified as 'basically negative.' In the 1980 survey only 29 percent gave a negative reaction to any and all forms of employee ownership that they could approve."[58]

revolution," and sociologist Daniel Yankelovich called it "an irrevocable watershed."[60]

The 1982 New York Stock Exchange survey estimated that worker participation programs had been adopted in 14 percent of all corporations, 11 percent of those with 100 to 499 employees, 33 percent of those with 500 and over, and 53 percent of those listed on the New York Stock Exchange. Moreover, 70 percent of corporations with 500 or more employees had some form of worker participation. Although 74 percent of these programs were less than two years old and 45 percent had had programs for less than a year, these companies were generally very positive about their experiences: 82 percent considered participative management to be "a promising new approach" and only 3 percent considered it to be "a fad destined to disappear."[61]

While there is no denying the flurry of worker participation activity in the United States and Europe, there is considerable doubt over whether this is a "passing fad," an "irrevocable watershed," the "third industrial revolution," or a "cultural revolution." Skeptics abound in labor and management circles. This skepticism is illustrated by the influential writings of Sar Levitan and Clifford Johnson, who consider the current focus on participative management and QWL to be a passing fad. The main impediment to cooperation in labor–management relations, they say, is the consistent rejection by large corporations of "the concept of collaborative decisionmaking and its implicit diffusion of responsibility and control." Despite the current spate of QWL programs, quality-control circles, and other cooperative processes, these authors see little evidence that corporate executives have taken any steps toward meaningful democracy in the workplace. Moreover, they find that "American labor traditionally has shown little interest in partnerships with management, and there is no evidence that workers are willing to pay the price that meaningful participation involves."[62]

These authors believe that "meaningful influence, authority, and a share of the ensuing profits" are frequently withheld by management under worker participation plans, so "such experiments may be rightly viewed by labor as shams, as sophisticated attempts at behavior modification." In view of these limitations, "The success of quality-of-work-life programs depends on the establishment of a fair exchange between labor and management, with workers gaining tangible rights and financial benefits in return for their greater level of commitment and responsibility within the enterprise. Few companies have managed to strike this balance, try as they may."[63]

Although the unmistakable trend toward greater worker participation has acquired sufficient momentum that it will probably continue, it is not at all clear what form it will take. There are many obstacles and considerable resistance, especially from midlevel management and union representatives who are committed to traditional systems. There also are a number of relationships that remain to be worked out, including whether worker participation can cause traditional American companies to become more competitive and the role of unions in worker participation. There are those who see conflict between the role of the unions as both protest organizations with a consumptionist philosophy and agents to improve productivity, flexibility, and competitiveness. This conflict is most evident in the anomalous position of worker representatives on corporate boards, who are both representing their fellow workers and participating in management. Similarly, some critics of all noncollective bargaining forms of labor–management cooperation stress the positive values of inherent labor–management adversarial relationships. Others see fewer problems in accommodating these roles. Indeed, some see worker participation as the logical outcome of trade union development. As one analyst put it: "Thus, the old trade union position of support for collective bargaining *or* other forms of workers' participation seems to be giving way to acceptance of collective bargaining *and* other forms of workers' participation."[64] As John Joyce put it, participation and cooperation are designed to increase profits and benefits, while collective bargaining is about how to divide profits and benefits. Any viable worker participation system probably requires workers to have some independent power, through organizations they control. Otherwise, management will emphasize information sharing and not power sharing. Supposed worker participation schemes during the twenties often failed and were converted to unions when management imposed arbitrary changes, despite strong protests from workers.

This new role, however, would probably require important changes in union structure, orientation, and degree of involvement. Local unions would be strengthened, members would probably become more active, and more extensive education and training would have to be provided to enable employees or members to participate more effectively.

Thus, how well various forms of economic democracy and worker participation perform in achieving their promise of making American companies more democratic and competitive remains to be seen. My own belief is that companies with a high level of participation will become more important and be more competitive than those that attempt to retain the traditional authoritarian model with "scientific" management.

A significant determinant of the growth of economic democracy and worker participation will be the extent to which these arrangements are compatible with existing labor laws, especially the 1935 National Labor Relations Act (NLRA). The NLRA's implicit assumption was that labor relations were essentially between clearly defined adversaries, labor and management. The act's implicit model was a large manufacturing plant with predominantly blue collar workers who had fairly homogeneous interests and who needed unions to help counteract the power of large corporations.

Although the model never really fitted nonmanufacturing companies very well, a number of features caused the NLRA to function reasonably well until the sixties. For one thing, in industries like construction and printing, where unions were strong, employers accepted and even preferred to work with unions. Indeed, in these industries many employers had been union members and often continued their membership when they became managers. Even most large manufacturing companies, the managers of which were generally hostile to unions, nevertheless accepted the workers' legal right to bargain.

These matters began to change during the sixties, when employer resistance to unions intensified. In some cases, management's resistance was benign in that it took the form of providing relatively good wages and working conditions, causing employees to see little need to organize. However, this kind of employer was rarely the subject of union organizing drives. The more important cases were those in which a company's wages and working conditions were such that workers wished to organize but were prevented from doing so by active employer opposition. In these cases, unions usually succeeded in signing up a majority of a company's employees and then petitioning the National Labor Relations Board for an election. "At this stage, management sets out on a vigorous campaign to make union representation an *unpalatable* prospect for its employees. Of course, the [National Labor Relations] Act does make many of these tactics clearly illegal," but the penalties are so weak and legalistic tactical delays so debilitating to the union that a growing number of employers decided to disobey the law. A study by Paul Weiler of the Harvard Law School documented this trend. He found that "in the early fifties, unions won elections covering about 80% of the workers in potential bargaining units, and obtained contracts from nearly 90% of those units.... By 1980, though, American unions were winning certifications covering less than 40% of the potential members, and then translating these hard-won certifications into contracts not more than half the time."[65]

Weiler found that the incidence of "discriminatory discharges and other forms of tangible reprisal against union supporters" increased 350 percent from 1955 to 1980. The proportion of charges against employers found to be "meritorious" by the NLRB rose by one-third during this period. The Board "secured reinstatement in 1980 for more than 10,000 illegally fired workers, more than 10 times the number in the mid-fifties. When one puts this figure side by side with a total of 200,000 workers who voted for union representation elections that year, the current dimensions of such employer actions are damaging indeed." Weiler calculated that in 1980 and 1981 the NLRB "obtained either reinstatement or position on a preferential hiring list for an illegally-discharged employee(s) in roughly one-third of the representation cases of those years." On the basis of his and other studies, Weiler believes that "All in all we are safe in relying on our common sense intuition that so many employers would not have invested so much resources in fighting unions in representation campaigns without that having had a pronounced favorable impact on the overall struggle."[66] It is little wonder, therefore, that a 1986 Department of Labor study concluded that "over time, many employers and their agents have become adroit at manipulating the labor laws to delay and obstruct unionization."[67]

Another problem with our labor laws is their inflexibility with respect both to different conditions at any given time and to the changes in workplace conditions since 1935. According to former Secretary of Labor John Dunlop, labor laws often "yield results that defy practical experience," are sometimes delusions, and are "an invitation to fakery."[68] The inflexibility Professor Dunlop describes extends particularly to the newer forms of worker participation. One example was the legal challenge to the UAW–GM Saturn agreement mentioned earlier. Although NLRB regional directors refused to issue complaints against this agreement in 1986,[69] "the possibility that such charges could be seriously considered under present law has the potential to deter parties from attempting dramatic and innovative cooperative initiatives in the future."[70]

Other examples of the negative potential of the NLRA for labor–management cooperation include uncertainty over whether workers with some managerial responsibility lose legal collective bargaining protection,[71] whether various kinds of labor–management committees violate the NLRA's prohibition against company-dominated unions,[72] or whether support for cooperative labor–management arrangements is "illegal support" under the NLRA.[73]

Worker participation arrangements raise legal issues for unions as well as for employers. For example, does a union violate its duty (under the NLRA and the Railway Labor Act) to represent all workers fairly—the duty of fair representation—when it delegates part of its authority to a labor-management committee? This issue has not been resolved, but presumably a worker within the bargaining unit could sue the union if that worker thought his or her fair representation rights had been violated. Similarly, union representation on company boards of directors raises a number of unresolved questions under present laws. Is it legal, for example, for a union to elect its president to the board of directors of a corporation when that union also represents the employees of competing companies for collective bargaining purposes? This issue arose when the UAW's president, Douglas Fraser, was elected to Chrysler's board. In response to a charge that Fraser's board membership represented an unfair labor practice, the NLRB Division of Advice concluded that such a charge should be dismissed because of insufficient evidence of a conflict of interest in this case.[74]

There is also an unresolved question of whether union representation on competing boards of directors violates other laws. The UAW raised this question with several federal agencies in 1981 after Doug Fraser was elected to the Chrysler board and when the union was seeking another representative on the American Motors (AMC) board. The Department of Labor and the Federal Trade Commission saw no problem with this arrangement, but "The Justice Department . . . declined to state unequivocally that the proposed arrangement would be legal and noted that the proposal raised 'serious antitrust questions,' and left open the possibility that such an arrangement could be found to violate antitrust laws. Not surprisingly, in the face of intergovernmental uncertainty, AMC and the UAW decided to forego their efforts to place a union representative on the company board of directors."[75]

Because both the right of workers to bargain collectively and greater worker participation are in the national interest, high priority should be given to amending labor and other laws to remove these legal obstacles. The penalties for violating the NLRA should be strengthened and the NLRB election procedures should be expedited to avoid purely tactical delays. Where the union has signed up, say, 55 or 60 percent of an employer's work force, the NLRB should hold an election within a reasonable period of time, say ten to fifteen days. If employers have legal questions, the votes could be counted after these questions are resolved. Similarly, legal restrictions on strikes to achieve a first contract should be relaxed. It would be particularly helpful to allow strikers to be reinstated if a dispute is settled within six months and to permit strikers to appeal to other workers not to cross picket lines or to otherwise help the struck employer.

It also would be very useful to develop consensus among labor, management, and public officials for the complete overhaul of national labor and antitrust laws to make them compatible with the realities of the international information world. As John Dunlop observes:

> We have inherited a legal framework of industrial relations that is destructive of our economic future.
>
> Our legal framework teaches that some functions exercised in the enterprise are management's exclusive rights and prerogatives and other matters are within the realm of collective bargaining. . . . A sharp line is drawn and the board and the courts police that line with ever more detailed and trivial requirements. . . .
>
> The needs of the country require joint study, joint discussion, joint development of the facts, and joint problem solving (and sometimes tripartite consultations).

He believes a good place to start building consensus over a new labor policy more suitable for the realities of the 1990s is the following statement adopted by the private Labor–Management Group, which he chairs:

> The uniqueness of America lies in the vitality of free institutions. Among these a free labor movement and a free enterprise economy are essential to the achievement of political and economic stability and economic prosperity for all. It is destructive to society and to business and organized labor, if

in our legitimate adversarial roles, we question the right of our institutions to exist and perform their legitimate functions. In performing these legitimate functions, we recognize that both parties must respect deeply held views even when they disagree.[76]

America's economic performance probably depends at least as much on reforming our industrial relations and management systems as it does on modernizing our economic policy making processes, though both are needed.

A major obstacle to improved labor relations in the United States is employer hostility to the right of workers to organize and bargain collectively and the excessively adversarial relationships between labor and management. As noted earlier, conflicts of interest are natural and serve important positive social functions. But conflict based on an unwillingness to accept the legitimacy of the other party or institution will inevitably be debilitating. The endangered institution now might appear to be the union, but a weak labor movement will mean a weak free enterprise system. The last thing any thoughtful business executive should want is a union-free America. It would therefore be in the national interest to develop consensus on the basic principles outlined by the Labor–Management Committee and to proceed from there to reduce functionless conflict and build consensus on the broad areas of common labor–management interests. Since I doubt this is likely to be done spontaneously in the present environment—at least without a national crisis—the federal government should take the lead in building consensus for labor law reform. As John Dunlop emphasizes, without consensus no legal framework is likely to be very effective.

Chapter VII

Forging a National Consensus

AS SHOWN in the last chapter, there is considerable evidence that processes to improve worker participation in and ownership of enterprises can improve economic performance. Indeed, greater worker ownership and involvement in production processes are probably *required* to make enterprises more competitive in the global information world. But effective participation requires that employees have real power to influence decisions and to protect their interests. Industrial and economic democracy concepts are closely related to political democracy and are based on the same logic—that the best decisions are those that reflect the interests of all major groups who will have to live with them. Many of our economic problems today are due to the lack of balance among these various economic interests. In particular, economic policies in the

United States and in the international organizations in which it participates reflect too much the ideas of orthodox economists and financial experts and gives inadequate attention to the concerns of workers and even to nonfinancial business—such matters as employment and unemployment, labor standards, human resource development, real productivity and production, efficiency, equity, and technology are neglected in the pursuit of short-run outcomes.

The major trends—especially internationalization, technological revolutions, and demographic changes—have reduced the effectiveness of traditional national economic policy and enterprise management systems. Indeed, our economic problems are due at least as much, if not more, to economic policy failures as to the failure of management, industrial relations, or other private institutions. A consensus-based policy with worker participation could improve economic policy making at the national or industry level just as worker participation improves management.

There are several examples of such consensus processes on a large scale. Austrian economic policy processes and the Concerted Action program in Germany (a voluntary consensus process that, at least until recently, helped that country have one of the most successful economic policies of any industrialized society) are two such. There have also been developed certain consensus mechanisms in the United States, for example, the Carter administration's Steel Tripartite Committee, which can provide some lessons for consensus mechanisms in the American context. The role of consensus in Japan's economic policy, with emphasis on industrial policy, will be examined later on.

Austria

Austria has the longest lasting, most successful example of a national consensus-building mechanism.* A formal organization of representatives from government, business, labor, and agriculture—the Joint Price and Wage Commission (JPWC)—has administered a comprehensive incomes policy since 1957. The Commission has no statutory base, and compliance with its decisions is voluntary (though the government has statutory backup power to regulate prices).

To a great extent, the success of Austria's system is due to the fact that economic interests are centrally organized, and so policy differences can be resolved through negotiation. Five major organizations represent business and labor: the Chamber of Labor, the Federal Chamber of Trade and Industry, the Chamber of Agriculture, the Federation of Trade Unions (Oesterreichischer Gewerkschaftsbund, OeGB), and the Industrialists' Association. The Chambers of Trade and Industry, Labor, and Agriculture were established by law, with compulsory membership and expenditures raised by taxes. No comparable system exists in any other country.

The principal Austrian labor organization is the OeGB, which represented roughly 65 percent of the nation's employees in the seventies.[2] The OeGB's ability to enforce a wage solidarity policy has been the major reason why government and business have had to deal with that organization. The federation's ability to main-

---

*During the 1970s, Austrian unemployment was 2 percent or below. The inflation rate was 3.7 percent in 1979 and 6.4 percent in 1980. At the same time, the economic growth rate was 5.2 percent and 3.5 percent, respectively. From 1966 to 1979, prices doubled but wages tripled. Finally, Austria's GNP per capita increased from 60 percent of the United States' in 1970 to 87 percent in 1981.[1]

tain unusual internal discipline is enhanced by the fact that its principal officers have a measure of independence from rank-and-file pressures: they are elected by union representatives, who are selected by works councils within plants, rather than through local unions. Finally, Austrian workers have been unified by a desire not to repeat the tragedies of the thirties, which allowed the Fascists to come to power, due in part to conflict between Socialist and Christian unions.

In addition, Austrian interest groups were unified by the problems facing the country in the fifties. It was clear to labor leaders that inflation, noncompetitiveness in international markets, and external turmoil threatened their members' real incomes and jobs. In 1956, for example, Austria suffered declining investment, rapidly rising prices, and stagnant productivity and output. These experiences convinced the OeGB's leaders that voluntary cooperation with other groups was preferable to the use of strict financial controls (like monetarism) as a means of deliberately increasing unemployment or reducing real wages, or both, as the principal means of checking inflation. As a consequence, the JPWC was established with the understanding that the labor federation would limit wage demands if business enterprises moderated price increases and the government reduced tariffs and strengthened antimonopoly enforcement. The OeGB viewed the Joint Commission as a step toward the creation of a mechanism to give workers a greater voice in national economic matters—one of the federation's basic objectives.

The Joint Price and Wage Commission

The JPWC reviews all requests for wage and price changes. It was proposed by a cabinet resolution, but has no legal authority. The federal chancellor chairs the com-

mission and the secretaries of interior, trade, and labor
attend commission meetings, but do not participate with
the private interest representatives in wage and price
decisions. All commission decisions must be unanimous,
requiring participants to work to achieve compromise. In
short, the system is designed to produce consensus, not to
impose solutions; it is therefore an exercise more in per-
suasion than in the use of power. To facilitate the consensus process, the presidents of the private interest organizations meet informally prior to the JPWC's monthly
meetings and try to reach agreement on the issues.

A number of features account for the Austrian incomes
policy's relative success. The first is that the JPWC does
not restrict its flexibility by relying on fixed quantitative
wage and price guidelines, as has happened in the United
States and other countries. Similarly, the commission has
considerable discretion concerning the order and timing
of wage and price increases—an enormous advantage in
preventing such potentially inflationary processes as
whipsawing and leapfrogging, which have been troublesome for decentralized industrial relations systems like
the American one.

In the Austrian system, control is maintained by two
subcommittees of the JPWC—one for wages, the other for
prices. The wage subcommittee cannot directly affect the
substance of wage agreements but has the power to determine when a union starts negotiations. If unanimity is
impossible after six weeks from the receipt of a request,
the issue is sent back and forth between the JPWC and the
wage subcommittee until a unanimous vote is reached.
The negotiated contract is eventually submitted to the
whole commission for approval, which is usually granted
without changes.

The OeGB is the real wage control agent in Austria. All
wage revisions must be submitted to the federation's
committee on wage policy prior to consideration by the

JPWC. The OeGB analyzes the wage proposal's impact on the national economy and its compliance with the federation's overall wage policy. Wages negotiated by unions are automatically justifiable and can be passed on, but wages negotiated by the works councils generally are not approved, which probably explains why wage drift* is not as serious a problem in Austria as in some other countries. If the proposal is approved, it is submitted with the OeGB's priorities to the JPWC. This process encourages coordination of wage demands by affiliated unions and the resolution of disputes by the OeGB before the JPWC is involved.

In an internationalized information world, even the best domestic policies can be frustrated by the requirements of the internationalized economy, over which domestic interests have little control. In order to deal with this problem, Austrian trade unions suggested, with the concurrence of employers, that the schilling be tied first to a basket of currencies and later to the West German deutschmark. This requires the unions to accept real compensation adjustments parallel to productivity changes; otherwise, the important export sector would have competitive problems. The acceptance of this so-called "hard currency" option—which implies a willingness to accept real wage cuts if necessary—required considerable self-restraint and discipline by the unions. Labor organizations in other countries have opted for at least some protection rather than accept real wage reductions and subjection to international markets.

The subcommittee on prices, made up of representatives from the major economic interests and the government, originally tried to review all price changes, but administrative difficulties forced the list to be reduced to about 200 standard articles, or about one-third of all con-

---

*"Wage drift" means that the actual wages paid in tight labor markets tend to be higher than negotiated wages.

sumption expenditures. But an additional 25 percent or so of consumer spending is controlled directly by the Austrian government, which imposes price ceilings on certain basic foods, energy, and public services.[3]

The procedures of the subcommittee on prices are similar to those of the subcommittee on wages. Proposals for price increases are screened by the Chamber of Trade and Industry before going to the subcommittee, which must act within six weeks or send the request to the full commission. A key requirement in this process is that price increases will be allowed only if justified by cost increases that cannot be recouped by productivity gains, which ordinarily means the wage increases sanctioned by the wages subcommittee. Requests based only on favorable market conditions are not considered. This requirement puts great pressure on companies to keep prices down. Finally, the Austrian government has the legal power (though it has never been used) to impose sanctions on businesses that raise their prices above the approved level or that do not submit their price increases to the JPWC for approval.[4] This threat clearly makes the "voluntary" system more effective. Irreconcilable wage and price problems are sent by the JPWC to the Presidents' Conferences (comprising the presidents of the three chambers and the head of the OeGB).

To provide a means of moving beyond wage and price issues, in 1963 the JPWC created a third subcommittee— the Economic and Social Advisory Board—consisting of three representatives of each of the four main interest groups (industry, commerce, agriculture, and labor), one representative from the employers' association, and experts from the Austrian Institute for Economic Research. This well-staffed board focuses on such broad economic and social policy questions as changes in fiscal and monetary policy and investment, taxation, and the labor market. Like the other two subcommittees, the advisory board has no enforcement power, but its activities provide the factual and analytical bases for consensus on economic policy.

The JPWC was strengthened by success in several initial challenges to its ability to prevent price increases in anticipation of increased costs. It has successfully limited price hikes to increases in actual costs and persuaded firms to postpone some price rises and absorb some increased costs. At the same time, it also experienced some initial resistance when a number of businesses, especially hotels and caterers, refused to observe price agreements, causing union and consumer representatives to conclude that it could not rely on self-discipline from the business community. The JPWC overcame this problem by legislation strengthening the penalties for price violations. As noted, these sanctions have not been used, but their availability encourages compliance. After these early challenges, the work of the JPWC became more routine.

Unanimity and Discipline

Austria's relatively successful experience with consensus-based incomes policies is due to a unique set of circumstances: a very powerful labor movement whose leaders are somewhat insulated from rank-and-file pressures; a clear need for internal economic discipline because of international trade's importance to the nation's economy; the relatively small size and homogeneity of the population; and the economic sophistication of the principal economic actors who, because of serious economic problems in the fifties, had strong motives to avoid the adverse impacts of inflation, the loss of investment, and stagnating productivity and output.

The government's voluntary participation in the JPWC is very important. Even though the government is not involved directly in negotiations, the parties usually assume that taxes and social insurance legislation will prevent real losses to wage earners who practice restraint. They also know the government has more powerful tools at its disposal if voluntarism fails. Unanimous decisions limit the tendency for disgruntled parties to withdraw, making this a classic case of the importance of consensus over authority.

Any incomes policy, whether based on consensus or not, has to be administered, so wage or price standards must be set—a very difficult task in a complex, dynamic economy. It is *technically* difficult to establish price standards, without which it is hard to win union support for wage controls. The Austrians were able to avoid precise quantitative guidelines and therefore achieved sufficient flexibility to make the system work reasonably well. Because there are no clearly articulated price standards, there is some debate about the effectiveness of price controls in the Austrian system. Nevertheless, this process has considerable political and psychological effect in inducing workers to abide by wage increases limited to changes in productivity and the discipline of international markets. The Austrian wage and price system was also probably helped by the fact that the labor movement's egalitarian income redistribution objectives were channeled into the political process, relieving the collective bargaining system of the strains these objectives inflict on other European industrial relations systems.

The Austrian system has avoided the strong rank-and-file revolts that characterized centralized bargaining in other countries during the sixties and seventies. There was some wage drift, but no widespread wildcat strikes or wage explosions. Rank-and-file rebellions, along with wage drift and revolts by white-collar and skilled workers who object to wage-leveling policies, have from time to time weakened the incomes policies of most other European countries.[5]

West Germany

The West German Concerted Action experience provides an example of a different kind of consensus process designed to support national economic policy making, which produced a decade of cooperation among government, business, and labor. Though boycotted by the trade unions since 1977, this system continues informally. Because German conditions are closer to those in the United States than Austrian ones, the Concerted Action experience provides more lessons for an American consensus-building process.

Concerted Action was established in 1967 by the "Law to Promote the Stability and Growth of the Economy," which outlined four national economic goals—price stability, high employment, international equilibrium, and adequate growth—and specified that "in cases where one of the goals is endangered . . . the federal government will provide orientation data for simultaneous, coordinated behavior (concerted action) of local authorities, trade unions, and employers' associations in order to achieve these goals."

As in other countries, the German decision to adopt a consensus-building process reflected the conditions of its present and recent past. The disastrous social conflict and inflation of the twenties made Germans unusually sensitive to the need for national unity in order to prevent any recurrence. The immediate impetus for Concerted Action was the economic recession of the sixties and an increasing number of unofficial strikes in 1966 and 1967. Although neither was serious compared with the experiences of other countries, the fear of a return to the disastrous economic conditions of the Weimar Republic made the Germans feel threatened by a slight reduction in the GNP, a 3.5 percent inflation rate, and 2.1 percent unemployment. A series of small wildcat strikes that would have gone virtually unnoticed in other countries represented a qualitative change in what had been relatively peaceful labor relations in postwar Germany. Both of these developments challenged the consensus that had characterized the nation's industrial relations and economic policy after World War II. The establishment in 1966 of a Christian–Social Democratic coalition government, which reinforced the Keynesian approach to economic policy, also facilitated the creation of Concerted Action.[6]

Concerted Action (CA) was recommended by the Council of Economic Experts (CEE)* in 1965. The CA was a tripartite (government–labor–business) mechanism intended to address the problems created by the recession and increased labor strife of the sixties. This system was designed to remedy the sectionalist, short-term perspective of the economic interest groups, which, the CEE thought, led to pointless conflicts over the distribution of wealth and power and would, in the long run, not only be detrimental to the national economy but also prevent any individual group from improving its economic power. To avoid such a stalemate, the CEE argued that the state should provide information and projections on future economic developments. Concerted Action was designed to encourage coordination of business and labor policies with the government's macroeconomic goals by "moral suasion."

The Social Democratic–Christian "Grand Coalition" government adopted Concerted Action in 1967. Initially, unions were more supportive of Concerted Action than

---

*The council consists of five members, usually professors, appointed for five-year terms. It is completely independent of the government and makes annual recommendations on policies to maintain Germany's basic economic objectives.

employers. The Federation of Trade Unions (Deutscher Gewerkschaftsbund, DGB) hoped to use it to give labor a greater voice in national economic policy decisions. The DGB also thought concerted action would allow the government to gain greater control over the economy. Business representatives were less enthusiastic about the new framework; they favored a voluntary body to discuss general economic trends, but opposed a statutory mechanism, which they feared would increase union influence over national economic policy. Concerted Action was the product of these hopes and fears; it was designed to provide greater coordination of private and public policies through an exchange of information among government, business, and labor. Because Concerted Action required a united response from each interest group, the existence of central organizations of trade unions (DGB) and employers (BDA) greatly facilitated the process. The participants met several times a year to discuss the government's economic plans and forecasts. Attendance at these meetings was voluntary, no votes were taken, and no group had to commit itself to any particular course of action. Originally only representatives of the Economics Ministry, business, and labor participated in Concerted Action, but this group soon expanded to include participants from the ministries of Finance and of Labor, the Federal Bank, the Federal Cartel Office, and the CEE. Eventually representatives of commerce, small businesses, and farmers were included.

The procedural rules adopted at the outset had important implications for Concerted Action's success. After each meeting a communiqué was agreed to by all of the participants. Although this requirement was eventually relaxed, the communiqués originally created a morally binding policy commitment from all participants. As Economics Minister Schiller put it, "Obviously jointly approved orientation data change the situation. No one can act any longer as if they didn't exist."[7] In order to avoid

needless controversy, preliminary meetings were sched-
uled between staff members of the main participating
groups to ensure that the issues in conflict were explained
to all parties beforehand and either excluded from debate
or formally acknowledged. Finally, because Concerted
Action did not create an independent bureaucracy, each
participating group had to rely on its own specialists to
prepare for the meetings. As a result, the heavily staffed
Economics Ministry initially exerted inordinate influence
over the process.

These procedural rules and the reliance on the government for data, forecasts, and analyses put the labor representatives at a disadvantage. The DGB had some
very good technical experts, but it was no match for the
government agencies—especially with respect to data
sources. Throughout 1968, for example, both the CEE and
the government predicted that the low economic growth
rate would allow only moderate wage increases. These
forecasts turned out to be too pessimistic, leading to faster
than expected economic growth and causing wages to lag
behind profits—which naturally made the DGB's members dissatisfied with Concerted Action. Union leaders
became concerned that Concerted Action did too much to
hold wages down and not enough to give labor a greater
voice in national decisions.

There is no agreement about the actual effect of the
government's orientation data either on wages or on the
wage policies of the negotiating committees. But it seems
clear that Concerted Action restrained wages, which
union leaders were willing to accept if they achieved
greater participation in national economic policy making.
As long as they relied on the government's forecasts, the
unions were also willing to exercise wage restraint in
order to protect their members' jobs.

The faster than projected growth in both profits and
economic activity caused rank-and-file union members to

press for higher wage increases in 1969 than had been stipulated by the eighteen-month agreement negotiated the previous spring. After a series of spontaneous work stoppages in key industries in September 1969, IG Metall agreed to an 11 percent wage increase, making it possible for other unions to negotiate increases averaging 3.5 percent above the rates agreed upon earlier that year. Thus, after three years of wage restraint, nominal (12.1 percent) and real (8.1 percent) wage increases reached their highest levels in twenty years.[8]

As might be expected, Concerted Action's record in the first two years caused a shift in labor's attitude about the process. This new mood was to resist Concerted Action's being used mainly as a wage-control process; it was reflected in a motion adopted at the 1969 DGB Congress: "macroeconomic goal predictions simply provide orientation data. It can in no way be the task of Concerted Action to bind union wage bargaining to so-called wage guidelines. [The] Congress will resolutely oppose any attempt to limit indirectly or directly bargaining autonomy or even to abolish it." The Congress also insisted that DGB leaders begin to develop their own economic projections and not merely react to the proposals and initiatives of other groups.

Following the debate at the 1969 DGB Congress, union representatives developed their own plans and took a much more aggressive posture in Concerted Action meetings. They held a press conference after the May 1970 session, for example, to indicate that the post-meeting communiqué should not be taken to mean that the parties had agreed on all issues, especially wage restraint. The DGB also made a serious attempt to include profits, prices, and investments as proper topics for discussion and demanded that debate focus on medium- and long-term trends such as company mergers and codetermination:

What the unions were demanding, in effect, was that Concerted Action should not be a framework in which the government attempted to win compliance from the unions, and
to a certain extent from the employers, for its immediate
policy initiatives, but a forum to which unions and employers could learn about medium- and long-term government
thinking and have the chance to influence future national
economic policy.[9]

In short, consensus would require comprehensive decision sharing; it could not be just a mechanism to constrain
wage increases.

Subsequent events thwarted the DGB's objectives. In
October 1970, the new government, headed by Willi
Brandt, suggested an 8 percent limitation on wage increases. The DGB, noting that the government had
agreed not to publish wage guidelines, declared its opposition to wage orientation data. By publicly express-
ing dissatisfaction with Concerted Action, DGB leaders
adhered to their members' demands for greater independence and demonstrated their willingness to abandon
the consensus-building process if it ignored their interests. Concerted Action received another setback in 1972,
when Helmut Schmidt became Economics and Finance
Minister and developed an indirect incomes policy in
which changes in income taxes, national insurance, and
sickness contributions were exchanged for wage restraints. The government also sought to constrain wages
by exerting strong pressure on public-sector wage
negotiations.

As a consequence of these developments, the union
representatives eventually perceived Concerted Action
meetings as primarily information-sharing processes, not
the decision mechanism they had hoped for. Nevertheless, information sharing had its value: it strengthened
regular public and private decisions by greatly improving

the quality of information available to all parties and by narrowing differences based on disagreements about the facts, forecasts, and analyses.

A number of developments led to the DGB's formal withdrawal from Concerted Action. The government's apparent inability to deal with the recession following the first oil price shock in 1973 and 1974 created growing union disenchantment with labor's limited influence on government policies. Many union leaders were also unhappy with the government's position on the 1976 Codetermination Law and what they considered to be the administration's plans to weaken social programs. The immediate cause of labor's withdrawal from the formal joint consensus process, however, was the employers' decision to challenge (unsuccessfully) the constitutionality of the 1976 Codetermination Law, which gave workers greater representation on the boards of all major German companies, not just coal, iron, and steel, where workers had had equal representation since 1951. The DGB regarded the employers' action as a betrayal of trust and a refusal to continue to rely on the consensus approach to economic policy making. The trade unions withdrew from Concerted Action in July 1977; the government continued the consensus process, but not on a joint and formal basis.

Although the West German experience was less successful as a decision process than its advocates had hoped, Concerted Action demonstrated that government, business, and labor could work together on national economic policies, at least in the German setting. Other institutions that require consensus building within the enterprise—like codetermination and workers' councils—have been more successful as decision processes, and there is general agreement on the need for national consensus-building processes. Concerted Action demonstrated both the limitations and value of these mechanisms.

The Organization for Economic Cooperation and Development

Since most OECD countries consider consensus to be a desirable component of economic policy making, the OECD studied the experiences with these mechanisms in five countries (France, West Germany, the Netherlands, Norway, the United Kingdom) to see what general lessons could be learned. This study defined consensus as "free and broad agreement among unions, employers, and governments on the nature and extent of a nation's principal economic and social problems, the policies to surmount them, and the operation of collective bargaining in the context of these policies, with each party being willing to play a part in carrying forward the policies to an extent which has been agreed."[10] The report points out that consensus is not always possible, but when it is achieved it has four main advantages: it furthers the democratic tradition of decision making in pluralistic societies; it affords all parties a chance to achieve at least some of their policy objectives; it can be more equitable than a nonconsensus-based policy, in which weaker groups have no voice in decision making; and it facilitates compliance with policies—agreement by the leaders of all important interest groups should pressure their constituents to comply.

The OECD study identified several terms commonly used in consensus processes. The basic term is "participation," which includes *all kinds of activity by unions and employers that directly concern national policy questions . . . be it actual joint decision-making, consultation with governments, or administration of policy decisions that have already been taken.*" The study was primarily concerned with consultation and joint decision making. Consultation is "a dialogue, a two-way exchange of information in which each party represents its position on an issue or a given range of issues and discusses these questions with the other participating groups. Generally, consultation is discussion with a view to taking a decision by one or more of the parties, normally the government, in the area of national policy." Another term, "concertation," commonly has a number of meanings, but for the OECD it is a form of consultation. It differs from simple consultation in that its initiators—normally governments —emphasize the goal that national policy decisions be agreed upon by such discussion:

> Concertation is meant to involve a process of mutual education by parties leading to an appreciation of the needs and problems of each and (ideally) a willingness to change opinions by all concerned to reach an agreed perception of the general interest. However, the other parties are not necessarily *responsible* for the action taken—only the party—usually the government taking the action has responsibility.[11]

Joint decision making is different from consultation in that the parties to joint decision share responsibility for it. The outcome of successful joint decision making is ordinarily a package representing trade-offs. The outcome does not necessarily represent agreement on what constitutes the common interest, but rather a shared view that any alternative package would be less equitable for some parties.

In practice, the distinctions are not always as clear as the definitions imply, and sometimes processes shift from one to the other. In Norway, for example, a process considered to be fairly successful started as consultation but became joint decision making.

The OECD report concludes that there are advantages and disadvantages to all parties for participation in consensus processes, "the costs tending to be greater for the unions than for employers and for both than for governments, but with potential benefits outweighing potential costs for all three."[12] The main cost for the union is potential conflict between leaders and rank-and-file members over concessions to the other parties. The main cost to employers and political leaders is that they might be pressured into making concessions not warranted by their relative power positions. The gains for all can be better information, economic stability, and the avoidance of unnecessary conflict. All parties incur the resource cost for involvement, which is usually a greater burden for unions than for either governments or employers, though a benefit for the unions is often a stronger research and analysis capacity.

As might be expected, the success of the participatory process varies with the underlying level of consensus in a country. In addition, "where effective consensus has been achieved it has been through joint decision making and bargaining rather than consultation, normally involving a considerable degree of unstructured interaction." Finally, and "more important in the outcome of these discussions than the particular structures in which they take place is the underlying power relationships existing between the parties."[13]

All participants in these processes felt they derived important benefits, but (not surprisingly), unions and employers were rarely able to shape government policies as much as they had hoped. The Norwegian experience is the main exception, where the system evolved into joint decision making and where unions and employers have had more influence on policy. Governments, too, have been disappointed, though they have received the greatest benefits from the process, including a useful source of informed advice and help in implementing decisions. Moreover, participation by unions and management has raised the level of public debate, though in some cases the length of time it takes a consultative body to deal with an issue has muted public debate "if the government does not wish to deal with it immediately."[14] Governments have been disappointed with these mechanisms mainly in cases where public officials hoped to structure the process fully; structured processes have not done away with the need for unstructured interactions among the parties.

Consensus Building in the United States

The Steel Tripartite Committee

The United States has had a number of experiences with consensus-building mechanisms. We can learn from these as well as from foreign experiences. One of the most recent was the Carter administration's Steel Tripartite Committee (STC). The STC was cochaired by the secretaries of Labor and Commerce and created on the recommendations of an Interagency Task Force on the Steel Industry. The December 1977 report of this task force not only recommended the establishment of the STC but also emphasized the need for the modernization of steel-making facilities, the installation of new technologies, the commitment to environmental protection measures (in which some steel companies were seriously deficient), and a trigger price mechanism to deal with the problems of dumping (selling at less than production costs) from international competitors. The basic idea behind this trigger price mechanism was to take the Japanese cost of production as the minimum price at which steel would be permitted to enter the United States. The Japanese prices were used for triggers because it was generally agreed that the Japanese were the world's most efficient steel producers. American steel companies had argued that they could compete at fair prices, but not if the Japanese companies were either subsidized or were selling below their costs of production. The problem was that it was very difficult to determine Japanese costs, and because the steel market is international, other countries—over 35 percent of whose steel capacity was state-owned—could dump at Japanese prices.

However, the task force report and the STC made it clear that the problems confronting the steel industry went far beyond international trade. It soon became apparent that a major problem in this case was the internationalization of an industry that had looked mainly to the large internal market and had not been very competitive. The industry's oligopolistic pricing arrangements were strengthened by the high capital requirements for entry. The industry tended to have prices that were relatively inflexible downward, and the absence of competition had made it possible to develop a collective bargaining system that shared oligopolistic prices with the workers in the form of higher wages. But the intensification of international competition made the companies vulnerable to import penetration because threats of strike and actual strikes had caused steel buyers to turn to foreign sources. Indeed, major surges of steel imports coincided with strikes, especially the 111-day strike of 1959 and 1960. This loss of markets motivated the companies to maintain labor peace, giving the union greater short-run bargaining power. American labor costs became even less competitive because of the cost-of-living adjustment and annual improvement factor in the 1973 steel agreement, which caused wages to increase more rapidly than in other industries during the accelerating inflation of the late seventies. Indeed, during the seventies, when most wages declined in real terms, steel wages increased 27 percent more than inflation.[15]

Foreign competition had a number of features that made it difficult for the American industry to compete through traditional pricing arrangements. For one thing, because of its importance to both development and national prestige, governments in the developing countries made building steel capacity one of the top priorities in industrialization, causing steel capacity to bear very little relation to economic costs. For another, the size and importance of the steel industry required governments to be heavily involved in the steel business, whether or not capacity was publicly owned. Government involvement in the United States frequently took the form of prohibiting price increases during periods of prosperity, when the companies could have made greater profits. The poor public image of American steel companies made them inviting targets for elected officials and regulators, intensifying the adversarial relations between the industry and the government. At the same time, though, government involvement was encouraged by the industry itself, which decided in the sixties to opt for a political strategy of preventing foreign imports as a way to maximize short-run profits and fully depreciate obsolete facilities, while foreigners were modernizing both their facilities and their management systems.[16]

The industry's lack of competitiveness in international markets made it an inviting target for foreign producers, whose mills were more modern and productive and who had lower labor costs. The economics of the American industry and its heavy dependence on equity financing caused some larger companies to ignore long-run technological viability. They continued to invest in obsolete open hearth furnaces while the Japanese were building more efficient basic oxygen furnaces. Japanese firms relied mainly on low-interest bank financing, which could be guaranteed by the government, so Japanese managers could take a much longer view.

In addition, the Japanese flexible consensus-based system gives them a competitive advantage. The Japanese practice of maintaining production during recessions makes them reliable suppliers and enables them to meet rising demand much faster than their oligopolistic American competitors, who are forced to rebuild capacity during upturns. Because their variable costs (and therefore liquidation costs) are lower, the greater fixed costs from wages, interest, and capital equipment give the Japanese a competitive advantage during downturns, even if their total costs are the same as those of American producers. Large Japanese companies also became formidable competitors because they are not profit maximizers, but seek to increase their size and market share. American companies have higher profit thresholds and thus tend to abandon the field or demand protection in the face of stiff competition from the Japanese and other Pacific basin countries that have adopted the Japanese system.

These realities confronting the STC made it clear that the problem went much deeper than dumping. The government had to help develop a strong and economically viable world-class steel industry and to promote an equitable sharing of the costs of adjustment among the uncompetitive components of that industry. The STC differed from many such committees in the United States in that the participants were very actively involved. The principals rarely missed meetings. The chief executive officers of the companies and the president and principal officers of the United Steelworkers attended the meetings along with the secretaries of Labor and Commerce and senior officials from the Treasury, the Environmental Protection Agency, and the office of the Special Trade Representative. Other senior government officials attended occasionally, depending on agenda items. These discussions were based on extensive joint staff work between meetings and the thorough preparation of the principals.

On the basis of the task force's report, the STC determined that the main problems confronting the industry included: modernization and capital formation; labor and community adjustment assistance; environmental protection; research and development; and international trade. STC working groups were established in each of these areas with the mandate to undertake careful assessments and make recommendations to the full committee and ultimately to the president.

It soon became clear that the joint factual and analytical staff work was an important part of the consensus process. It is very important to agree on the facts before allowing recommendations to be made—otherwise there is a strong tendency to develop facts to fit the recommendations. But labor, management, and government professional staffs had less difficulty agreeing on the facts than one might have assumed. This careful staff work made it possible very early to dismiss an area of controversy that is endemic in public statements—assigning responsibility for the steel industry's problems. It was easy to agree that there was enough blame to go around and that assessing blame was not likely to do much to strengthen the industry. They also realized that labor, management, and government had each functioned in rational terms in the separate systems within which they operated and within the economic context of the fifties and sixties, but that this had produced results incompatible with the realities of the seventies and beyond. It was equally clear that changing these systems and subsystems would require joint action on some matters and joint sacrifices, even though each party had to adapt its own systems to the more competitive internationalized information world.

After a year and a half of intensive study and debate, consensus emerged on a comprehensive program for the steel industry, which included a number of recommendations. First, tax measures should be introduced to encourage investment in plant and equipment modernization. (There was agreement that a "targeted refundable" tax credit would do more to strengthen the steel industry, but the companies naturally favored general tax credits and depreciation allowances, which they subsequently got from Congress and the Reagan administration and which were more favorable to the companies whether or not they remained in the steel business or modernized their plant and equipment.) Similarly, there should be measures designed to promote the development of advanced steel technology. A trigger price mechanism needed to be reinstated and improved to govern dumping of foreign steel in the American market. Amendments to the Clean Air Act would have to be made to give the industry more time for compliance. Finally, the committee made proposals for improved worker and community adjustment assistance, and recommended the rechartering of the STC.

The STC did not survive the Carter administration, but the Clean Air Act amendments were approved by Congress on the condition that the industry modernize, and the trigger price mechanism was carried over into the Reagan administration. Despite strong support from labor and management, the STC and the cooperative concept on which it was based initially received little encouragement from the Reagan administration—probably partly for political reasons but also because of deep ideological aversion to nonmarket approaches to decision making. The administration apparently believed that its supply side and monetarist economic policies would cause a broad revitalization of the economy, which would also revitalize the steel industry. However, President Reagan finally yielded to industry and labor pressures and in August 1983 announced the reestablishment of a tripartite steel committee.

The Benefits of Teamwork

There were a number of lessons learned from the STC experience. The first was that each party gained greater understanding of the others as a result of the interaction. The government representatives gained a much more realistic appraisal of the problems confronting the industry. Unlike most countries, the United States has no sector-specific government agencies to gain expertise and information on particular industries. The STC forced government agencies to come together to acquire this knowledge. It was particularly important for the government to realize that existing motivations and systems would not guarantee the economic viability of the steel industry, even if profits were the same as those of other countries; higher profits in some other types of production would tempt profit-maximizing firms to abandon the industry. Industry representatives soon realized that their efforts to blame the government for their problems would have little credibility in view of their own operating procedures. By the same token, there was no question that government regulators were often antagonistic to the industry and that government actions had created an unrealistic depreciation schedule for tax purposes, had intervened to prevent the industry from maximizing profits during periods of prosperity and relatively full employment, and had not enthusiastically enforced trade laws designed to protect the industry from unfair practices of foreign producers.

The government similarly acquired some valuable lessons about how to conduct worker adjustment programs from a demonstration project jointly mounted by the commerce and labor departments to show how to work with industry, labor, and communities to adjust to mass layoffs and plant closings. The need for such adjustment efforts will be a serious problem of the eighties and beyond. On the basis of the STC experience, the Carter administration launched a number of similar demonstration projects. Unfortunately, the Reagan administration continued only one of these—the Downriver Community Conference Economic Readjustment Activity Program in Michigan—which preliminary evaluations show to have been successful.

The STC had other accomplishments: its comprehensive analyses revealed that the various factors causing the steel industry's problems are interrelated, and it achieved consensus among the parties. As the late Lloyd McBride, president of the United Steelworkers of America, argued:

> This is not simply accommodation. It is a process of persuasion, education, compromise, and the search for feasible alternative solutions. Consensus-building suggests that each party has an area of responsibility in the resolution of issues and must integrate its own actions and interests with those of other parties. In this kind of tripartite forum, government is not a mediator. It is an active participant in the policy formulation process, because it has a constituency—the American public—which is adversely impacted by most solutions. We must rid ourselves of the notion that government is somehow a disinterested third party or "above the battle."

McBride found other advantages of the STC, including the opportunity it provided for taking a long-term look at the industry's problems:

> This was inevitable, given the nature of the problems; but it was a process that evolved. The R&D Working Group is a case in point. Discussion began with the simplistic notion that there was nothing to discuss in R&D because new technology in steel is virtually instantaneously available worldwide. The issue was getting the capital funds to install existing technology. So, in the beginning, R&D was perceived as a capital formation issue. This was a premature judgment. In

the final analysis, the R&D Working Group saw the need for further development of technologies in formed-coke, sensors in control systems in steelmaking, coal-based direct reduction and recycling technology. A planned, coordinated and financed approach to remedying these technological deficiencies in steelmaking was recommended.[17]

Some critics argue that tripartite mechanisms ignore the public interest. Experiences with the STC suggest that while this danger must be guarded against, in the American system there are built-in protections for the public interest. Indeed, the tripartite process tends to safeguard the public interest through government participation and by making the public interest more informed and explicit than is likely to be possible through the usual special interest lobbying, which usually takes place out of public view. If anything, formal American processes lean over backward to protect the public interest. Environmentalists and consumer groups, for example, monitored the STC's activities very closely and were quick to criticize actions they considered inimical to their concerns. Since these tripartite arrangements tend to be advisory only, other groups have adequate opportunity to express themselves during legislative deliberations. In a democracy, the public interest is more likely to be served by making decision processes more open and the trade-offs more explicit than by abandoning those processes to the behind-the-scenes lobbying efforts of special interests.

I do not mean to imply that the STC was without its faults and false starts or that everything proceeded smoothly. But it was a joint learning process and was evolving into a better working relationship when it was abandoned in 1981. As the committee gained more experience with joint problem solving, the government could have used its leverage to extract concessions from the companies and unions. Clearly, the unions and companies should have been required to improve their productivity and reduce their costs in exchange for tax credits, trade protection, and regulatory relief. Unfortunately, these matters were never adequately followed through. The Carter administration's main interest in the committee was to achieve that consensus and then to work with the industry to develop a joint plan to deal with its problems.

Other Tripartite Committees

In 1980, the Carter administration and the AFL-CIO entered into a national accord, which outlined principles of cooperation between the administration and the federation on economic policy—especially "to deal effectively with inflation in an equitable manner" by assuming "that the austerity arising from battling inflation is fairly shared" and to "pursue our established national goals of full employment, price stability, and balanced growth." The accord also called for a tripartite Economic Revitalization Board cochaired by Lane Kirkland and Irving Shapiro, chief executive officer of DuPont. The board's purpose was to advise the president on a broad range of economic issues, including the establishment of an industrial development authority to provide financial assistance for the economic revitalization of areas affected by high unemployment and economic dislocation.

The Carter administration also established tripartite commissions to deal with other industry problems, including the very successful President's Commission on Coal, chaired by Governor (now Senator) John D. Rockefeller IV of West Virginia, and an Automobile Industry Committee modeled after the tripartite steel committee. The latter was not established until 1980 and therefore did not have much time to work, but the plan was that, like the STC, it would bring top industry, labor, and government representatives together to discuss the long-term prospects for the industry and its workers and to undertake joint efforts to manage the adjustment process associated with plant closings or mass layoffs that had significant community impact.

Finally, the administration strengthened Construction Coordinating Committees in a number of cities, modeled after a successful Chicago committee that had been established in 1973 primarily to work cooperatively on the problem of seasonal work availability. Since governments are responsible for about one-third of the construction in major cities, cooperative efforts were able to spread out the contracting throughout the year instead of the usual practice of concentrating contracts at the beginning of the year; to stabilize employment; and to provide more employment, less upward pressure on wages, greater choice to builders. In other words, coordination at very little cost produced benefits for everybody. Moreover, experience in tripartite problem solving about seasonality was quickly transferred to other areas of common interest to workers, employers, and the public. Unfortunately, despite very successful experiences, the Reagan administration abandoned these committees.

Pros and Cons and Some Cautions

Despite the problems associated with these efforts, consensus-building coordinating mechanisms (CBMs) have growing support among people with widely differing political persuasions, who see a need for processes to moderate adversarial relationships and to supplement public and private decision procedures with participatory mechanisms at various levels.

Those who advocate CBMs point to a variety of advantages. They recognize that while governments and markets have legitimate and central roles to play in the economy, there are areas of joint responsibility requiring common perceptions of facts and an understanding of the attitudes and reactions of the principal economic actors. As the German CEE concluded, in the absence of consensus between the economic actors there are likely to be conflicts over the distribution of wealth and power which could reduce the growth of productivity and total output and therefore make it impossible for the major interest groups to improve their relative economic positions. The underlying assumption for CBMs is that the commonality of interests in a system outweighs the differences and that concentration on areas of agreement can minimize conflict and improve regular decision processes.

Consensus processes can facilitate adjustment to change by clarifying both the economic limits confronting an enterprise, industry, area, or country and the relative power positions, attitudes, and institutional requirements of the various participants.

Policies developed from consensus are likely to improve the performance of the whole system. Agreed-upon objectives are superior to those imposed by the government or by one interest group. Proponents of CBMs believe a common error of some economic and management theorists is to assume that there is one "best" economic or management policy and that the function of management is to impose that policy on the enterprise or the economy. They do not believe there is a single optimal policy that can be determined with present analytical tools; the best rules for any particular enterprise, industry, or country consequently depend on the unique resources, institutions, customs, entrepreneurs, innovators, and leaders. Participation clarifies objectives, facilitates communication and understanding, and smooths the adjustment to change.

Moreover, they argue that a national CBM in the United States could overcome one of our main disadvantages relative to our stronger world competitors and adversaries—a lack of continuity and coordination. Continuity would be provided because members from the private sector could continue even when governments change. Representation from the Congress, the White House, the Federal Reserve, and other appropriate agencies could provide for better coordination. CBMs would complement, not replace, collective bargaining, market forces, legislative action, or other decision mechanisms. Proponents believe these processes will improve regular decision processes by providing more accurate information and isolating areas of agreement and disagreement. The success of the process might require the transfer to legislative or collective bargaining processes the most difficult issues on which consensus could not be reached, as happened with the Austrian incomes policy.

Experience suggests two major guidelines for a consensus-building organization. First, the process should include the main economic interests in the economy or industry, especially representatives of labor, management, financial institutions, and branches of government concerned with economic policy. Agricultural or other interests could be included as the need for their inclusion is demonstrated.

Second, consensus-building processes have some essential elements, including ongoing dialogue among the various parties; the ability to conduct off-the-record as well as formal discussions; continuing cooperative staff work; and the understanding that while information can be shared, consensus is not likely on every issue. A common theme is the CBM's tendency to produce better information and to improve the factual and analytical bases available to all actors involved. The process usually requires a convergence of the competence of the technical staffs that support the different participants—as happened in the German Concerted Action program.

In all cases, it is clear that the procedural rules, along

with the nature and history of relations among the parties, will influence the effectiveness of the CBM. They seem to be most effective where there has been a history of self-defeating conflict as there had been in Germany, Austria, and Japan; the groups are well organized and have internal cohesion; the parties are unified by common purpose, mutual dependence, or external threats; the parties make a good-faith effort at flexible arrangements that emphasize consensus and not the exercise of power; and finally, the parties recognize the need to let the process evolve to adjust to changing circumstances. As John Dunlop, who has had considerable experience with these mechanisms, puts it, a consensus-building process can "provide a sense of direction, smooth social conflict and speed formal processes. The consensus building process can often be extraordinarily constructive; policies emerge which were not envisaged initially by any participant. Thus, initial processes . . . should be treated as tentative, to be tested and perfected by discourse."[18]

The arguments against public–private CBMs include the belief that such organizations would be undemocratic because in the United States (unlike other countries, where functional interests are better organized and decisions are more centralized) there are no representative functional organizations. For example, unions and workers' associations represent only about one-fourth of the work force and there is no representative business or employer organization. Who would represent consumers, small businesses, environmentalists, nonunion workers, and the like?

Detractors also feel that participatory CBMs might actually intensify conflict because if no consensus were achieved, the process might simply become an arena for conflict.

In the American context, critics warn, CBMs would inevitably lead to political decisions that would impair economic efficiency by sustaining politically popular but uneconomical activities. CBMs would also cause governmental instruments (such as international trade or procurement processes) to be used for inappropriate purposes simply because they are available.

According to some views, the effectiveness of CBMs in other countries either has been exaggerated or has been due to conditions not likely to be duplicated in the United States. Most of these mechanisms have fallen apart because of political problems. For example, the German Concerted Action program was discontinued when the DGB boycotted meetings to protest German employers' challenge to the constitutionality of the Codetermination Law of 1976. Several labor–management committees in the United States have also failed because of political conflicts. Moreover, each participant, especially the unions, would have internal problems if it made concessions for the common good that were unpopular with its members. The most successful CBMs have been in Austria and Japan; but Austria has had an unusual degree of organization by different interest groups and an unusual degree of political insulation by the leaders of the OeGB from rank-and-file union members—and such conditions are unlikely to prevail in most other countries. Moreover, the Japanese and Austrian systems were unified by the need to rebuild their economies and to be competitive in international markets.

The structures of the American government and society are not conducive to CBMs. Adversarial relationships between business and government are deeply entrenched in the United States, as are relations between unions and management. American business leaders are more likely than their foreign counterparts to view unions as necessary evils and to use legal and illegal means to avoid collective bargaining. We are not likely to develop cooperative relations between actors who do not accept the right of the other participants to exist. Employers in other industrialized countries are more likely to view unions as social partners and essential components of free societies. The other side of this coin is that American unions have typically viewed worker participation schemes as subterfuges to achieve the business objectives of a union-free environment. Despite the development of some cooperative labor–management activities, adversarial relations continue to dominate labor–management relations in the United States. Finally, the American government is weaker and more fragmented than the centralized governments of most other industrial economies. In parliamentary systems, there is much more unity and centralization of decision making—which facilitates consensus. In the United States, Congress is separated from the executive branch, and the Federal Reserve Board is relatively independent of both the Congress and the White House.

These criticisms of consensus mechanisms raise important problems, which must be carefully considered in the establishment of consensus processes at every level. The relative weakness of American unions is a serious problem and makes it very difficult for workers' interests to receive adequate expression in policy-making processes. Because the expression of workers' concerns is so important, serious attention should be paid to strengthening the workers' ability to organize and bargain collectively. The principles of exclusive bargaining rights and majority rule embodied in the National Labor Relations Act are sound. It is especially important to change National Labor Relations Board procedures to avoid tactical delays in representation elections and to strengthen the penalties for violating that law—the penalties are currently so weak as to be almost meaningless.

The evidence suggests that increased employer opposition is an important reason American workers are having so much trouble organizing, but it is not the only one. The unions need to do more to change their image as narrow, inflexible special interest organizations led by people who pay little attention either to their members' or the public interest. These images are based on heavy publicity given to a few bad examples and on inadequate public understanding of the role and function of unions in democratic societies; but the evidence suggests that public opinion is a very important determinant of the unions' ability to organize. Public policy should be flexible enough to protect the workers' rights to make a timely decision and prevent unfair labor practices, but it is up to the unions to bring their policies and practices into conformity with the viability conditions of the global information world; to convince the public of the legitimacy of their role in society; and, most important, to convince workers that they have something to gain from unionization.

Despite real problems, however, the advantages of consensus processes outweigh the disadvantages and help minimize or avoid the most serious problems. Indeed, in the United States CBMs are probably more essential to overcoming the defects in both public and private decision processes. Better cooperation is needed in order to develop and sustain effective economic policies and productive work environments, independent of short-term, profit-maximizing interest groups. Without such mechanisms, in the long run the United States will have great difficulty in realizing its economic potential, restoring productivity growth, or sustaining our competitive position in a world where our principal competitors have more unity of purpose, coordination, and governmental continuity. As with any innovation, it is important not to set the stage for disillusionment by promising too much. CBMs will not work miracles, but they can improve understanding and communication and help eliminate some causes of governmental and economic ineffectiveness.

Chapter VIII

The Japanese Make It Work

AS HAS BEEN demonstrated earlier, the Japanese have been the main winners in the international competitiveness race. They, and the "little Japans" of the Pacific rim, have gained market share at the expense of the United States and Europe. The Japanese have accomplished what is generally referred to as the "Japanese Miracle" while maintaining relatively low levels of unemployment, rising real wages, the highest levels of productivity growth in the industrialized world, and a relatively equal sharing of the benefits of economic growth.

There are many reasons for Japan's successes. In certain targeted industries, Japanese companies have developed management systems that combine quality and price much better than most of their American competitors. Because they have been so successful and because their successes have been at the expense of American companies, it is very important that we understand how the Japanese system works, with special focus on the roles played by consensus-based policies and strategies. To do so we must examine the nature of the Japanese cost advantage and analyze Japanese governmental and corporate strategies.

Why Are Costs Lower in Japan?

The Japanese have significant labor and capital cost advantages over the United States. Japanese wages were only 50 percent of U.S. wages in 1984, and Data Resources, Inc. (DRI) estimated that the net after-tax cost of capital was only 0.1 percent in Japan between 1973 and 1983, compared with 5.3 percent for the United States. Productivity increases are much faster in Japan than here, and in the key automobile and other manufacturing industries Japanese productivity is higher. As a consequence, according to a 1985 DRI study, the Japanese are able to underprice U.S. companies by 20 to 50 percent in every market sector.[1]

The nature of the Japanese cost advantage can better be understood by examining a particular industry. If we look at automobiles—a high-wage, highly unionized industry in both America and Japan—it becomes very clear that the popular belief that union wage rates are mainly responsible for America's competitive disadvantage is a myth. In fact, according to a 1984 study by Telesis, an independent economic consulting firm, completely eliminating the wage differential for hourly workers would reduce the $1,900 cost gap between U.S. and Japanese subcompact cars only by about $500, or about 25 percent.[2] The Telesis study also found that a large part of the hourly labor cost differential was due to much higher costs of fringe ben-

efits in the United States. The hourly compensation cost
of $22.67 often cited as the average "wage" of American
auto workers actually contains wages of only $15.79—the
other $6.89 is for fringe benefits. Japanese hourly com-
pensation costs are $11.30, but $9.81 of this is wages and
only $1.49 is for fringes.

Despite the higher costs of fringe benefits in America,
Japanese benefits are superior to those of American auto
workers in every area except pensions—which cost $2.41
an hour in the United States and $0.75 in Japan. Even
though health care costs are $2.47 an hour here and only
$0.39 in Japan, Japanese workers get better coverage,
partly because of governmental subsidies but also because
doctors are paid only $20,000 to $30,000 a year in Japan
and over $100,000 here. Similarly, unemployment com-
pensation costs $0.70 an hour in America and only $0.08
in Japan, mainly because Japanese economic policy keeps
unemployment very low.

Japanese unit labor costs (ULCs) are even lower relative
to those of U.S. companies because of higher Japanese

TABLE 8.1

Unit Labor Costs for Subcompact Cars, United States and Japan

	Compensation Costs		Productivity (hours per car)		Unit Labor Costs		Ratio, Unit Labor Costs
	U.S.	Japan	U.S.	Japan	U.S.	Japan	U.S.–Japan
Hourly	$ 22.67	$ 11.30	56.5	43.0	$1,281	$434	2.95
Wages					892	377	
Fringes					389	57	
Salaried	27.41	12.82	28.5	19.5	781	250	3.12
Outside	12.00	7.00	70	70	840	490	1.71
Total Unit Labor Cost					2,902.04	1,174.09	2.47

SOURCE: Derived from Telesis, Inc., data presented in United Auto Workers Research Department, "Choices for American Industry: Autos," unpublished paper, 1986.

productivity. The total U.S.–Japan hourly pay ratio is
2.01, but the ULC ratio is 2.95. Moreover, the U.S. salaried
productivity and labor cost disadvantages are greater than
those for hourly workers (see table 8.1). Note also that the
Japanese gain a wage advantage for using more low-wage
outside contract labor.

The main conclusion to be drawn from these comparisons is that given present policies, it is unlikely that
American automobile companies will be able to compete
with the Japanese for many years to come. Indeed, with
present Japanese policies and no trade restraints by the
United States or Japan, the Japanese could eventually put
American automobile companies out of business, even if
hourly wage differentials were eliminated completely.

These cost differentials are the consequence of carefully
developed corporate and government strategies. It is well
known that these strategies have given the Japanese important advantages in basic industries like automobiles
and steel. What is not as well known is the fact that the
Japanese are using the same basic strategy in high-tech
areas like microelectronics and telecommunications that
they used in certain manufacturing industries. It is therefore very important for American policy makers to understand this strategy.

The Consensus Strategy

The first important difference between U.S. and Japanese
policy making is the absence of an explicit consensus
process in America, whereas in Japan consensus building
is central to decision making at every level—firm, industry, related industry groups, and the national economy.

Japanese consensus building is ordinarily initiated with a tentative proposal of some kind, which is then discussed at great length by all interested parties before a decision is made. There also are formal consensus committees in which agreements are ratified, but much preparation has already been made before matters come before these committees. If consensus is not reached, the process continues through additional fact finding in order to promote greater agreement. According to Ezra Vogel, "The Japanese assume that differences of opinion can best be resolved not by adversary procedures and brilliant argument, but by further gathering of information."[3] The Japanese call this consensus-building process *nemawashi* or "root trimming," after the careful preparation of the roots before moving a tree. The extensive discussions involved in the consensus-building process help all parties involved to identify with the decision reached, to understand it well enough to form the basis for their actions in the matter and for each party to contribute its specialized knowledge to the common effort. The Japanese typically take considerable time to reach a decision but act quickly to implement it; decision makers in the United States make decisions faster, but have slower and less effective implementation.

The consensus process assumes a common goal that transcends the interests of individuals and groups. Indeed, Japanese government officials frequently appeal to the common interest to force consensus among the various interest groups. As one student of Japan puts it: "Invoking the national interest, whether pretended or real, tends to screen out *ad hoc* programs and solutions inconsistent with the shaping of generally coherent overall national policies."[4] Indeed, according to Vogel, Japanese business leaders "expressed surprise at the extent to which American businessmen were ill-prepared to consider business problems from a broader perspective, let alone negotiate agreements on complex issues."[5]

By making all agreements tentative, the consensus process avoids embarrassing the participants; preliminary discussions are extensive, nonbinding, and as discreet as possible. The rules developed by this process are likely to be intentionally vague in order to make them adaptable to a wide variety of circumstances. Indeed, the consensus process makes it possible to avoid the extensive litigation over government regulations common in the United States.

While consensus building became pervasive after World War II, Japan's economic history is one of conflict as well as cooperation. Following World War II, Japanese leaders, after extensive discussions, debate, and conflict, made a conscious choice for consensus and cooperation. In a time of uncertainty, when the country had to be rebuilt, the consensus process provided more national unity, relative security for enterprises, and much better information for decision making purposes.

The use of consensus processes can be illustrated by the role they play in the formulation of Japan's very successful economic policies. Economic strategy in Japan is comprehensive, as well as coordinated between the public and private sectors and between government agencies. For example, industrial policy is closely related to macroeconomic policy and long-run economic forecasting, or "indicative planning."*

Macroeconomic policy is of major importance in Japanese economic policy. In most countries macroeconomic policies are used to smooth out the business cycle; but in Japan, macroeconomic tools have been used primarily to achieve balance-of-payments equilibrium, to generate investment funds for economic growth, and to stimulate selected industries and sectors.

---

*In Japan industrial policy is designed to strengthen productivity and economic efficiency by encouraging the growth of strategically important sectors and facilitating adjustment of resources out of sectors judged by consensus systems to be noncompetitive.

Macroeconomic policy is developed mainly by the Ministry of Finance and the Bank of Japan, which emerged in the postwar period as an arm of the Ministry of Finance to implement monetary policy. Throughout most of the postwar period the basic objective of monetary and fiscal policy has been to promote rapid real growth in targeted activities by keeping interest rates relatively low, controlling commercial bank loans, and allocating foreign exchange to priority uses.

Long-range aggregate planning, another major element in Japanese policy, is pursued by the Economic Planning Agency, created in 1955. Indicative plans, which contain growth projections for the overall economy as well as for particular sectors, form the basis for consensus building; before these are adopted by the Cabinet, they are thoroughly discussed by all major economic groups. These plans thus form the framework within which the various economic actors make their specific decisions, and are flexible and noncoercive: the private actors are provided incentives to operate within the planning framework, but are not compelled to do so. The basic assumption underlying the Japanese consensus process is that each group contributes specialized knowledge about its own resources, capabilities, and intentions and acquires much better information from the process for its own decisions, but no one is compelled to abide by the consensus decisions.

The third element of Japan's comprehensive economic plan is industrial policy to achieve various sectoral goals, which is the responsibility of the Ministry of International Trade and Industry (MITI). MITI attempts to find the best way to encourage the growth of, or adjustment out of, particular sectors. The specific tools available to MITI have included credit rationing; allocation of foreign exchange; organization of industry groups or cartels either to pool resources for desirable objectives (like developing new technology) or to agree on each company's share of total output during recessions or periods of structural change; and controlling technology transfer through foreign exchange allocations, licensing, international trade controls, taxes, and subsidies.

MITI's principal consensus-building mechanism is the Industrial Structure Council, made up of representatives of business, labor, government, academia, and others as appropriate. It helps MITI develop its long-range plans or "visions." These plans differ from those of the Economic Planning Agency in that MITI's visions provide much more detail on both the targeted sectors and the means to be used to achieve sectoral objectives. MITI's visions and the consensus process involved in their formulation are critical to the success of Japanese industrial policy. As a U.S. General Accounting Office study concluded:

> Dialogue between government and industry to achieve consensus on goals and mechanisms is critical to the effectiveness of industrial policy. The role of industry and trade associations, individual firms, *ad hoc* government committees, subgroups of the various ministerial agencies, etc. cannot be overemphasized. The cooperative working relationship which develops through government–industry interaction is equally critical to the success of industrial policy in Japan.[6]

Consensus-building mechanisms and processes are used to coordinate various Japanese plans and forecasts. Close coordination between the Ministry of Finance, MITI, and other ministries is very important because the financial system is pivotal to Japan's economic strategies; this system socializes risk by making it possible for firms to rely heavily on debt financing, which is guaranteed in targeted activities by the Bank of Japan. For this reason only about 11 percent of the financing of Japanese industry between 1966 and 1970 came from equity, and the proportion of financing raised through debt was about twice as great as it was in other OECD countries.[7]

The Japanese system illustrates the way coordination of various policy instruments can achieve such national objectives as high savings levels, efficient and flexible production systems, and the growth of both exports and national output. By keeping interest rates low, the Japanese ensured that demand for funds would exceed supply, which gave the banks considerable control over private companies. This system also gave the government considerable control over the banks. Securities markets were less developed because credit was cheaper through the banks, which were encouraged both to grant loans to favored activities and to underwrite government bond sales. Control of international financial transactions enabled the government to prevent outside influences from having much impact on the system, making it possible to keep interest rates and the value of the yen relatively low in order to discourage imports and stimulate exports. Similarly, the banks were forced to rely heavily on the Bank of Japan for loans to finance their operations. Since these loans were backed by the government, the Bank of Japan was able to maximize the credit available for growth by being overloaned—in other words, its external liabilities were greater than its total deposits. This system was reinforced by the banks' close interest in borrowing firms in which they held equity interests, a practice prohibited by law (the Glass–Steagall Act) in the United States. Indeed, most of the stock in Japanese corporations is held by closely related banks and corporations, and a relatively small percentage is held by individuals.

The system is also reinforced by measures to discourage consumption and encourage savings, including poorly developed social security and consumer credit systems, the semiannual bonus compensation system, relatively high prices for consumer goods, tax incentives for savings through either the banks or the postal system, and limited alternative investment opportunities for savings.

Japanese economic objectives have changed over time, altering the effectiveness of various policy instruments. In the fifties and early sixties the primary objectives were to achieve economic independence, to promote reconstruction, and to catch up with the developed countries. Between 1965 and 1974 social development became more important and economic activity shifted more to urban and regional development; to improvements in the public environment, health, and safety; to housing; and to the development of domestic computer and technology capability. After 1975 the policy focus shifted more to the stable development of the economy and the industrial focus shifted to the development of sophisticated technology and further improvements in the standard of living.

As might be expected, the relative importance of various policy instruments and the ability to achieve consensus changed as the Japanese economy developed and became more competitive in international markets. Monetary and fiscal policies became less restrictive with economic development, and trade and industry policies were liberalized. It also became more difficult to build consensus as groups diversified and became more independent of the government in an increasingly affluent society. Companies tended to become more independent as they accumulated internal resources, and the government's control of financial markets loosened as the Japanese economy became more internationalized. The sectoral targets became less obvious as the Japanese exhausted the pools of foreign technologies that could be quickly exploited. The need evolved for the Japanese to develop their own technology. Similarly, Japanese success with restrictive trade policies brought protests from their international trading partners, especially in the United States.

In the late sixties and early seventies it became clear to Japan's leaders that continued economic progress would depend on the shift of resources into high technology and high value-added activities, and out of some older industries in which Japan was no longer competitive with the less developed and newly industrializing countries, especially those in the Pacific basin. During the seventies the disintegration of the international financial and trading system, the oil crisis, and worldwide inflation caused the Japanese to shift their primary objective to stable economic growth instead of rapid growth.

These developments changed both industrial policy and MITI's power to carry out its objectives. So MITI shifted its focus to stress moving up the technological ladder and easing the adjustment of workers displaced from non-competitive industries. The economic problems of the seventies increased the Japanese budget deficit, so it was harder for MITI to acquire the resources to implement its programs, and the liberalization of trade and financial markets loosened MITI's control of credit and international trade. Ironically, MITI was forced to rely more heavily on moral suasion and to put a greater premium on consensus building at the very time its reduced economic power made it more difficult to achieve consensus.

While its functions and powers have changed, it would be a serious mistake to argue, as some have, that MITI no longer plays an important role in Japanese economic policy. The Ministry of Finance plays an important role in MITI's consensus-building discussions. It cannot propose projects or funding levels but can reject projects proposed by MITI and can modify funding levels. While MITI and the Ministry of Finance attempt to achieve consensus, there have been areas of disagreement, such as their ongoing conflict over the aircraft industry. Similarly, companies have not always accepted MITI's advice, as illustrated by the famous case in which the government tried to dissuade Honda from producing automobiles. Nor does MITI always accept industry advice: on one occasion, it successfully pushed for the creation of a robot leasing company, despite opposition from the Japan Industrial Robot Association.

Adjustment to a Changing Economic World

Japanese policy during the seventies and eighties turned increasingly to helping companies and workers move out of declining industries. Labor, business, and community representatives and the government participate jointly in these adjustment activities. The basic approach is to make public assistance depend on worker and community adjustment action.

The Japanese positive adjustment program is controlled by special industry-specific legislation and the Structurally Depressed Industries Law of 1978. If industries are designated as depressed (initially, open-hearth steel, shipbuilding, aluminum refining, and synthetic fiber production), the ministry responsible for that industry works with management and labor representatives to develop a basic stabilization plan to reduce capacity, improve the industry's operations and stabilize employment. To be designated as depressed, more than half the industry's firms must be having financial trouble, there must be unusual excess capacity, and two-thirds of the firms in the industry must sign a petition asking for this designation. This requirement means that the industry must first develop its own consensus.

After being designated a structurally depressed industry, the responsible ministry develops a detailed industry analysis and forecast in consultation with the industry advisory commission, unions, and the Fair Trade Commission, whose approval is required in order to exempt the plan from the Antimonopoly Law. To improve indus-

try-wide efficiency a joint fund is established with resources from the Japan Development Bank and from private sources. The ministry is authorized to restrict further
investment in the depressed industry and to encourage
firms to shift to other activities. The worker adjustment
programs for depressed industries and geographic areas
are administered by the Ministry of Labor and include
unemployment compensation, retraining, and job search
allowances.

The Japanese have developed sectoral and macroeconomic policies to deal with cyclical as well as structural
changes. Cartels are created to deal with short-term cyclical disruption by making price and production-sharing
agreements. There is evidence that Japanese approaches to
handling both structural and cyclical problems have been
successful in strengthening industrial competitiveness,
for example, in the textile and shipbuilding industries.

Such adjustment is not necessarily carried out smoothly
or without political opposition, because MITI has rarely
been able to repair declining industries as much as its
economic calculations predicted. In particular, the Japanese government has allowed some excess capacity to
remain for political reasons, though it has resisted demands by such declining industries as textiles for import
restrictions. Its theory is that continued imports accelerate
adjustment when decline is inevitable, while its consensus-building process promotes the general recognition by
all parties involved that adjustment is necessary and helps
obtain agreement on the most appropriate means for
facilitating adjustment. On the positive side, however,
the Japanese experience shows that the private employers,
especially in large firms, have considerable flexibility in
helping dislocated workers if they wish to do so, or are
required to do so by their restructuring agreement. In the
Japanese textile and shipbuilding industries, for example,
private firms assumed primary responsibility for retraining and relocation to other activities or industries.

National Economic Strategies

A very important difference between the United States and Japan has been the theoretical or conceptual framework upon which policies and strategies are based. For reasons discussed in chapter 4, many American companies focus too narrowly on short-run profit maximizing and not enough on long-run strategic considerations. The same theoretical underpinning creates ideological opposition to national economic strategies on the grounds that strategies cannot improve on the free market. Japanese officials, by contrast, have specifically rejected such static, orthodox economic theories. A high-ranking MITI official explained:

> Should Japan have entrusted its future, according to the theory of comparative advantage, to these industries characterized by intensive use of labor? [Had Japan] chosen to specialize in this kind of industry, it would almost permanently have been unable to break away from the Asian pattern of stagnation and poverty. . . . [MITI] decided to establish in Japan industries which require intensive employment of capital and technology, such as steel, oil refining, petrochemicals, automobiles, aircraft, industrial machinery of all sorts, and later electronics, including electronic computers. From a short-run, static viewpoint, encouragement of such industries would seem to conflict with economic rationalism. But, from a long-range viewpoint, these are precisely the industries where income elasticity of demand is high, technological progress is rapid, and labor productivity rises fast. It was clear that without these industries it would be difficult to raise [our] standard of living to that of Europe and America; . . . whether right or wrong, Japan had to have these heavy and chemical industries.[8]

Japanese corporate policy is likewise much more nationalistic than American; most Japanese business policies reflect national interests, whereas American policies rarely do. In part, the lack of coordination between business and government policy in the United States is responsible. Moreover, a Japanese corporation derives important strategic advantages from being a Japanese company, while an American company has few unique advantages not available to foreign companies operating in the United States.

In addition, Japanese companies have developed global strategies to gain market share by relying on their manufacturing superiority, while American companies pay much less attention to manufacturing. Indeed, American neoclassical economic thought sees no strategic advantage in manufacturing; but the Japanese believe that whoever controls manufacturing has a strategic economic advantage. Part of the Japanese strategy has been to gain ultimate competitive advantage by first entering into joint ventures with American companies that can no longer compete in price, quality, technology, or all of these. The Japanese take advantage of the American companies' tendency to respond to competitive challenges by shifting manufacturing to other countries in search of lower costs instead of by improving productivity through mechanization and better management. This has happened, for example, with cameras, hi-fi equipment, and video recorders, and is under way in many other industries, including automobiles, aircraft, computers, microelectronics, and steel. Such "outsourcing" is frequently the first stage in the loss of market share by American companies—this happened to RCA, when it entered into an agreement with Matsushita to produce RCA VCRs in Japan. After it acquired the technology, Matsushita started undercutting RCA by selling its own VCRs, which were very similar to RCA's, at substantially lower prices. RCA has now turned to Hitachi to manufacture its VCRs, but it suspects that before long it will have the same problem with them. RCA, unfortunately, has little choice because it lacks the manufacturing expertise to compete with the Japanese companies.

Other U.S. companies have had similar experiences. The 3M company made an agreement with Toshiba to produce copying machines, but in 1985 Toshiba started marketing similar machines in the United States for 20 percent less than 3M's copier. In the fifties and sixties, Bell & Howell marketed Canon's cameras in America, but in 1971 Canon canceled the arrangement and started marketing on its own in the United States. Bell & Howell's chief executive officer, Donald N. Frey, explained: "The Japanese pattern is very clear: Get an American involved to build the business and then get rid of the American."[9]

IBM developed a more effective strategy. In order to launch its personal computers quickly and at competitive prices, IBM had components made overseas. But as it gained market share with these computers, IBM was investing hundreds of millions of dollars in automated factories to make components in America. Having a stronger commitment to manufacturing and a well-developed global strategy, IBM managers realized that foreign manufacturers could encroach on its market if it remained dependent on them for manufacturing expertise. They also recognized that in the long run cheap foreign labor is not competitive with automated plants, which gain tremendous advantage from being located in the markets where final products are to be sold. But, most importantly, as Patrick Toole, IBM's vice-president for manufacturing, explained, "Unless you own the technology you can't be in the game for long."[10]

Some senior Japanese executives have warned their American counterparts of the dangers of abandoning too much manufacturing too fast. According to Sony chairman Akio Morita, "unless U.S. industry shores up its manufacturing base, 'it could lose everything.' . . . American companies have either shifted output to low-wage

countries or come to buy parts and assembled products
from countries like Japan that can make quality products
at low prices. The result is a hollowing of American industry. The U.S. is abandoning its status as an industrial
power."[11]

Microelectronics: A Classic Case

Japanese industrial strategies can best be illustrated by
the use Japanese companies have made of them to gain
market share in microelectronics, though they applied
strategies here that had already been perfected in other
industries, such as shipbuilding, steel, and autos. MITI
has made its motives for moving into the high-tech industries fairly explicit:

> It is extremely important for Japan to make the most of her
> brain resources, which may well be called the nation's only
> resource, and thereby to develop creative technologies of its
> own. . . . Possession of her own technology will help Japan
> to maintain and develop her industries' international superi-
> ority and to form a foundation for the long-term develop-
> ment of the economy and society. . . . This spirit of basing
> national development on technology should be our aim in
> the 1980s.[12]

The components of Japan's national strategy for establishing a comparative advantage in knowledge-intensive
industries were fivefold. The cornerstone was closing the
Japanese market to foreign competitors, except on a limited basis to acquire technology and know-how. Protectionist policies gave Japanese companies important strategic advantages. Japanese companies could test products
and achieve cost-effective, large-scale production without
their competitors exposing product weaknesses. Domestic
companies could also develop financial resources for fur-

ther research and product development, sometimes by charging higher prices in the domestic than in foreign markets. Moreover, state-owned companies, like Nippon Telephone and Telegraph, could provide guaranteed markets at premium prices.

Second, in carrying out its export-oriented industrial policy, MITI chose industries that could expand overseas sales because of cost or other advantages over foreign companies. American oligopolies were particularly vulnerable, not only because of their inherent inefficiencies but also because of their attempts to hold prices high and lay off workers during recessions. Japanese companies often established a toehold in the American market, and later enlarged their share through aggressive competition. A preferred strategy was "capital blockage," whereby Japanese firms cut prices very aggressively to deny American companies the opportunity to regain their development costs and finance the creation of new products. This strategy was particularly important in the memory chip competition.

The government's third component of its long-term strategy was to promote some competition in Japanese markets to stimulate efficiency, but controlling it within a framework of cooperation, coordination of effort, and specialization to strengthen technology and foreign market share. Finally, two of its financial priorities contributed: providing a dependable low-cost supply of capital through the banking system, and helping Japanese companies acquire and develop world-class technologies.

In short, the Japanese government's basic approach was to serve as doorman and promoter; to limit foreign competition and promote domestic industries. This strategy had worked to promote rapid development of the automobile industry in the seventies. In 1960, Japanese automobile production was only 120,000 vehicles. By 1970 it had jumped to 3.1 million, and by 1980 to more than 8 million. Earlier, similar progress was achieved in the steel industry, where production went from 5 million net tons in 1950 to 24 million in 1960 and more than 100 million in 1970, over 40 percent of which was exported.[13] The Japanese government refined its basic development strategy very successfully to move from a very weak position in the semiconductor industry in the sixties to very strong competitive positions in components, telecommunications, and computers in the seventies and eighties. In order to do this, MITI and Nippon Telephone and Telegraph agreed in 1975 to combine their research activities with private companies in a very large-scale integrated circuit research and development project funded at between $250 and $350 million over four years. The government provided $150 million of this money, and the rest came from private industry. Since a major objective of this project was to overtake the United States in integrated circuits, the Japanese spent 25 to 35 percent of their resources acquiring advanced semiconductor manufacturing and test equipment from the United States.

The Japanese moved quickly during the seventies to establish a strong position in American markets, where by mid-decade they had developed a solid marketing and distribution system. American firms, whose production and investment decisions were dictated mainly by short-run product and financial market considerations, were very vulnerable to this strategy. For example, during the 1974–1975 recession, American firms had cut their capacity. As the economy began to recover, they could not meet demand; so the Japanese moved quickly to capture 40 percent of the U.S. market for 16K RAM chips. During the late seventies and early eighties, they achieved important victories with the 64K RAM, and during the 1981–1982 recession, they strengthened their capacity and were ready to capture over 90 percent of 256K RAM sales, while consolidating their position in the 64K RAM market. Thus, after each American recession, Japanese companies have emerged with a larger market share.

In achieving their competitive successes in the semiconductor and other industries, the Japanese had a number of advantages. First of all, semiconductor production in Japan is concentrated in six large integrated companies, which accounted for 79 percent of sales in 1979, even though semiconductors accounted for a much smaller percentage of each company's sales than was true of their American competition. The ratio of semiconductors to total sales for the American companies ranged from 31 percent to 89 percent; for Japanese companies the range was 2.3 percent to 17.8 percent.[14] In 1985, Japanese companies accounted for 90 percent of semiconductor sales in Japan.[15]

Second, the Japanese companies were aided by the government's help in coordination of effort within the industry so that specialization permitted each company to achieve cost-effective, large-scale production in its specialty. Internal consumption by each company was therefore relatively low: 21 percent for the largest ten companies and 10 percent for the top four in 1979.[16]

By controlling large shares of semiconductor production and consumption, the largest companies effectively controlled the market and therefore could limit foreign competition—a role performed earlier by the government. During the seventies, for example, the Japanese stepped up their imports from the United States in advanced products the Japanese did not produce, but American imports leveled off and then declined as Japanese firms became competitive in these items. When the Japanese were building market share in the United States during the seventies, they actually increased both their imports from and their exports to the United States, which simultaneously improved their American market share and diverted American production into the Japanese market, where the

Japanese companies had sufficient control to reduce imports when they wanted to. Japanese competitiveness in the U.S. market was not just on the basis of price: they also sold higher quality products, so they could increase their market share while avoiding the charge of dumping. Thus, even after the Japanese government liberalized trade restrictions, control functions were taken over more informally by the large Japanese electronic companies. The multiproduct, integrated nature of these large firms also gives them greater resources than their smaller American merchant competitors and permits them to cross-subsidize—in other words, profits in some areas can subsidize developing products until they become competitive.

Aside from their advantages of scale, Japanese companies also have important market structure advantages. Each Japanese company is not only a larger integrated company than its American competitors, but is also part of a stabilizing and reinforcing conglomerate industrial and financial group, or *keiretsu*. These groups are ordinarily organized around a bank or large industrial firm; in addition, they contain large trading companies to facilitate overseas sales, distribution, and financing. There is cross-ownership and interlocking management within the *keiretsu*. These industrial and financial conglomerates thus provide an additional internal market to enhance economies of scale, create barriers to market penetration by outsiders, and provide financial and market stability.[17]

In an increasingly capital-intensive area like semiconductor technology, the ready availability of capital at lower rates is an enormous competitive advantage,* which has allowed Japanese firms to rely much more heavily on debt than on equity. American companies, by contrast, rely more heavily on retained earnings and eq-

*In the early seventies, the rate of capital investment per unit of wafer fabrication was 1:15, but for the 64K RAM chip it was 1:2.5.[18]

uity. Most Japanese semiconductor firms have debt–equity ratios of between 150 and 400 percent, compared with 5 to 10 percent for U.S. companies. Equity is ordinarily controlled by other firms in the *keiretsu,* who have more of a business than an equity interest in the semiconductor firms.

There are various consequences of this financial structure. A Japanese semiconductor company is able to pursue a long-run competitive strategy, while its American competitors are more vulnerable to short-run stock market fluctuations, which do not necessarily coincide with the companies' capital needs. This long-term strategy permits Japanese companies to take advantage of American vulnerability to market cycles. In this manner, the Japanese became reliable suppliers of quality chips, while their more volatile American competitors were acquiring reputations for unreliability because of their typical American "feast and famine" procedures, dictated by unstable American markets and the tyranny of Wall Street.

The *keiretsu* system is made possible, of course, by the coordinated and comprehensive economic and financial policy generated by the teamwork of the Bank of Japan and the Ministry of Finance. The government's ability to steer capital to favored industries means that private lending is likely to follow. As Richard Caves explains, the fact of "government concern with the well-being of a favored sector, like semiconductors, is taken as an implicit guarantee of loans made to them."[19] The Japanese system in general, therefore, greatly reduces the risks for Japanese companies through the active involvement of the government working through the Bank of Japan to provide financial security, protection from external competition, and strategic help with technology and information. Companies can take advantage of long-term strategic opportunities with less fear than their American competitors of foreclosure and financial collapse.

Prior successes in market penetration in the United States, together with long-term economic and financial stability, have made it possible for Japanese firms to devote a much larger proportion of their revenues to capital investment and process innovations. Japanese companies regularly spend at least 50 percent of their semiconductor revenues on research and development, about twice as much as their most aggressive American competitors. The Japanese spent more in absolute terms on capital investment and research and development in 1984 than U.S. merchant companies; according to the *New York Times* (March 24, 1985), the Japanese spent $3.2 billion compared with $2.3 billion for U.S. firms.

Underlying all of these advantages are the close (though changing) relations between the Japanese public and private sectors, in sharp contrast to U.S. experience, where policy is uncoordinated and simplistic, and often inflicts considerable damage on American companies and workers. For instance, after 1981 U.S. macroeconomic policy greatly increased real interest rates and economic instability. Similarly, America's passive, inchoate trade policy is an open invitation to the active predatory practices of foreign firms and governments. While American policy attempts to convert the world to Adam Smith, other countries are gaining competitiveness by pursuing a carefully orchestrated combination of policies to strengthen domestic, economic, and trade policies in order to achieve national goals.

The debilitating effects of the naïve commitment to the ghost of Adam Smith is nowhere illustrated more clearly than in the U.S. government's treatment of the semiconductor and telecommunications industries. In August 1985, long after its decision was irrelevant to the strategic victory of the Japanese in the next generation of memory chips, the U.S. International Trade Commission ruled that the Japanese were guilty of dumping 64K RAM chips by selling them in the United States at about half the cost of production.[20] Moreover, when the administration almost simultaneously announced plans to charge the Japanese with dumping the 256K RAM chip, Japanese companies could negate this action by raising prices. Since they had gained over 90 percent of the world market for this chip, they could increase their profits while avoiding dumping charges.[21] This case was resolved, at least temporarily, in August 1985 when Japan agreed to establish a price monitoring system and to give American companies greater access to the Japanese market. As in the steel case, however, this belated arrangement could set prices at a level to permit dumping by other countries, especially Korea.

At the same time, the U.S. policies were destabilizing the American telecommunications industry by forcing the breakup of AT&T, generally regarded as the cornerstone of the most efficient communications system in the world. The breakup of Bell Labs will deprive the country of an important public source of research and development. Naïve and ineffective trade policies unilaterally opened the American telecommunications market to Japanese equipment manufacturers while allowing the Japanese market to remain virtually closed to more efficient American producers. The Japanese have announced the partial privatization of Nippon Telephone and Telegraph, but only the most innocent really expect the Japanese to provide equal access voluntarily to American producers. As Department of Commerce trade expert Lionel Olmer put it, Japan's position on telecommunications is "inherently discriminatory."[22] Japanese "liberalization" of official trade restraints usually comes only after the private structures are in place to continue to bar those things the Japanese wish to exclude.

Japan's reluctance to open its markets is well documented. Applications by American companies, like IBM, to operate in Japan were delayed while Japanese compa-

nies could strengthen their competitiveness. Even though
IBM Japan is a Japanese-managed company, it is considered an "outsider." According to another *New York Times*
article (August 9, 1985), Japanese companies wishing to
purchase IBM equipment have been required to explain
why they were buying "foreign computers."

Japan apparently responds no faster to national agreements. In the 1981 Nippon Telephone and Telegraph
agreement, for example, Japan promised to open its markets to U.S. telecommunications equipment. However, as
Robert B. Wood testified to the Senate Subcommittee on
International Trade on May 3, 1985, between 1981 and
1984, the Japanese purchased $61 *million* in telecommuni-
cations equipment from American companies, but sold
$1.95 *billion* in the United States ($941 million of which
was in 1984 alone). This is a ratio of $1 of exports to Japan
for every $32 of imports from that country. It is, more-
over, hard to argue that U.S. companies, with by far the
world's most advanced technology, are "noncompetitive"
in telecommunications. It is thus not surprising that the
1980 U.S. trade surplus in telecommunications equipment
of $874 million was converted to a deficit of $660 million
in 1983. The real value of exports in this industry increased modestly from $1 billion in 1978 to $1.3 billion in
1983; imports increased from $426 million to $2 billion.

These developments are critical because of the importance of the telecommunications industry. The worldwide
proliferation of public and private communications net-
works will provide enormous markets for telecommunications equipment for the next twenty years; the telecommunications sectors' use of microelectronics will do much
to determine the future competitiveness of *both* sectors, as
well as of the entire U.S. economy.

Thus, a major problem for the future competitiveness of
the American semiconductor and telecommunications industry has been inadequate government policies, not the
industries' inherent inability to be technically innovative

and economically competitive. In a really free and open market system, Japanese telecommunication equipment and semiconductor manufacturers would have had great difficulty surviving. As Michael Borrus and his colleagues at the Berkeley Roundtable on the International Economy point out on the basis of thorough studies of both the semiconductor and the telecommunications industries:

> In the dynamically unstable, strategic competitive market environment . . . government has critical roles to play. Yet, U.S. policy has become increasingly directionless, committed to deregulation and market competition but pushed toward international protectionism by the imports and market adjustments that are the very consequences of its commitment. . . .
>
> Yet, coherent and strategic policy matters crucially in this sector. . . . Policy matters because producers . . . create economically strategic impacts on related sectors, most critically computing and microelectronics. . . . And policy matters because the combination of foreign interventionist policies and closed markets threatens to undermine the current competitive advantages of U.S. firms in open markets.[23]

There can be little doubt about the basic strength of American semiconductor, computer, and telecommunications equipment companies. U.S. microelectronics components firms, nevertheless, have seen their share of the world market shrink from 63 percent in 1978 to 50 percent in 1984, while the Japanese share was increasing from 24 percent to 38 percent. The Japanese have succeeded in gaining control of the strategically important memory chip business, but U.S. companies still have a commanding lead in microprocessors, for which in 1984 Japan held 30 percent of world market shares, the United States held 63 percent, and Europe held 7 percent.[24]

As noted earlier, however, the Japanese want to win in computers, not just chips and microprocessors—though microprocessors are a key to their success in computers generally. The Japanese have also increased their research and development and capital expenditures in an effort to seize market share in other areas where U.S. firms hold commanding technological positions—especially the final systems, computer, and telecommunications markets.

It will be more difficult for the Japanese to take over these sectors of the information industry, however, where their international competitors are strong, well-entrenched firms like IBM, AT&T, Northern Telecom, Ericson, and Hewlett-Packard. There is now much more awareness of Japanese strengths and strategies and, with appropriate public policies, these companies can hold their positions. IBM, for example, holds an almost unassailable lead in large mainframe computers, even though it has slipped to third place in the Japanese market, which its chairman characterizes as "one of the most closed markets in the world."[25] According to the March 11, 1985, issue of *Forbes,* U.S. producers also still have over 50 percent of the chipmaking machine market, while the Japanese have 41 percent. In fact, most of the worldwide gains in semiconductors by Japanese companies have been at the expense of the Europeans, who occupy very weak positions in these sectors. European producers' world market share in semiconductors declined from 13.9 percent in 1978 to 8.6 percent in 1984.[26]

The Legacy of Protectionism and Stability

While there is no question about the Japanese economic successes, there is considerable disagreement about their causes, their applicability to other countries, and Japan's ability to sustain this growth in the more restrictive economic environment of the eighties. There will be greater resistance to Japan's export-driven economic policies, and Japan will have to develop its own technologies and contend with both a growing demand by its citizens for domestic improvements in the standard of living and an aging work force. In addition, Japanese micro, industrial, and macro systems, which were geared to an era of fairly rapid growth, will have to adapt to slower growth in the eighties—even though Japan's performance has been superior to that of other OECD countries on most change indicators.

While Japan's management systems and corporate strategies have played important roles in their economic successes, their consensus-based economic policies have also contributed significantly to the Japanese "economic miracle." This is particularly true of industrial policy, which many critics argue played no role at all. In some sense, however, the arguments over industrial policy spring from preconceived biases, which create caricatures of what industrial policy is and what it is intended to achieve. Few of its advocates believe that industrial policy *alone* would be sufficient for economic policy purposes. There is general agreement among its supporters that industrial policy complements, rather than replaces, markets and macroeconomic policies. Macroeconomic policy is generally conceded to be the main instrument for countercyclical policies, while industrial policy is designed to complement monetary and fiscal policies and deals more effectively with the specific problems and opportunities in selective sectors. As noted, however, the close complementary (even synergistic) interrelationships between selective and general economic policies make it difficult to measure the impact of each.

Because of these complexities, it is impossible to resolve the issue of how effective Japanese industrial policy has been. But there is considerable evidence that Japanese industrial policy was an important cause of Japan's superior economic performance. Clearly, it has not been perfect nor always achieved its objectives, but it would be difficult to examine the Japanese experience industry by industry and not conclude that it has been largely successful.[27] Critics point to examples such as MITI's failure to persuade Honda not to produce automobiles as evidence of the government's inability to pick winners, but that is an example of the system's *success*. In a planned economy (which critics accuse industrial policy supporters of advocating), Honda would not have been allowed to produce cars if the planners hadn't wanted them to. Fortunately, infallibility is not a precondition for relatively successful policy making, or we would all be doomed.

It is sometimes argued that the Japanese government failed in its efforts to develop the automobile industry. However, this argument will not withstand careful scrutiny. The Japanese government in fact played a key role in helping it become a strong international competitor. The Japanese auto industry grew from second in the world with three million vehicles to first place in 1980 with eleven million vehicles. This was achieved until the seventies by stiff tariff barriers, and thereafter by onerous standards, customs procedures, and other nontariff barriers. As in other industries, the Japanese government gave preferential credit to auto companies and prevented foreign auto companies from investing in Japan until the seventies, when foreigners were permitted to have minority interests. The auto industry also benefited from MITI policies to improve technology and reduce the costs of steel, robotics, and machine tools.

Because scale economies are so important to international competition in this industry, MITI had visions of consolidating a dozen Japanese auto companies into two very large ones producing several million vehicles apiece. Although MITI failed with this consolidation, its "vision" was fulfilled on schedule. Toyota and Nissan (with its *keiretsu* partner Fuji, maker of Subarus) each produced over three million vehicles in the early eighties, and three other companies (Toyo Kogyo, Mitsubishi, and Honda) also produced over a million vehicles each.

One tactic used by its critics is to pose artificial definitions of industrial policy. For example, critics usually define industrial policy as an effort to "pick winners and losers" by substituting economic planning for the free market and by using government revenues to accelerate the winners and prop up the losers. This is obviously a caricature that few careful analysts would support; it certainly does not define Japanese industrial policy. As the Japanese use the term, industrial policy is simply designed to affect a particular industry or industries. As one Japanese expert observes:

> The central lesson of the Japanese industrial policy experience is not, as some Americans argue, that government 'guidance' of industry works better than traditional market economies. Unfettered supply and demand determine the direction of growth in Japan at least as much as they do in the United States. The lesson of Japan is that a government can truly aid private industry if and only if it coherently plans *its* ordinary activities on the basis of a vision of the economy's future.[28]

The main point here is that the government uses its *regular activities* to help private economic activity to achieve agreed-upon objectives.

MITI does not pick winners and losers; its visions predict "which industries will be able to grow and which will shrink because international competition is too tough for them." Moreover, these visions are developed on the basis of consensus processes involving labor, management, and other groups, so the government does not develop its predictions in isolation.

> Businessmen . . . can expect more sympathy from officials if they try to produce things that the projections indicate the country needs, but the government rarely becomes coercive. . . .
>
> In the United States policies are developed either with no clear vision of the future or with conflicting visions held by the people approving and implementing the policies . . . the corresponding groups in Japan may have differed too, but the discipline of helping MITI produce an official vision at least forced them to think through their own ideas. They had to consider their policies in the light of other policies that were likely to be adopted. Japan's Environmental Protection Agency, for example, has always had to think about how industry will pay for the environmental improvements the agency proposes.[29]

Despite the consensus-building process, which helps all parties avoid mistakes, any forecast may turn out to be wrong. But in Japan, when errors are made all parties involved in constructing the original view understand why it was wrong, or at least how the prediction was put together. For example, a faulty 1974 economic growth forecast caused an overproduction of steel, but those government officials involved understood the industry's problems and were better able to cooperate in the adjustment process to reduce overproduction. The faulty forecast in the early seventies was worldwide, requiring most steel-producing countries to reduce capacity. For whatever reason, the Japanese reduced capacity with a good deal less hardship and conflict than was true of, say, the United States, the United Kingdom, or France. It even reduced capacity more easily than the Germans—where different consensus processes (codetermination and Concerted Action) facilitated adjustment.

One cannot examine Japanese economic success in much detail without concluding that their public policies have been a major source of their success. It is hard to imagine that Japanese auto or microelectronics companies would have ever become important international competitors without active government involvement to protect them from more competitive American companies, provide technological and financial help, and maintain a very supportive economic environment. Japanese leaders themselves concur in this conclusion.

I do not mean to imply by anything in this chapter that we should either condemn or emulate the Japanese. Japanese strategies are perfectly rational when compared to the irrationality of American policies. But while we can learn from the Japanese experiences, our conditions are different and policies must therefore be adapted to the American environment and economic history. While the Japanese economy has made great progress and is rapidly catching up to the United States, ours remains the world's strongest economy. Nevertheless, our policies can be modified to improve our performance, as my recommendations in the *next* chapter will show.

Chapter IX

We Too Can
Make It Work

THIS BOOK has demonstrated that the performance of the American economy has been weakened by poor economic policies and inefficient, obsolete management systems. America's policy problems, in turn, are due partly to the absence of mechanisms to balance the concerns of workers and other major economic interests. Although it remains the world's strongest economy, the productive potential of the United States is being eroded, its companies are losing their competitiveness, and the gap between our economy's potential and its actual performance is growing. These developments have ominous implications for America's national power and for the welfare of its people. The United States is losing its ability to project its values and defend its global interests. Poor economic performance means, in addition, declining real incomes for American families, increasing joblessness, serious social pathologies, and a diminished standard of living for most Americans. These problems are camouflaged by the rising incomes of the wealthy, who get most of their income from property and not from work, and by the fact that so much of our current consumption is financed by heavy borrowing, much of it from abroad. Indeed, many of America's prominent economists and political leaders exhibit the kind of hubris—an overwhelming self-confidence and arrogance about what they perceive to be the "American way"—that usually afflicts the leaders of a declining civilization. They assume that, because we are rich and our policies and institutions have "worked" in the past, they are working now and will work in the future. Unfortunately, the erosion of America's economic might is a slow, cancerlike process whose full consequences might not be sufficiently obvious to gain political attention until they have become irreversible.

The tragedy is that America's loss of economic power is unnecessary. We have the resources to reverse our economic decline, but we lack the policies and institutions. Worker participation can contribute importantly to management systems and can help create economic policies that are more balanced and therefore more effective. The domination of economic policy making by economists, politicians, and bankers causes them to minimize the importance of such matters as employment, real wages, human capital, long-run economic competitiveness, and equity—all of which are essential to sound economic performance.

The technological and economic changes of today and tomorrow—especially internationalization—require that we give more attention to human capital and worker participation. We are not likely to have enduring prosperity and growth in a democratic society without an equitable sharing of the benefits and the costs alike of change. Our current economic policies not only create instability and make us less competitive; they also shift most of the benefits of limited growth to nonworkers and most of the costs to workers.

I do not mean to argue, of course, that worker participation *alone* will solve our problems. We need to do more. But I do believe that greater worker involvement and a full employment, human resource oriented economic strategy would be much better than the strategies (or nonstrategies) that currently dominate U.S. economic policy. I hope to outline here a more democratic alternative that gives greater weight to workers' concerns.

Transforming the American System

Internationalization, especially competition with the Japanese, has exposed weaknesses in American management, industrial relations, and public policy-making systems. These changes have spawned a variety of new forms of cooperative worker participation, sometimes to complement and sometimes as a substitute for collective bargaining. Many see the new trends as part of the inevitable transformation of democratic processes—from political, to industrial and social, and now to economic democracy.

There is, however, considerable debate about whether these new participation forms are a basic trend or a passing fad. The evidence suggests that many of those processes are very superficial and so will not last, but that genuine worker participation is here to stay. In the global information world, genuine participation and cooperation provide significant competitive advantages. Similarly, increased worker ownership could improve employee incentives as well as help prevent the polarization of income distribution. And worker ownership could help halt the export of jobs by profit-maximizing multinationals and might create more competitive business organizations. While the trends and potentials are unmistakable, the magnitudes of these changes are still too small to give much indication of their future impact.

Worker involvement and sound economic policies are also important in making the most effective use of information technology, the development and proper use of which is essential to the competitiveness of American industry. There is the danger that this technology will be used to displace workers and make work more hazardous and degrading—finally realizing the objectives of scientific management to give managers complete control over workers, fragment work, and make it dull, dangerous, and boring—or it can be used to create jobs and to make work more interesting and challenging. Worker participation in the planning and use of the technology can maximize the latter outcome and minimize the former. Unfortunately, the traditional authoritarian management system has a bias toward reducing worker participation in order to strengthen management's control. This bias, if unchecked, may continue to weaken the competitiveness of American industry relative to more participative competitors in other countries.

It should be emphasized, however, that while genuine participation makes labor–management relations less adversarial, it does not eliminate conflict. Indeed, collective bargaining and other adversarial processes serve the important positive functions of protecting legitimate differences. What is required, therefore, is to prevent purposeless conflict, which only makes all parties worse off. It is perfectly natural for cooperative and adversarial relations to coexist. Cooperation strengthens production; adversarial processes contest the best way to share the gains of a common enterprise. The evidence suggests, moreover, that participation is not likely to be very effective or enduring unless workers have the ability to form strong independent organizations to protect their workplace and societal interests.

It is not widely recognized in the United States that providing worker participation in public policy making can strengthen those policies. The workers' perspective is needed to balance the ideas of academic economists and commercial and financial interests. Worker representation will focus on human resource development, which is the main source of improved productivity and competitiveness. Workers will emphasize the need for jobs, real output, and employment, and those too are in the national interest. Nonlabor interests are, moreover, likely to deemphasize equity. While there can be conflict between equity and efficiency, in the long run, a just society is a more efficient society.

Public Policy

As I have emphasized throughout this book, private systems alone will not restore competitiveness and real wage growth; our public policy defects are at least as serious as the shortcomings in our management and industrial relations systems. A major problem for American policy makers is the absence of a consensus-building process that balances labor and nonlabor interests. Consensus mechanisms based on the principles outlined in chapter 7 could therefore improve U.S. economic policy making.

Of course, consensus mechanisms alone will not solve our problems. Solutions—or even improvements—will require comprehensive economic policies geared to the realities of the global information world. The remainder of this chapter outlines the public policy goals and policies that I would recommend to a consensus-building group if we had one.

Full employment should remain our main economic objective. Employment is the main way workers participate in the economy. Work is the way most adults organize their lives, identify themselves, and contribute to the community. Despite the emergence of two-income families and unemployment compensation, unemployment still exacts heavy human and material costs. Most unemployed workers do not receive unemployment compensation, and declining real wages make it difficult for the families of the unemployed to make it on one income. Besides its benefits to individual workers, lower unemployment would ease many of our social and economic problems. In fact, the full employment dividend of at least $200 billion a year could provide resources to fund pressing national needs.*

Stronger growth would facilitate economic adjustment, reduce national disunity, and help restore the kind of optimism, self-confidence and generosity of spirit that infused many of our policies in the fifties and sixties. Strong growth would also help combat the dangers of degenerating protectionism, which usually results from rising unemployment and slow growth. In fact, strong growth in the United States would help with both the federal deficit and the problems associated with the depressed global economy. Slow growth in productivity and output has created serious problems for American workers, despite the growth in jobs. Our goal should therefore be rising wages and family incomes, both of which have been declining since the sixties. The problem is particularly serious for young families:

> When two wages do not seem to bring a family the same standard of living one wage did 15 years ago, when young couples fight to be able to afford their first home, . . . and

*Brookings Institution economist Ed Denison has demonstrated that the American economy has experienced a widening gap between actual and potential output; the gap averaged only 0.9 percent from 1948 through 1969, but jumped to 4.2 percent from 1970 through 1973, to 6.5 percent from 1975 to 1979, and to 9.8 percent from 1980 through 1983.[1]

when 55 percent of children living in single parent families are brought up in poverty, it is no wonder that this generation thinks more about themselves than their neighbors. Our challenge is to broaden both their income opportunities and their field of vision.[2]

Because of these problems, we must be concerned about economic justice and equity, as well as growth. Many people see a conflict between efficiency and equity, but our history, along with the contemporary experiences of countries like Germany and Japan (whose growth in both productivity and total national output has been greater than ours), make it clear that the degree of inequality that we have today is not necessary for economic efficiency and growth. This does not mean, of course, that we must redistribute incomes by transfer payments or welfare— though these programs must be provided for those who cannot or should not work. Rather, a fair economy is one in which people have adequate opportunity to develop their human potential, where everyone who is willing and able to work has an opportunity and an incentive to do so, where rewards are distributed mainly on the basis of work, and where those who are willing to work can earn decent incomes.

My recommendations are founded on five principles for economic policies. First, policies should be *comprehensive*, since the causes of our economic problems are long standing, deeply entrenched, complex, and international in scope. Unless policies are comprehensive and mutually reinforcing, they are likely to be ineffective or even contradictory. The problems confronting the American economy are sufficiently serious to require urgent attention from labor, management, and government alike.

Second, policies should be *relevant to current conditions*. The policies and institutions that contributed significantly to the longest period of growth and widely shared prosperity in our history between 1945 and 1965 have many features that remain viable, and are much better than the monetarist and supply side alternatives. Nevertheless, they need to be modified to fit the realities of the internationalized information world. Labor and management as well as governments must adapt their policies and institutions to modern realities.

Third, policies should recognize *the logical division of labor between governance mechanisms.* Markets are the principal allocative mechanisms in a democratic industrial economy. Experience shows markets to have important efficiency advantages. However, markets also have important limitations. In particular, markets tend to become uncompetitive and to generate instability and inequalities in wealth and income. Similarly, they are not very good at achieving such critical objectives as research and technological innovation, safe and healthful workplaces, a clean environment, equity, and human resource development. Moreover, market mechanisms will not protect American producers or consumers from the predatory activities of foreign governments or corporations. To be effective, therefore, national and international markets must operate within the framework of rules, policies, and institutions that correct for these market failures and defects.

Fourth, there are rough *logical divisions of labor between the public and private sectors and among levels of government.* Many of the things that need to be done—especially those relating to human resource development—are properly the functions of state and local governments. Indeed, at a time of political stalemate and confusion in Washington, many states have demonstrated the kind of creative pragmatism needed to address the problems America faces in a global information era. Several states, for instance, are developing consensus-based industrial policies anchored in human capital strategies. These states recognize the futility of strategies based on tax subsidies to attract marginal, low-wage industry that is on its way to the Third World. Unfortunately, however, the states cannot solve the trade, finance, and national economic instability problems responsible for most of our economic difficulties.

Finally, there should be means for *full participation by all major economic interests* at every level, state and local, national and international. Governments at any level have major responsibilities for building consensus between diverse organizations and interests. Governments also have a responsibility to protect the public interest and to promote economic justice for the powerless. The main purpose of consensus mechanisms should be to focus attention on common interests and avoid functionless conflict. In the absence of consensus, policies are likely to be erratic and uncoordinated and to serve already powerful interest groups. Properly structured consensus processes at every level reduce conflict and can provide all parties with better information about limits and about individual and collective options. At the same time, consensus processes must not be substitutes for markets, enterprise and organizational decisions, collective bargaining, regulations, or legislation; but they can improve all of these activities.[3]

The components of comprehensive economic policies, to restore competitiveness and real wage growth, should include coordinated, balanced macroeconomic policies; dynamic policies that can adapt readily to changing conditions; enforceable minimum international labor standards; and the capability to intervene selectively on the national front to deal with specific sectoral problems.

Our aim in macroeconomic policy making should be to give high priority to promoting balanced economic growth and relatively full and efficient utilization of human and physical resources. These goals should be united with active policies to promote a relatively open and expanding international trade, finance, and development system within the framework of negotiated, realistic, and enforceable rules. An expanding international economy contributed importantly to economic growth and prosperity between 1945 and 1965, but since 1975, the international economy has stagnated and international institutions are in disarray. As the strongest economy in the world, the United States has a major responsibility to initiate the processes that can restore the health of the global economy. In order to achieve more effective international economic cooperation, the United States should strengthen the coordinating functions of such international organizations and processes as the OECD and the annual economic summits by encouraging much greater business and labor representation in these activities. We should, in addition, take the lead to modernize other international economic institutions, including the General Agreement on Tariffs and Trade, the International Monetary Fund, and the World Bank. These international institutions are in distress in part because they are based on the realities of the forties, not of the eighties and beyond. It is especially important to have better coordination of macroeconomic policies; prevent wide exchange rate fluctuations; provide stronger mechanisms to bring discipline to international financial markets; broaden participation in international institutions; and modernize the rules for international trade to make them more realistic and enforceable. Realism requires the inclusion of important activities like services and labor standards.

Enforceable minimum international labor standards would protect workers, strengthen management, improve international competitiveness, and promote human resource development. It is unrealistic to assume that a uniform international minimum wage could be enforced, but other standards that most countries have already accepted as part of their involvement in the International Labor

Organization could be enforced. These include freedom of association, occupational safety and health, and freedom from discrimination and forced labor. It is particularly important to strengthen workers' ability to organize in order to protect and promote their interests. The United States has taken the first steps toward international labor standards in the 1984 extension of the Generalized System of Preferences, the Overseas Private Investment Corporation Reauthorization Act of 1986, and the 1983 Caribbean Basin Initiative, which linked trade preferences and political risk insurance to the establishment and protection of internationally recognized worker rights. International labor standards should be included in the General Agreement on Tariffs and Trade rules. These standards could overcome worker resistance to a more open trading system, as well as protect labor standards, which are likely to be neglected by traditional economic policy makers. Such protection is necessary because depressed working conditions in other countries give international and foreign companies competitive advantages, violate the human rights of workers in those countries, and make it difficult to enforce labor standards in countries with generally acceptable practices.[4]

At the national level there should be selective interventions to deal with specific sectoral problems that cannot be reached very efficiently or equitably by macroeconomic policies. For example, a selective anti-inflation policy should be developed *before* inflation becomes a problem again. A comprehensive anti-inflation policy should combine four basic inflation-fighting strategies: first, a balanced general economic policy aimed at steady growth, strong investment in physical and human capital, and full employment of human and physical resources; second, targeted sectoral programs designed to increase supply, reduce costs, and improve efficiency in inflation-leading sectors; third, equitable wage–price policies developed cooperatively and founded on a fair sharing of the sacrifices needed to prevent inflation or bring it under control; and fourth, policies to insulate the American economy as much as possible from external exchange rate, financial, energy, and commodity price shocks. In the last half of the eighties, for example, a massive buildup of oil reserves at low prices could do much to prevent future energy price shocks. Without such measures to develop stockpiles and alternative sources of supply, the U.S. economy is virtually certain to have new energy price shocks in the nineties that could be much worse than those of the seventies. Similarly, without interventions to stabilize volatile exchange rates, the U.S. economy could continue to lurch back and forth between stagnation and inflation.

Selective labor market policies are essential to strengthen public and private systems for job training; to improve the operation of labor markets, especially through better information and other means of encouraging labor mobility; and to provide greater public support for public and private job creation for targeted groups not likely to be absorbed in the private sector at reasonable unemployment levels by macroeconomic policies alone without unacceptable levels of inflation. Experiences in the United States and elsewhere demonstrate that selective labor market policies are needed to complement macroeconomic policies, and they can be very cost effective public investments. Macroeconomic policies to promote growth must be the main instruments of a full employment strategy, but selective labor market policies can reduce unemployment more efficiently and equitably and thus should play a much larger role in economic policy.

A lifelong education and training and a human resource development strategy would establish a system of worker training entitlements to foster the upgrading of workers' skills. This system could be used for education, training, and a variety of related activities, and could be modeled after the GI Bill, one of our most successful human resource development programs. Tax incentives for investment in human capital should be at least as attractive as those for investment in physical capital.

Similarly, there should be selective industrial policies, one important component of which being an adjustment program to provide a more equitable sharing of the benefits and costs of change, promote the adjustment of resources from noncompetitive into more competitive industries, and strengthen the competitiveness of all industries that have a realistic chance to become competitive. Similarly, it should be required that employers give adequate notice of plant closings and large-scale layoffs. A public investment bank should be created to meet important investment needs not likely to be financed by private credit markets. Such a bank could bring together present disorganized federal credit activities and encourage the investment credit activities already under way in a number of states. The Glass–Steagall Act should be repealed, in order to permit equity interests in companies by commercial banks. Finally, civilian research and development should be increased in order to promote innovation—including process innovation to improve productivity.

We should also continue to encourage worker participation in the ownership and management of enterprises by providing greater worker control of pension funds and improving the usefulness of employee stock ownership plans (ESOPs), according to the principles outlined in chapter 6. And since worker participation is not likely to be very effective unless workers have the right to form organizations that they control, workers' right to organize and to bargain collectively through representatives of their own choosing should be strengthened by stiffening the penalties for violation of the National Labor Relations Act and by streamlining the National Labor Relations

Board's procedures regarding representation elections and unfair labor practices. The National Labor Relations Act should also be modernized to bring its provisions more into conformity with the requirements of an internationalized information world. Like many of our labor market institutions, it is based on the assumptions of the thirties, when most workers were involved in the production of goods for the domestic market, managerial functions were fairly distinct from those of workers, labor–management relations were almost exclusively adversarial, and work forces were more homogeneous. The National Labor Relations Act needs to be revamped to accommodate the needs of the service and information occupations, temporary and part-time workers, greater job mobility within companies, more cooperative and participative arrangements, and the blurring of distinctions between employees and management. Present National Labor Relations Board rules tend to perpetuate fragmented, adversarial relations and are not flexible enough to accommodate highly mobile and dynamic work relationships. Moreover, increased employer violations of the law, combined with weak penalties and procedures that permit long-time delays, have greatly weakened legal protections for collective bargaining. This is a serious hazard because worker participation is not likely to be very effective unless workers have the ability to form independent organizations in the workplace as well as in the larger society.

Lastly, we need to rebuild our public infrastructures, which are in such serious disrepair that they impair the efficiency of the economy. A shelf of public works projects in specific areas to be used to counteract rising unemployment in those areas is an effective way to prevent the waste of human resources through unemployment. These public works activities could be financed through loans from a public investment bank.

A full exploration of all the items in this outline is

beyond the scope of this chapter, but certain of the major points should be expanded.

Macroeconomic Policies and International Coordination

As has been demonstrated throughout this book, many of our economic problems are due to macroeconomic policy failures. Coordinated monetary and fiscal policies must therefore be the main instruments for placing the economy on path toward full employment. Federal budget deficits must be reduced and monetary constraints loosened in order to reduce real interest rates. But budget deficits should be reduced by raising revenues, not by further cuts in vital human resource development programs (such as health, education, and training).

Effective national macroeconomic policy requires much better international economic cooperation. During the first half of the eighties, the expansionary U.S. fiscal policy has been counteracted by restrictive policies in other industrialized countries. These countries had the political freedom to practice fiscal constraint because the unprecedented stimulus resulting from U.S. budget deficits and an overvalued dollar enabled them to export to relatively open U.S. markets instead of stimulating their own economies. Thus, a large part of the increase in demand here was met with foreign imports.*

The United States should take the lead in reestablishing an open and expanding international trading system that would be in the interest of all countries. Strong and steady growth in the American economy would help, but this requires internationally coordinated macroeconomic policies, at least among the major industrial countries. It would be useful for the United States to loosen its restric-

---

*From the first quarter of 1981 to the third quarter of 1984, the foreign share of increased demand was 56.1 percent for all goods, 67.6 percent for durables, 35.9 percent for nondurables, and 94.7 percent of nonresidential capital goods.[5]

tive monetary policies as fiscal policy becomes more restrained. Other industrialized countries, especially Japan
and Germany, should help increase global demand by
stimulating their economies. In order to enhance coordination of world monetary policy, we should work with
the central banks of other countries to manage the key
exchange rate relationships. We must also take the lead to
make international cooperation more effective. As a
prerequisite, our political leaders must have better understanding of how the global economy works, become more
actively involved in international economic matters
(which are far too important to be left to economists and
bankers), and should seek to establish permanent international cooperative processes, with much greater participation by business and labor representatives.

Industrial Policy

Support for more effective U.S. economic policies is
based on a conviction that the American economy has
serious problems that have not been solved either by
Reaganomics or by traditional pre-Reagan economic policies. We are willing to look for new approaches, and looking abroad we see that America's more successful rivals—
especially Germany and Japan—owe much of their success to better coordinated and more effective economic
policies.

Industrial policy consists of selective interventions designed to increase productivity and international competitiveness and to promote economic growth, full employment, and higher real incomes. Such policies are
needed to solve specific problems that cannot be ad-
dressed equitably or efficiently by macroeconomic policies alone. Within the larger context of comprehensive,
consensus-based economic policies, industrial strategies
play important complementary roles. Industrial policy is

not government "picking" winners and losers, allocating private capital, or undertaking detailed government planning. It implies a cooperative undertaking by public and private representatives to identify those kinds of activities best suited to their situation and goals. All countries already have industrial policies—ours are just not very well thought out, and the components are not very well coordinated with one another or with macroeconomic and other selective policies. Moreover, the best defense the government could have against being whipsawed by special interests is a coherent, long-run, consensus-based strategy. Industrial policy means that the government would use its regular functions in a more coherent way to strengthen competitiveness.

Critics argue that industrial policy is a "solution in search of a problem" and that there is no problem it could address that could not be solved with appropriate macroeconomic policy. There is, however, abundant evidence to the contrary. The United States has had a very serious problem of declining productivity growth for twenty years, which is clearly not cyclical and will not, therefore, be solved by macroeconomic policy alone. Declining competitiveness in international markets is partly related to declining productivity growth, but has also been exacerbated by erratic and uncoordinated economic policies.

While the government cannot solve these problems by itself, there is much that can be done through public–private cooperation, especially providing a more predictable and stable economic environment; making capital available on more reasonable terms and bringing real interest rates down; improving the quality of human resources through better training, health care, and education; supporting more civilian research and development, especially basic research not likely to be undertaken by the private sector; developing more supportive international trade policies; and strengthening collective bargaining and other democratic institutions.

A public investment bank is one of the most controversial industrial policy instruments. An investment bank could deal with a number of financial problems that private markets cannot solve. One major problem is that credit is allocated according to size, not according to productive efficiency. Large corporations unable to compete in their basic industries have little trouble financing unproductive corporate acquisitions and takeovers, while more efficient, smaller companies pay more for credit and have more trouble finding it. Similarly, the federal government is a preferred borrower because of its risklessness, not because of efficiency or the productive uses of that credit. Private financial markets provide inadequate sources of "patient" capital to finance longterm and risky research and development or public infrastructures; and there is no financial institution to broker concessions between government, workers, creditors, and companies in order to restructure degenerating enterprises (like Chrysler), which, with proper restructuring, can be salvaged. Financial institutions also have inadequate information about smaller, localized entrepreneurs, even if they were inclined to invest in them. Repeal of the Glass–Steagall Act to make it possible for investment or commercial banks to have equity interests in such enterprises would divert more capital to them.

As noted in the discussion of the competition between American and Japanese companies in chapter 8, American companies' heavy reliance on equity financing puts them at a competitive disadvantage with Japanese companies that have close relationships with their banks and rely more heavily on debt financing. Private investment or "merchant" banks could provide these advantages to American companies. Merchant banks could accept deposits, make equity investments in corporations, and help finance promising companies and restructure those that could no longer compete. Since these banks would have business (and not just investment) relations with companies, they would be more willing to make "patient" capital available for long-term corporate investments. It is significant that unproductive, hostile mergers that divert managerial energies and drive up the cost of existing assets are almost entirely American phenomena. This is at least partly because in other countries, banks with large equity interests in companies have sufficient voting power to prevent such unproductive activities. Merchant banks also could inject much more equity capital into businesses than can be made available by venture capitalists, who are important but very small participants on the American financial scene—with no more than $3 or 4 billion available in 1986. Many of America's fastest growing companies, those too big for the venture capitalists but not big enough for Wall Street, could benefit greatly from merchant banking.

The absence of effective merchant banking has not been too debilitating in the past because American companies have been able to finance investments out of high profits. Now, however, declining profit margins and intensified international competition will make it very difficult for American companies to finance their future investments from retained earnings, especially where better organized foreign companies can practice the kind of capital blockages discussed in the previous chapter.

It is not clear that the United States would need public investment or development banking if the Glass–Steagall Act were repealed and if we were to encourage private merchant banking. However, there are, in my judgment, stronger arguments for such an institution than against it. As noted, the federal government already has over $1 trillion in loans and loan guarantees, which undoubtedly could be much better coordinated. Moreover, some desirable activities might be too risky or too large for private institutions alone. As in other countries, a large public development bank could join with private investors in large ventures. In addition, a public investment bank could help negotiate the kinds of tradeoffs required to restructure sick industries.

The main argument against public investment banking is the justifiable fear of political (noneconomic) loans and favoritism. Although this is a legitimate concern, it would be possible to structure an investment bank in order to minimize these problems. There could, for instance, be a requirement that no project could have more than, say, half of its funds from the public bank. It therefore seems desirable to launch such a bank with a small capitalization —say $10 billion—to test the idea. A sunset provision of ten years would make it possible to discontinue the institution if it did not serve useful purposes. As Lester Thurow observes: "Given $1 trillion in outstanding lending and more than $100 billion per year in new government lending or loan guarantees, such a bank would neither constitute a noticeable extension of current government banking activities nor threaten the credit markets with its size."[6]

There are also serious defects in the system that currently controls pension funds. Pensions amounted to about $1.3 trillion in 1986 and were the largest external source of equity capital. These funds are properly viewed as deferred wages that belong to their beneficiaries, but, except for multiemployer funds in which workers have joint control, those beneficiaries in fact have little or no control of their funds. A public investment bank could use pooled pension funds much more effectively, and this could be done in a way to ensure the safety of pension funds for retirement purposes. Federal pension laws should be amended to give pension beneficiaries greater control.

The main economic role of financial institutions should be to support productive economic activities. Unfortu-

nately, financial institutions have acquired lives of their
own, and their activities are too often divorced from, and
often inimical to, productivity and real economic efficiency. A public investment bank, together with changes
in the pension laws and repeal or modification of the
Glass–Steagall Act, could do a lot to make the system
more concerned about economic growth and competitiveness.

Trade Policy

It is vitally important, in any plan to restore the competitiveness of the American economy, to have an active
international trade policy. Experiences in the United
States and elsewhere make it clear that the choice is not
between a "free" trade policy and "protectionism," but
between *active* trade policies like those of other countries, and the *passive* or reactive trade policies we have
had in the United States. A passive policy will ensure
that other countries with more active policies can determine the structure of American industry, and our competitiveness—in market shares, real wages, and profitability—will either continue to decline or remain below
potential levels.

An active trade policy is required to avoid negative
protectionism, which shields companies from international competition without requiring them to take action
to become more competitive. As noted, a coherent policy
is the best defense against the present system, whereby
well-organized and well-financed special interests whipsaw different agencies and branches of the federal government to achieve their purposes, regardless of compati-
bility with the public interests. Where American
companies have made good-faith efforts to become competitive, international trade arrangements—like the 1974
Multifiber Agreement (MFA)—can be used to limit im-

port surges that would inflict unacceptable damage on American companies.*

An active trade policy would be able to use the leverage of access to American markets as an important means of establishing acceptable trade rules. This leverage is destroyed when we take unilateral actions to grant access to the American market in such strategic areas as banking and telecommunications by firms in countries whose markets are closed to American products. An active trade policy would attempt to open foreign markets by counteracting predatory foreign activities as immediately and forcefully as possible and by developing realistic rules based on *outcomes,* not *processes,* to prevent damage to American economic interests. It is fairly easy for imaginative governments and companies to find ways to work around quotas and other trade restrictions, by shipping goods through countries that are free from these restrictions or by changing the value or content of products. It is usually preferable to use tariffs instead of quotas. Tariffs could equalize prices internationally, and the federal government would get the revenues instead of foreign producers and the importers of foreign products. Alternatively, the United States might auction quota rights

---

*The MFA is a master agreement that outlines a process for negotiating bilateral arrangements between countries, dispute settlement procedures, and so on. Recognizing the "importance of textiles to the developing countries," the MFA provides for orderly increases in import quotas (generally, 6 percent a year). The MFA thus stabilized industries in the developing countries, as well as affording orderly adjustments in the United States. A 1983 Congressional report concluded:

> The MFA is by no means perfect—and it is still evolving. But on balance it has been a success—bringing a degree of order to what had been an important but extremely chaotic and politically sensitive industry. In the U.S., the MFA has provided a framework within which the industry has been able to invest, retool, and innovate. As a result, an industry which fifteen or twenty years ago was widely considered moribund—a prime example of the kind of "sunset industry" the United States is supposed to relinquish in the "post-industrial age"—has been returned to a position of health and strength, not only domestically, but on the world market as well.[7]

to the highest bidder. Foreigners with quota rights to
export to the United States now frequently sell these
rights.

Human Resource Development

It is widely recognized that the quality of our work
force is a major determinant of productivity, flexibility,
and international competitiveness. Indeed, improved
knowledge and education are largely responsible for past
advances in output and productivity and are likely to be
even more important in the future.* We should recognize,
however, that our current education system is grossly
inadequate for world-class competition. Not only must
learning systems be improved, but we also need to
strengthen the quality of teachers and their role in education and training systems. We must recognize that learning is a lifetime process and not restricted to the first
two-and-one-half decades of life. The improvements
suggested here will require more resources; but much can
be done to improve the productivity of the present system, which costs $453 billion a year, $210 billion of which
is provided by private companies.[9] In the long run, it will
be very costly *not* to make these changes.

The American economy has serious problems that will
not be solved by the present elitist "trickle down" economic policies, based mainly on the ideas of conservative
economists and financial experts. Nor will our problems
be solved by a return to the more participative Keynesian

*Anthony Patrick Carnevale concludes, on the basis of a review of various
economic analyses: "People, not machines are the well-spring of productivity.
Since 1929, growth in on-the-job retraining, and increased labor quality
through education, training, and health care consistently have accounted for
more than three-quarters of productivity improvements and most of the job
growth of national income. By comparison, over the same period, machine
capital has contributed a consistent and disappointing 20 percent or less."[8]

policies that served the United States and other industrialized market economy countries so well between 1935
and 1965. These Keynesian policies had inflationary
biases, assumed closed national economies, and gave too
little attention to productivity, flexibility, and efficiency.
On the positive side, they did provide the intellectual and
programmatic support for collective bargaining, the only
important form of worker participation until after World
War II. But the new global information world requires the
revitalization and modernization of international financial
institutions, coordinated macroeconomic policies between countries, and selective anti-inflation, labor market, and industrial policies—all of which must be based
on participation by the principal actors affected by those
policies.

Most of all, we need a burst of creative pragmatism to
restore the American economy to a path of strong and
steady growth in order to reduce unemployment. At the
same time, we must be concerned about the quality of
jobs, economic opportunity, and equity, not just the number of jobs created.

The quality of jobs is measured mainly by the level and
growth of real wages. The United States is a high-wage
country and should try to stay that way. Many policy
makers give inadequate attention to the maintenance of
real wages because of a belief that high real wages will
cause unemployment; but higher real wages need not necessarily produce unemployment in the United States or
elsewhere.[10] The main objective should be to increase
wages through improving productivity, thus avoiding inflation *and* unemployment.

Since there are no longer any necessary connections
between what is good for an "American" company and
what is good for American workers or communities, U.S.
policies should protect the national interest by giving
more weight to a human resource development strategy.

A full employment policy is a major element of this strategy, but there is more to it. It also includes education, training, worker adjustment, and worker participation and ownership. A human resource development strategy requires, in addition, a strengthening of organizations to represent grassroots interests, especially of workers. We should be particularly concerned about the weakening of labor organizations since the sixties, because we are not likely to have a free and democratic society without a free and democratic labor movement. Trying to have economic democracy without unions is like trying to have political democracy without political parties. The strengthening of unions, however, is up to the workers and union leaders. Public policy should back neither the unions nor the employers—it should serve the needs of the workers. Unfortunately, our present labor relations policies do more to support the interests of employers than to protect the workers' right to decide for themselves whether they want to be represented by unions. Public policy should protect this right with timely representation elections and stiff penalties for violation of the workers' rights by unions, employers, or their representatives. We should also reexamine our labor relations laws to be sure they reflect the realities of the eighties and beyond, not those of the thirties and forties.

In order to achieve these objectives, a global information world requires the restructuring of management and industrial relations systems. Greater attention must be given to sophisticated manufacturing, technological innovation, and human resource development. Otherwise, industrialized countries like the United States will see a continued decline in real wages and family incomes and a flight of industry to other countries with lower wages or more attractive policies.

NOTES

Chapter I
The Context: The Global Information World

1. New York Stock Exchange, *U.S. International Competitiveness: Perception and Reality* (New York: NYSE, 1984).

2. International Monetary Fund, Finance and Development Editorial Staff, "The Realities of Economic Interdependence," *Finance and Development: Quarterly Publication of the International Monetary Fund and the World Bank* (March 1984):30.

3. U.S. House of Representatives, Committee on Energy and Commerce, *Industrial Import Shock: Policy Challenge of the 1980s,* staff report, August 1985.

4. J. Steven Landefeld and Kan H. Young, "The Trade Deficit and the Value of the Dollar," *Business Economics* (October 1985): 11.

5. Michael J. Piore and Charles F. Sabel, *The Second Industrial Divide: Possibilities for Prosperity* (New York: Basic Books, 1984).

6. Donald Tomaskovic-Devey and S. M. Miller, "Can High-Tech Provide the Jobs?" *Challenge* (May–June 1983): 57–63.

7. Edward Fergenbaum and Pamela McCorduck, *The Fifth Generation* (Menlo Park, Calif.: Addison-Wesley, 1983).

8. British high-tech developer Clive Sinclair, quoted by Peter Ornos, "Hi-Tech Wizard Sees Brave New World in '90's," *Washington Post* (March 6, 1983), p. A-1.

9. Quoted in Harlan Cleveland, "Information as a Resource," *The Futurist* (December 1983): 34; italics are mine.

10. Sar Levitan and Clifford Johnson, "The Future of Work: Does It Belong to Us or to the Robots?" *Monthly Labor Review* (September 1982): 10–14.

11. N. D. Grundstein, quoted in *Industry Week* (May 30, 1983), p. 33.

12. The High Tech Research Group, *Massachusetts High Tech* (Somerville, Mass.: The High Tech Research Group, 1984), pp. 22–23.

13. Wassily Leontief, "Technological Advance, Economic Growth, and the Distribution of Income," *Population and Development Review* (September 1983): 405.

14. Frederick W. Taylor, *Scientific Management* (New York: Harper Bros., 1947), p. 32.

15. Ibid., p. 104.

16. Cited by Sudhir Kaker, *Frederick W. Taylor: A Study in Personality and Innovation* (Cambridge, Mass.: M.I.T. Press, 1970), p. 146.

17. Harley Shaiken, *Work Transformed: Automation and Labor in the Computer Age* (New York: Holt, Rinehart & Winston, 1985), p. 26.

18. In "The Machine Tools That Are Building America," *Iron Age* (August 30, 1976), p. 158.

19. Shaiken, *Work Transformed*, p. 5.

20. Ibid., p. 14.

21. Daniel P. Yankelovich, *Putting the Work Ethic to Work* (Washington, D.C.: Public Agenda Foundation, 1983).

Chapter II
The Problem: Adapting to International Competition

1. See W. W. Rostow, *The Barbaric Counter-Revolution: Cause and Cure* (Austin: University of Texas Press, 1983).

2. Ray Marshall et al., *An Economic Strategy for the 1980's* (Washington, D.C.: Full Employment Action Council, National Policy Exchange, 1982).

3. Robert Eisner, "Are Things Really Better After Four Years?" *New York Times* (July 8, 1984), p. F-3.

4. Peter T. Kilborn, "American Savings Less Now than Before the 1981 Tax Act," *New York Times* (September 6, 1983), p. A-1.

5. George Johnson, "Capital Formation in the United States: The Postwar Perspective," in Board of Governors of the Federal Reserve System, *Public Policy and Capital Formation* (1981).

6. Ibid.

7. Bob Kuttner, "Savings, Investment, and Distribution: Lessons from Abroad on Capital Formation," in Robert S. McIntyre, ed., *Growth with Fairness* (Washington, D.C.: Institution of Taxation and Economic Policy, 1983), p. 8.

8. Arthur Okun, "The Invisible Handshake and the Inflationary Process," *Challenge* (January–February 1980): 5–12.

9. See Sar Levitan and Robert Taggart, *The Promise of Greatness* (Cambridge, Mass.: Harvard University Press, 1976); John E. Schwarz, *America's Hidden Success* (New York: W. W. Norton, 1983); Neil Gilbert, *Capitalism and the Welfare State* (New Haven, Conn.: Yale University Press, 1983); Sar Levitan and Clifford Johnson, *Beyond the Safety Net* (Cambridge, Mass.: Ballinger, 1984).

Chapter III
People: The Key to Competitiveness

1. U.S. Department of Commerce, International Trade Administration, *U.S. Competitiveness in the International Economy* (October 1981).

2. President's Commission on Industrial Competitiveness, *Global Competition: The New Reality* (Washington, D.C.: Government Printing Office, 1984).

3. Bruce Scott, "Toward Greater U.S. Competitiveness," *New York Times* (November 25, 1984), sec. 3, p. 3.

4. Bruce Scott, "National Strategy for Stronger U.S. Competitiveness," *Harvard Business Review* (March–April 1984): 77.

5. New York Stock Exchange, *U.S. International Competitiveness: Perception and Reality* (New York: NYSE, 1984), p. 12.

6. Otto Eckstein, Christopher Caton, Roger Brinner, and Peter Duprey, *The DRI Report on U.S. Manufacturing Industries* (New York: Data Resources, Inc., McGraw-Hill, 1984); J. Steven Landefeld and Kan H. Young, "The Trade Deficit and the Value of the Dollar," *Business Economics* (October 1985); Roger Brinner, "The United States as an International Competitor," testimony before the Joint Economic Committee, March 12, 1985.

7. Charles L. Schultze, "Industrial Policy: A Dissent," *Brookings Review* (Autumn 1983): 3; Robert Lawrence, *Can America Compete?* (Washington, D.C.: Brookings Institution, 1984).

8. Stephen Cohen, David Teece, Laura Tyson, and John Zysman, "Competitiveness," working paper for the President's Commission on Industrial Competitiveness, November 8, 1984.

9. Ibid., p. 32.

10. Eckstein, Caton, Brinner, and Duprey, *The DRI Report,* pp. 79, 102.

11. Herbert Stein, "Don't Fall for Industrial Policy," *Fortune* (November 14, 1983), pp. 64–78, and "Industrial Policy à la Reich," *Fortune* (June 13, 1983), pp. 201–8.

12. Cohen, Teece, Tyson, and Zysman, "Competitiveness," p. 6.

13. Ibid., p. 7.

14. Paul Lewis, "A Fight on Trade in Services," *New York Times* (October 2, 1985), p. D-1.

15. Lester Thurow, *The Zero Sum Solution* (New York: Simon & Schuster, 1985).

16. Economic Policy Council of the United Nations Association of the United States of America, Productivity Panel, *The Productivity Problem: U.S. Labor–Management Relations* (New York: United Nations Association of the U.S.A., 1983).

17. Brinner, "The United States as an International Competitor."

18. Zvi Griliches, "R & D and the Productivity Slowdown," National Bureau of Economic Research, Working Paper no. 434, January 1980; N. E. Terleckyj, *Effects of R & D on the Productivity Growth of Industries: An Exploratory Study* (Washington, D.C.: National Planning Association, 1974); J. W. Kendrick, "Total Investment and Productivity Developments," paper presented at the Joint Session of the American Finance Association and the American Economic Association, New York, December 30, 1977.

19. See Frederick H. Harbison, *Human Resource as a Wealth of Nations* (New York: Oxford University Press, 1973); Frederick H. Harbison and Charles Myers, *Education, Manpower, and Economic Growth* (New York: McGraw-Hill, 1964); Theodore W. Schultz, *Human Resources*, Fiftieth Anniversary Colloquium of the National Bureau of Economic Research, Atlanta, 1971 (New York: Columbia University Press, 1972).

20. Anthony Patrick Carnevale, *Human Capital: A High Yield Corporate Investment* (Washington, D.C.: American Society for Training and Development, 1983), pp. 8–9.

21. President's Commission on Industrial Competitiveness, *Global Competition,* sec. 2, p. 9.

22. See Barbara Lerner, "American Education: How Are We Doing?" *Public Interest* (Autumn 1982): 64.

23. William C. Brainard and George L. Perry, "Editor's Summary," *Brookings Papers on Economic Activity* 1 (1981), p. vii.

24. Thomas E. Weisskopf, Samuel Bowles, and David M. Gordon, "Hearts and Minds: A Social Model of U.S. Productivity Growth," *Brookings Papers on Economic Activity* 2 (1983), p. 382.

Chapter IV
The Role of Management

1. Adolf A. Berle, Jr., and Gardiner C. Means, *The Modern Corporation and Private Property* (New York: Macmillan, 1933), p. 6.

2. Robert H. Hayes and William J. Abernathy, "Managing Our Way to Economic Decline," *Harvard Business Review* (July–August 1980): 67.

3. Hayes and Abernathy, "Managing Our Way," p. 74.

4. Seymour Melman, "Managers' Debacle," *New York Times* (November 4, 1983), p. A-27.

5. Ibid.

6. Quoted by Peter Behr, "American Management: Playing It Safe, and Losing Out," *Washington Post* (January 17, 1982), p. A-1.

7. Arnold Judson, "The Awkward Truth About Productivity," *Harvard Business Review* (September–October 1982): 93.

8. Anthony G. Athos and Richard T. Pascale, *The Art of Japanese Management: Applications for American Executives* (New York: Warner Books, 1982); Charles L. Schultze, "Industrial Policy: A Dissent," *Brookings Review* (Autumn 1983): 3.

9. Gene Bylinsky, "Japan's Ominous Chip Victory," *Fortune* (December 14, 1981), p. 56.

10. B. Bruce-Briggs, "The Dangerous Folly Called Theory Z," *Fortune* (May 17, 1982), pp. 41–43.

11. Masanori Hashimoto and John Raisian, "Employment Tenure and Earnings Profiles in Japan and the United States," *American Economic Review* (September 1985): 732.

12. Andrew Weiss, "Simple Truths of Japanese Manufacturing," *Harvard Business Review* (July–August 1984): 119–25. Quote on p. 124.

13. William P. Sommers, "Are We Still Managing Our Way to Economic Decline?" unpublished paper, Booz, Allen and Hamilton, 1985.

14. Peter Drucker, *Managing in Turbulent Times* (New York: Harper & Row, 1980), p. 24.

15. Quoted by James F. Bolt, "Job Security: Its Time Has Come," *Harvard Business Review* (November–December 1983): 118.

16. Ibid.

17. For a good discussion see Lester Thurow, *The Zero Sum Solution* (New York: Simon & Schuster, 1985), chap. 6.

18. Quoted by Mark Green and Bonnie Tenneriello, "Executive Merit Pay," *New York Times* (April 25, 1984), p. A-23.

19. Ibid.

20. Robert E. Lipsey and Irving B. Kravis, "The Competitive Position of U.S. Manufacturing Firms," *Banco Nazionale del Lavoro Quarterly Review* (1985): pp. 127–54.

Chapter V
The Role of Collective Bargaining

1. Ray Marshall, *The Negro Worker* (New York: Random House, 1967).

2. Ichiro Shioji, "Productivity and Labor–Management Relations," paper sent to author, 1985, p. 12.

3. Cited in ibid., p. 14.

4. Ibid.

5. Ibid., p. 20.

6. Ibid., p. 15.

7. Ibid., p. 16.

8. Case studies and econometric models have confirmed the positive impact of good industrial relations on productivity: see Kim B. Clark, "Unions and Productivity in the Cement Industry," Ph.d. diss., Harvard University, 1979; Thomas Kochan, *Collective Bargaining and Industrial Relations* (Homewood, Ill.: Richard Irwin, 1980); Conference Board, *Managing Labor Relations* (Washington, D.C.: Conference Board, Inc., 1979); Derek C. Bok and John T. Dunlop, *Labor and the American Community* (New York: Simon & Schuster, 1970); Richard B. Freeman, "The Exit-Voice Tradeoff in the Labor Market: Unionism, Job Tenure, Quits and Separations," National Bureau of Economic Research Working Paper, 1978; Irving Bluestone, "How to Put QWL to Work," speech delivered to the Work in America Institute, December 6, 1979; Richard E. Walton, "How to Counter Alienation in the Plant," *Harvard Business Review* (November–December 1972): 70–81; Ted Mills, "Altering the Social Structure in Coal Mining: A Case Study," *Monthly Labor Review* (October 1976): 3–10; and Karl-Olof Faxén, "Disembodied Technical Progress: Does Employee Participation in Decision Making Contribute to Change and Growth?" *American Economic Review* (May 1978): 131–34.

9. See William L. Batt, Jr., and Edgar Weinberg, "Labor Management Cooperation Today," *Harvard Business Review* (January–February 1978): 96–104; Dorothea DeSchweinitz, *Labor and Management in a Common Enterprise* (Cambridge, Mass.: Harvard University Press, 1949); National Center for Productivity and Quality of Working Life, *Directory of Labor–Management Committees* (Washington, D.C.: Government Printing Office, 1978); and R. A. Katzell, Penny Bienstock, and Paul Faerstein, *A Guide to Worker Productivity Experiments in the U.S., 1971–1975* (New York: New York University Press, 1977).

10. U.S. Department of Commerce, National Technical Information Service, *The Impact of Labor Unions on the Rate and Direction of Technological Change*, prepared for the National Science Foundation, Policy Research and Analysis, by the Institute of Labor and Industrial Relations, University of Michigan–Wayne State University, February 1979, PB-297-084.

11. Richard B. Freeman and James L. Medoff, *What Do Unions Do?* (New York: Basic Books, 1984), p. 58.

12. Albert Rees, "Improving Productivity Measurement," *American Economic Review* (May 1980): 340–42.

13. Charles Brown and James Medoff, "Trade Unions in the Production Process," *Journal of Political Economy* (June 1978): 355–78.

14. Robert Guenther, "Plan for Construction Productivity Stirs Industry, Takes Aim at Unions," *Wall Street Journal* (April 21, 1983), sect. 2, p. 35; Business Roundtable, *More Construction for the Money*, summary report of the Construction Industry Cost Effective Project (New York: Business Roundtable, January 1983).

15. D. Quinn Mills, "Reforming the U.S. System of Collective Bargaining," *Monthly Labor Review* (March 1983): 19, 20.

16. Marguerite Connerton, Richard Freeman, and James Medoff, "Productivity and Industrial Relations: The Case of U.S. Bituminous Coal," National Bureau of Economic Research Working Paper, December 1979.

17. Brown and Medoff, "Trade Unions."

18. Clark, "Unions and Productivity."

19. John Robert Frantz, "The Impact of Trade Unions on Productivity in the Wood Household Furniture Industry," thesis, Harvard University, 1976.

20. Steven Allen, "Unionized Construction Workers Are More Productive,"

Working Paper no. 9, Economics Department, North Carolina State University, February 1983.

21. Harry C. Katz, Thomas A. Kochan, and Kenneth R. Gobeille, "Industrial Relations Performance, Economic Performance, and QWL Performance: An Interplant Analysis," *Industrial and Labor Relations Review* (October 1983): 3–17.

22. J. R. Norsworthy and Craig Zabala, "Worker Attitudes, Worker Behavior, and Productivity in the U.S. Automobile Industry, 1959–1976," *Industrial and Labor Relations Review* (July 1985): 544–57.

23. Freeman and Medoff, *What Do Unions Do?* p. 180.

24. Daniel P. Yankelovich, *Putting the Work Ethic to Work* (Washington, D.C.: Public Agenda Foundation, 1983).

25. Clark, "Unions and Productivity."

26. Barry T. Hirsch, "Review Symposium," *Industrial and Labor Relations Review* (January 1985): 249.

27. Cathy Trost, "Labor Letter," *Wall Street Journal* (September 17, 1985), p. 1.

28. AFL-CIO Committee on the Evolution of Work, *The Changing Situation of Workers and Their Unions* (Washington, D.C.: AFL-CIO, February 1985), p. 5.

29. Thomas Kochan, Robert McKersie, and Harry Katz, "U.S. Industrial Relations in Transition: A Summary Report," M.I.T.: Alfred P. Sloan School of Management, Working Paper no. 1617–84, 1984, pp. 6–7.

30. Robert J. Flanagan, "Wage Concessions and Long Term Union Wage Flexibility," *Brookings Papers on Economic Activity* 1 (1984), pp. 183–221.

31. Kochan, McKersie, and Katz, "U.S. Industrial Relations in Transition," p. 9.

32. Ibid., pp. 10–11.

33. Audrey Freedman, *Managing Labor Relations,* report ser. no. 811 (New York: Conference Board, 1979), p. 3.

34. Noah M. Meltz, "Labor Movements in Canada and the United States," in Thomas A. Kochan, ed., *Challenges and Choices Facing the American Labor Movement* (Cambridge, Mass.: M.I.T. Press, 1985), p. 315.

35. Peter Drucker, "Are Unions Becoming Irrelevant?" *Wall Street Journal* (September 22, 1982), p. 30.

36. Ibid.

37. A management consultant quoted by Harry Bacas, "In Unions There Is Weakness," *Nation's Business* (April 1985): 73.

38. Audrey Freedman, "There's No Recovery in Sight for Unions," *New York Times* (January 20, 1985), p. F-2.

39. See *Now is the Time* (Atlanta: Southern Labor Institute, 1986).

40. Lane Kirkland, address to Brandeis University's National Fellows Conference, October 18, 1980.

41. George E. Barnett, "American Trade Unionism and Social Insurance," presidential address, American Economic Association, December 29, 1932, printed in *American Economic Review* (March 1933): 1.

Chapter VI
The New Thrust: Worker Participation and Ownership

1. Ted Mills, "U.S. and European Approaches to Improving Labor Productivity and the Quality of Worklife" (Washington, D.C.: American Enterprise Institute, 1982).

2. Guillermo Grenier, Jr., "Twisting Quality Circles to Bust Unions," *AFL-CIO News* (May 14, 1983), pp. 8–14.

3. Glenn E. Watts, statement to the Economic Policy Council of the United Nations Association, Washington, D.C., June 11, 1982, p. 7.

4. Ibid., pp. 8, 15–16.

5. Harry Bernstein, "Workers Have Their Say: Industrial Democracy Moves into Workplace," *Los Angeles Times* (October 23, 1980), p. 1.

6. Glenn E. Watts, remarks at the Third Annual Labor–Management Conference, University of Wisconsin, Milwaukee, November 16, 1983, p. 3.

7. Ibid., p. 4.

8. Kathy Sawyer, "Communication Workers Act to Ease Impact of Future Shock," *Washington Post* (March 29, 1983), p. A-3.

9. Thomas J. Murrin, remarks to the American Society for Quality Control Congress, Detroit, May 3, 1982.

10. Economic Policy Council of the United Nations Association of the United States of America, Productivity Panel, *The Productivity Problem: U.S. Labor–Management Relations* (New York: United Nations Association of the U.S.A., 1983).

11. Thomas W. Lippman, "Preaching Gospel of Productivity: The Sermon Works at Westinghouse," *Washington Post* (March 21, 1982), p. F-1.

12. Bernstein, "Workers Have Their Say."

13. Watts, Third Annual Labor–Management Conference.

14. Thomas Donahue, remarks to the International Conference on Trends in Industrial and Labor Relations, Montreal, Canada, May 26, 1976.

15. John Simmons and William J. Mares, *Working Together* (New York: Knopf, 1983), p. 260.

16. Paul Baicich and Lance Compa, "First You Cooperate, Then You're Coopted," *Washington Post National Weekly Edition* (December 16, 1985), p. 23.

17. Barbara Reisman and Lance Compa, "The Case for Adversarial Unions," *Harvard Business Review* (May–June 1985): 22, 36.

18. John T. Joyce, "Codetermination and Collective Bargaining in the U.S.," paper presented to the International Labor Organization Symposium on Worker's Participation, The Hague, May 5–8, 1981, pp. 2–3.

19. Ibid., p. 5.

20. Ibid., pp. 6–7.

21. Marc Stepp, speech to the Society of Automotive Engineers, February 29, 1984.

22. Thomas Miner, memorandum of understanding to Marc Stepp, September 16, 1982.

23. Ibid.

24. Ernest J. Savoi, "Statement to the President's Advisory Committee and Conciliation," September 16, 1986 (unpublished).

25. Ford Motor Company, Labor-Relations Staff, "The 1982 Ford–UAW Mutual Growth Agreement," special ed. for managers and supervisors of hourly employees, 1982, p. 1.

26. Ibid., p. 2.

27. D. Quinn Mills, "A New Cooperation Sweeps Detroit," *Wall Street Journal* (October 17, 1984), p. 18.

28. Ibid.

29. Warren Brown, "GM, UAW Consider Radical Salary Plan," *Washington Post* (June 23, 1985), p. G-1.

30. William Serrin, "Bold G.M. Pact Draws Praise, and Some Caveats," *New York Times* (August 3, 1985), p. 6.

31. Mark Paul, "Fremont Deal Could Hurt U.S. Industry," *Oakland Tribune* (April 15, 1984), p. 16.

32. Ibid., p. 15.

33. Ibid., p. 41.

34. Economic Policy Council, *The Productivity Problem.*

35. Jack Blasi and W. F. Whyte, "Worker Ownership and Public Policy," *Policy Studies Journal* (December 1981): 320–37.

36. Russell Long, "Unions and Employee Ownership," *Congressional Record* 129, no. 60, part 2 (February 2, 1982): 2, 3.

37. Ibid., p. 5.

38. Elizabeth M. Fowler, "Buyouts by Workers: Gains Cited," *New York Times* (August 29, 1984), p. D-20.

39. Richard Corrigan, "Workers at Weirton Steel See Only One Way to Save Their Failing Plant: Buy It," *National Journal* (August 13, 1983), pp. 1672–79.

40. Julian Morrison, "When Employees Get a Piece of the Action," *Nation's Business* (December 1983): 21.

41. Colin Leinster, "Can Pan Am Survive?" *Fortune* (April 15, 1985), p. 49.

42. Agis Salpukas, "The Long Fight for TWA: Unions Decided the Winner," *New York Times* (August 31, 1985), p. A-1.

43. T. R. Marsh and D. E. McAllister, "ESOPs Fables: A Survey of Companies with ESOPs," *Journal of Corporate Law* 6 (1981): 5–6.

44. Morrison, "When Employees Get a Piece of the Action," p. 20.

45. Marsh and McAllister, "ESOPs Fables."

46. Michael Conte and Arnold S. Tannenbaum, "Employee-Owned Companies: Is the Difference Measurable?" *Monthly Labor Review* 101 (1978): 27.

47. Corey Rosen and Katherine Klein, "Job-Creating Performance of Employee-Owned Firms," *Monthly Labor Review* (August 1983): 17.

48. Blasi and Whyte, "Worker Ownership and Public Policy."

49. Corrigan, "Workers at Weirton Steel."

50. IUD-AFL-CIO, *IUD Digest* (1986). Industrial Union Department, AFL-CIO, occasional paper.

51. Brian M. Freeman, "Why Employee Buyouts Often Fall Short of Hopes," *Wall Street Journal* (October 3, 1983), p. 30.

52. See Tamar Lewin, "Worker-Held Enterprises," *New York Times* (April 17, 1984), p. 28.

53. Peter Drucker, "Pension Fund 'Socialism,' " *The Public Interest* (Winter 1976): 3–4.

54. Jocelyn Gutchess, "Potential Outcomes of Joint Management of Pension Funds," paper presented at a Work in America Institute conference, February 18, 1983.

55. Lane Kirkland, quoted in William Serrin, "Labor Chief Seeks Investment Power," *New York Times* (November 16, 1981), p. 1.

56. Dale D. Buss, "GM Versus GM: Unions Say Auto Firms Use Interplant Rivalry to Raise Work Quotas," *Wall Street Journal* (November 7, 1983), p. 1.

57. William F. Whyte et al., *Worker Participation and Ownership* (Ithaca, N.Y.: ILR Press, Cornell University, 1983).

58. Ibid., p. 86.

59. Cary L. Cooper and Enid Mumford, eds., *The Quality of Working Life in Western and Eastern Europe* (Westford, Conn.: Greenwood Press, 1979).

60. Daniel P. Yankelovich, *New Rules: Searching for Self-Fulfillment in a World Turned Upside Down* (New York: Random House, 1981).

61. Ibid.

62. Sar Levitan and Clifford Johnson, "After Hard Times—What Hope for Labor–Management Cooperation?" *Daily Labor Report* (September 17, 1982), pp. E-1–E-3.

63. Ibid.

64. E. Cordova, "Workers' Participation in Decisions Within Enterprises: Recent Trends and Problems," *International Labor Review* (March–April 1982): 135.

65. Paul C. Weiler, in a speech before the National Academy of Arbitrators, May 30, 1985; printed in *Daily Labor Report* (June 11, 1985), p. E-3; italics are Weiler's.

66. Ibid., pp. E-3, E-4.

67. U.S. Department of Labor, Bureau of Labor–Management Relations and Cooperative Programs, *U.S. Labor Law and the Future of Labor Management Cooperation*, BLMR no. 104 (1986), p. 9.

68. John Dunlop, "The Labor Board at Mid-Century," *Daily Labor Report* (October 7, 1985), p. E-2.

69. *Daily Labor Report* (April 2, 1986), pp. A-4, A-5; "Labor Practices Charges Against GM, UAW Are Dismissed by the NLRB Counsel," *Wall Street Journal* (June 3, 1986), p. 7.

70. U.S. Department of Labor, *U.S. Labor Law,* p. 13.

71. Professors were denied legal collective bargaining protection in the Yeshiva case: *NLRB v. Yeshiva University,* 444 U.S. 672 (1980). However, in a 1984 case (*Loretto Heights College v. NLRB,* 742 F2d 1245), the Tenth Circuit Court of Appeals held that faculty members were not managerial employees under the law.

72. The Supreme Court upheld such a committee in the 1959 Cabot Carbon case, 360 U.S. 203, and the NLRB has upheld labor–management committees in other cases (such as Sparks Migget, Inc., 230 NLRB no. 43 [1977]; Mercy Memorial Hospital, 231 NLRB no. 182 [1977]; and General Foods Corp., 231 NLRB no. 122 [1977]); and committees were upheld by the Sixth Circuit Court of Appeals in *NLRB v. Streamway,* 691 F2d 288 (1982).

73. A number of Circuit Courts of Appeal have followed the Seventh Circuit in *Chicago Rawhide Manufacturing v. NLRB,* 221 F2d 165 (1955), in holding that it was not unlawful for employers to support cooperative labor–management activities.

74. H. Datz, Associate General Council, legal memorandum to B. Gottfried, director of NLRB region 6, October 22, 1980.

75. U.S. Department of Labor, *U.S. Labor Law,* pp. 28–29.

76. Dunlop, "The Labor Board at Mid-Century," p. E-5.

Chapter VII
Forging a National Consensus

1. U.S. Congress Joint Economic Committee, "Monetary Policy, Selective Credit Policy and Industrial Policy in France, Britain, West Germany and Sweden" (Washington, D.C.: Government Printing Office, 1981), p. 2.

2. Robert J. Flanagan, David W. Soskice, and Lloyd Ulman, *Unionism, Economic*

Stabilization, and Incomes Policies: European Experience (Washington, D.C.: Brookings Institution, 1983).

3. U.S. Congress Joint Economic Committee, "Monetary Policy."

4. Hans Seidel, "Incomes Policies in Austria," *Challenge* (September–October 1981): 59.

5. Flanagan, Soskice, and Ulman, *Unionism.*

6. Jon Clark, "Concerted Action in the Federal Republic of Germany," *British Journal of Industrial Relations* (July 1979): 249.

7. Quoted in ibid., p. 246.

8. Ibid., p. 249.

9. Ibid., p. 252.

10. Martha R. Cooper, *The Search for Consensus* (Washington, D.C.: OECD Publications Information Center, 1982), pp. 10–11.

11. Ibid., pp. 9, 10, 12 (italics are Cooper's).

12. Ibid., p. 8.

13. Ibid., p. 76.

14. Ibid., p. 51.

15. Robert Crandall, *The Steel Industry in Recurrent Crisis* (Washington, D.C.: Brookings Institution, 1981).

16. Michael Borrus, "The Politics of Competitive Erosion in the U.S. Steel Industry," in John Zysman and Laura Tyson, eds., *American Industry in International Competition* (Ithaca, N.Y.: Cornell University Press, 1983).

17. Lloyd McBride, statement to the Industrial Union Department's Industrial Policy Conference, Baltimore, July 21–22, 1983.

18. John Dunlop, "The Consensus: Process and Substance," in Michael L. Wachter and Susan M. Wachter, eds., *Toward a New US Industrial Policy?* (Philadelphia: University of Pennsylvania Press, 1981), p. 2.

Chapter VIII
The Japanese Make It Work

1. Roger E. Brinner, *Impact of the Dollar on U.S. Competitiveness,* U.S. Congress, Joint Economic Committee, Sub-Committee on Economic Goals and Interdevelopmental Policy, Hearings March 12, 1985, p. 12.

2. Cited in United Auto Workers Research Department, "Choices for American Industry: Autos" (1985), unpublished paper.

3. Ezra Vogel, *Japan as Number One: Lessons for America* (New York: Harper & Row, 1980), p. 27.

4. H. William Tanaka, statement before the Joint Economic Committee, 97th Congress, 1st Session, July 28, 1981.

5. Vogel, *Japan as Number One,* p. 115.

6. Comptroller General of the United States, *Industrial Policy: Japan's Flexible Approach* (Washington, D.C.: USGAO, report no. GAO/1D-82-32, June 23, 1982), p. 4.

7. Yoshio Suzuki, *Money and Banking in Contemporary Japan: The Theoretical Setting and Its Application* (New Haven, Conn.: Yale University Press, 1980).

8. Organization for Economic Cooperation and Development (OECD), *The Industrial Policies in Japan* (Paris: OECD, 1972), p. 15.

9. Kenneth Dreyfack and Otis Port, "Is American Knowhow Headed Abroad?" *Business Week* (March 3, 1986), p. 63.

10. Ibid., p. 62.

11. Norman Jonas, "The Hollow Corporation," *Business Week* (March 3, 1986), p. 57.

12. Industrial Structure Council, *Vision of MITI Policies in the 1980s* (March 1980), p. 136.

13. Michael Borrus et al., *Telecommunications Development in Comparative Perspective: The New Telecommunications in Europe, Japan, and the U.S.* (Berkeley: Berkeley Roundtable on the International Economy, University of California, Berkeley, May 1985).

14. Michael Borrus, James Millstein, and John Zysman, *International Competition in Advanced Industrial Sectors: Trade and Development in the Semiconductor Industry,* paper for the U.S. Congress Joint Economic Committee, February 18, 1982.

15. Susan Chira, "U.S. Chips Face Test in Japan," *New York Times* (August 13, 1986), p. 25.

16. Borrus, Millstein, and Zysman, *International Competition.*

17. Yoshikazu Miyazaki, "Japanese-Type Structure of Big Business," and Yusaku Futatsugi, "The Measurement of Interfirm Relationships," in Kazuo Sato, ed., *Industry and Business in Japan* (White Plains, N.Y.: M. E. Sharpe, 1980).

18. Borrus, Millstein, and Zysman, *International Competition,* p. 77.

19. Richard Caves, "Industrial Organization," in Hugh Patrick and Henry Rosovsky, eds., *Asia's New Giant: How the Japanese Economy Works* (Washington, D.C.: Brookings Institution, 1976), p. 488.

20. *Austin American Statesman* (August 3, 1985).

21. *New York Times* (December 4, 1985), p. 29.

22. *New York Times* (March 24, 1985), sect. 12, p. 12.

23. Borrus et al., *Telecommunications Development,* p. 25.

24. *Fortune* (July 8, 1985), p. 110.

25. *New York Times* (August 9, 1985), p. 25.

26. Borrus et al., *Telecommunications Development.*

27. Chalmers Johnson, *MITI and the Japanese Miracle: The Growth of Industrial Policy, 1925–75* (Palo Alto, Calif.: Stanford University Press, 1982).

28. Robert C. Wood, "Japan's Industrial Vision," *Asia* (January–February 1982): 8.

29. Ibid.

Chapter IX
We Too Can Make It Work

1. E. F. Denison, *Trends in American Economic Growth, 1929–1982* (Washington, D.C.: Brookings Institution, 1985), p. xvi.

2. David Obey, "Economic Policy and the American Economy: Lessons from the Past and Challenges for the Future," remarks to the U.S. Congress Joint Economic Committee's symposium on the fortieth anniversary of the Employment Act, Washington, D.C., January 16, 1986.

3. Ray Marshall, "Government, Markets, and Consensus-Building Mechanisms," *National Productivity Review* (Autumn 1982): 445–50.

4. International Confederation of Free Trade Unions, *Trade Unions and the Transnationals* (Brussels: ICFTU, March 1983).

5. U.S. House of Representatives, Committee on Energy and Commerce, *Industrial Import Shock: Policy Challenge of the 1980s,* staff report, August 1985.

6. Lester Thurow, *The Zero Sum Solution* (New York: Simon & Schuster, 1985), p. 280.

7. U.S. House of Representatives, Committee on Energy and Commerce, *The U.S. in a Changing World Economy: The Case for Integrated Domestic and International Commercial Policy,* staff report, 1983, p. 27.

8. Anthony Patrick Carnevale, *Human Capital: A High Yield Corporate Investment* (Washington, D.C.: American Society for Training and Development, 1983), p. 9.

9. Anthony Patrick Carnevale, "The Learning Enterprise," *Training and Development Journal* (January 1986): 18.

10. Jeffrey Sachs, "Real Wages and Unemployment in OECD Countries," *Brookings Papers on Economic Activity* 1 (1983): 255–304; Jacques Artus, "Are Real Wages Too High in Europe?" *Finance and Development* (December 1984): 10.

BIBLIOGRAPHY

AFL-CIO Committeee on the Evolution of Work. *The Changing Situation of Workers and Their Unions*. Washington, D.C.: AFL-CIO, February 1985.

Allen, Steven. "Unionized Construction Workers Are More Productive." Working Paper no. 9, Economics Department, North Carolina State University, February 1983.

Artus, Jacques. "Are Real Wages Too High in Europe?" *Finance and Development* (December 1984): 10–13.

Athos, Anthony G., and Richard T. Pascale. *The Art of Japanese Management: Applications for American Executives*. New York: Warner Books, 1982.

Bacas, Harry. "In Unions There Is Weakness." *Nation's Business* (April 1985): 29.

Baicich, Paul, and Lance Compa. "First You Cooperate, Then You're Coopted." *Washington Post National Weekly Edition*. December 16, 1985, p. 23.

Barnett, George E. "American Trade Unionism and Social Insurance." Presidential Address, American Economic Association, December 29, 1932, printed in *American Economic Review* (March 1933): 1.

Batt, William L., Jr., and Edgar Weinberg. "Labor Management Cooperation Today." *Harvard Business Review* (January–February 1978): 96–104.

Behr, Peter. "American Management: Playing It Safe, and Losing Out." *Washington Post,* January 17, 1982, p. A-1.

———. "American Management: Serving Only the Present." *Washington Post,* January 20, 1982, p. D-3.

Berle, Adolf A., Jr., and Gardiner C. Means. *The Modern Corporation and Private Property*. New York: Macmillan, 1933.

Berndt, Ernst R., and Dale W. Jorgenson. "How Energy, and Its Cost Enter the 'Productivity Equation.'" *IEEE Spectrum* 15 (October 1978): 50–52.

Bernstein, Harry. "Workers Have Their Say: Industrial Democracy Moves into Workplace." *Los Angeles Times,* October 23, 1980, p. 1.

Blasi, Jack, and W. F. Whyte. "Worker Ownership and Public Policy." *Policy Studies Journal* (December 1981): 320–37.

Bluestone. Irving. "How to Put QWL to Work." Speech to Work in America Institute, December 6, 1979.

Bok, Derek C., and John T. Dunlop. *Labor and the American Community*. New York: Simon & Schuster, 1970.

Bolt, James F. "Job Security: Its Time Has Come." *Harvard Business Review* (November–December 1983): 115–123.

Borrus, Michael. "The Politics of Competitive Erosion in the U.S. Steel Industry." In John Zysman and Laura Tyson, eds., *American Industry in International Competition*. Ithaca, N.Y.: Cornell University Press, 1983.

———, François Bar, Patrick Coyez, Anne Brit Thoreson, Ibrahim Worde, and

Aki Yoskekawa. *Telecommunications Development in Comparative Perspective: The New Telecommunications in Europe, Japan, and the U.S.* Berkeley: Berkeley Roundtable on the International Economy, University of California, Berkeley, May 1985.

————, James Millstein, and John Zysman. *International Competition in Advanced Industrial Sectors: Trade and Development in the Semiconductor Industry.* Paper for the U.S. Congress Joint Economic Committee, February 18, 1982.

Brainard, William C., and George L. Perry. "Editor's Summary." *Brookings Papers on Economic Activity* 1, 1981.

Brinner, Roger. "The United States as an International Competitor." Testimony before the Joint Economic Committee, March 12, 1985.

Brown, Charles, and James Medoff. "Trade Unions in the Production Process." *Journal of Political Economy* (June 1978): 355–78.

Brown, Warren. "GM, UAW Consider Radical Salary Plan." *Washington Post,* June 23, 1985, p. G-1.

Bruce-Briggs, B. "The Dangerous Folly Called Theory Z." *Fortune,* May 17, 1982, pp. 41–53.

Business Roundtable. *More Construction for the Money.* Summary report of the Construction Industry Cost Effective Project. New York: Business Roundtable, January 1983.

Buss, Dale D. "GM Versus GM: Unions Say Auto Firms Use Interplant Rivalry to Raise Work Quotas." *Wall Street Journal,* November 7, 1983, p. 1.

Bylinsky, Gene. "Japan's Ominous Chip Victory." *Fortune,* December 14, 1981, pp. 52–57.

Carnevale, Anthony Patrick. *Human Capital: A High Yield Corporate Investment.* Washington, D.C.: American Society for Training and Development, 1983.

————. "The Learning Enterprise." *Training and Development Journal* (January 1986): 18–26.

Caves, Richard. "Industrial Organization." In Hugh Patrick and Henry Rosovsky, eds., *Asia's New Giant: How the Japanese Economy Works.* Washington D.C.: Brookings Institution, 1976.

Chira, Susan. "U.S. Chips Face Test in Japan." *New York Times,* August 13, 1986, p. 25.

Chown, Paul, Bruce Poyer, Peter Guidry, and Joan Braconi. Letter to the Editor, *New York Times,* September 13, 1985, p. A-26.

Clark, Jon. "Concerted Action in the Federal Republic of Germany." *British Journal of Industrial Relations* (July 1979): 242–58.

Clark, Kim B. "Unions and Productivity in the Cement Industry." Ph.d. diss., Harvard University, 1979.

Cleveland, Harlan. "Information as a Resource." *The Futurist* (December 1983): 34–39.

Cohen, Stephen, David Teece, Laura Tyson, and John Zysman. "Competitiveness." A working paper for the President's Commission on Industrial Competitiveness, November 8, 1984.

Comptroller General of the United States. *Industrial Policy: Japan's Flexible Approach.* Washington, D.C.: USGAO, Report no. GAO/1D-82-32, June 23, 1982.

Conference Board. *Managing Labor Relations.* Washington, D.C.: Conference Board, Inc., 1979.

Connerton, Marguerite, Richard Freeman, and James Medoff. "Productivity and Industrial Relations: The Case of U.S. Bituminous Coal." National Bureau of Economic Research Working Paper, December 1979.

Conte, Michael, and Arnold S. Tannenbaum. "Employee-Owned Companies: Is the Difference Measurable?" *Monthly Labor Review* 101 (1978): 23–28.

Cooper, Cary L., and Enid Mumford, eds. *The Quality of Working Life in Western and Eastern Europe.* Westford, Conn.: Greenwood Press, 1979.

Cooper, Martha R. *The Search for Consensus.* Washington, D.C.: OECD Publications Information Center, 1982.

Cordova, E. "Workers' Participation in Decisions Within Enterprises: Recent Trends and Problems." *International Labor Review* (March–April 1982): 125–40.

Corrigan, Richard. "Workers at Weirton Steel See Only One Way to Save Their Failing Plant: Buy It." *National Journal,* August 13, 1983, pp. 1672–79.

Crandall, Robert. *The Steel Industry in Recurrent Crisis.* Washington, D.C.: Brookings Institution, 1981.

Denison, E. F. *Trends in American Economic Growth, 1929–1982.* Washington, D.C.: Brookings Institution, 1985.

DeSchweinitz, Dorothea. *Labor and Management in a Common Enterprise.* Cambridge, Mass.: Harvard University Press, 1949.

Donahue, Thomas. Remarks to the International Conference on Trends in Industrial and Labor Relations. Montreal, Canada, May 26, 1976.

Dreyfack, Kenneth, and Otis Port. "The Hollow Corporation: The Decline of Manufacturing Threatens the Entire U.S. Economy." *Business Week,* March 3, 1986, pp. 60–63.

Drucker, Peter. "Are Unions Becoming Irrelevant?" *Wall Street Journal,* September 22, 1982, p. 30.

———. *Managing in Turbulent Times.* New York: Harper & Row, 1980.

———. "Pension Fund 'Socialism.' " *The Public Interest* (Winter 1976): 3–46.

Dunlop, John. "The Consensus: Process and Substance." In Michael L. Wachter and Susan M. Wachter, eds., *Toward a New US Industrial Policy?* Philadelphia: University of Pennsylvania Press, 1981.

———. "The Labor Board at Mid-Century." *Daily Labor Reports,* October 7, 1985, p. E-2.

Eckstein, Otto, Christopher Caton, Roger Brinner, and Peter Duprey, *The DRI Report on U.S. Manufacturing Industries.* New York: Data Resources, Inc., McGraw-Hill, 1984.

Economic Policy Council of the United Nations Association of the United States of America, Productivity Panel. *The Productivity Problem: U.S. Labor–Management Relations.* New York: United Nations Association of the United States of America, 1983.

Eisner, Robert. "Are Things Really Better After Four Years?" *New York Times,* July 8, 1984, p. F-3.

Faxén, Karl-Olof. "Disembodied Technical Progress: Does Employee Participation in Decision Making Contribute to Change and Growth?" *American Economic Review* (May 1978): 131–34.

Fergenbaum, Edward, and Pamela McCorduck. *The Fifth Generation.* Menlo Park, Calif.: Addison-Wesley, 1983.

Flanagan, Robert J. "Wage Concessions and Long Term Union Wage Flexibility." *Brookings Papers on Economic Activity* 1, 1984, pp. 183–221.

———, David W. Soskice, and Lloyd Ulman. *Unionism, Economic Stabilization, and Incomes Policies: European Experience.* Washington, D.C.: Brookings Institution, 1983.

Ford Motor Company, Labor-Relations Staff. "The 1982 Ford–UAW Mutual Growth Agreement." Special ed. for managers and supervisors of hourly employees, 1982.

Fowler, Elizabeth M. "Buyouts by Workers: Gains Cited." *New York Times,* August 29, 1984, p. D-20.

Frantz, John Robert. "The Impact of Trade Unions on Productivity in the Wood Household Furniture Industry." Thesis, Harvard University, 1976.

Freedman, Audrey. *Managing Labor Relations.* Report ser. no. 811, New York: Conference Board, 1979.

———. "There's No Recovery in Sight for Unions." *New York Times,* January 20, 1985, p. F-2.

Freeman, Brian M. "Why Employee Buyouts Often Fall Short of Hopes." *Wall Street Journal,* October 3, 1983, p. 30.

Freeman, Richard B. "The Exit-Voice Tradeoff in the Labor Market: Unionism, Job Tenure, Quits and Separations." National Bureau of Economic Research Working Paper, 1978.

———. "The Impact of Collective Bargaining: Illusion and Reality." In Jack Stieber, Richard D. McKersie, and Daniel Q. Mills, eds., *U.S. Industrial Relations, 1950–1980: A Critical Assessment.* Madison, Industrial Relations Research Association, 1981, pp. 47–97.

———, and James L. Medoff. *What Do Unions Do?* New York: Basic Books, 1984.

Futatsugi, Yusaku. "The Measurement of Interfirm Relationships." In Kazuo Sato, ed., *Industry and Business in Japan.* White Plains, N.Y.: M. E. Sharpe, 1980.

Gilbert, Neil. *Capitalism and the Welfare State.* New Haven, Conn.: Yale University Press, 1983.

Green, Mark, and John F. Berry. *The Challenge of Hidden Profits.* New York: Morrow, 1985.

Green, Mark, and Bonnie Tenneriello. "Executive Merit Pay." *New York Times,* April 25, 1984, p. A-23.

Grenier, Guillermo, Jr. "Research Expenditures and Growth Accounting." In Bruce Rodda Williams, ed., *Science and Technology in Economic Growth.* New York: Wiley, 1973, pp. 55–95.

———. "Twisting Quality Circles to Bust Unions." *AFL-CIO News,* May 14, 1983, pp. 8–14.

Griliches, Zvi. "R & D and the Productivity Slowdown." National Bureau of Economic Research, Working Paper no. 434 (January 1980).

Guenther, Robert. "Plan for Construction Productivity Stirs Industry, Takes Aim at Unions." *Wall Street Journal,* April 21, 1983, sect. 2, p. 35.

Gutchess, Jocelyn. "Potential Outcomes of Joint Management of Pension Funds." Paper prepared for Work in American Institute conference, February 18, 1983.

Hall, Robert E. "The Importance of Lifetime Jobs in the U.S. Economy." *American Economic Review* (September 1982): 716–24.

Harbison, Frederick H. *Human Resource as a Wealth of Nations.* New York: Oxford University Press, 1973.

———, and Charles Myers. *Education, Manpower, and Economic Growth.* New York: McGraw-Hill, 1964.

Hashimoto, Masanori, and John Raisian. "Employment Tenure and Earnings Profiles in Japan and the United States." *American Economic Review* (September 1985): 721–35.

Hayes, Robert H., and William J. Abernathy. "Managing Our Way to Economic Decline." *Harvard Business Review* (July–August 1980): 67–77.
High Tech Research Group. *Massachusetts High Tech.* Somerville, Mass.: The High Tech Research Group, 1984.
Hirsch, Barry T. "Review Symposium." *Industrial and Labor Relations Review* (January 1985): 247–50.

Industrial Structure Council. *Vision of MITI Policies in the 1980s.* March 1980.
International Confederation of Free Trade Unions. *Trade Unions and the Transnationals.* Brussels: ICFTU, March 1983.
International Monetary Fund, Finance and Development Editorial Staff. "The Realities of Economic Interdependence." *Finance and Development: Quarterly Publication of the International Monetary Fund and the World Bank* (March 1984): 28–32.

Johnson, Alan. "Recovery Is on the Way in Executive Paychecks." *Nation's Business* (December 1983): 57–58.
Johnson, Chalmers. *MITI and the Japanese Miracle: The Growth of Industrial Policy, 1925–75.* Palo Alto, Calif.: Stanford University Press, 1982.
Johnson, George. "Capital Formation in the United States: The Postwar Perspective." In Board of Governors of the Federal Reserve System, *Public Policy and Capital Formation,* 1981.
Joyce, John T. "Codetermination and Collective Bargaining in the U.S." Paper presented to the International Labor Organization Symposium on Worker's Participation, The Hague, May 5–8, 1981.
Judson, Arnold. "The Awkward Truth About Productivity." *Harvard Business Review* (September–October 1982): 93–97.

Kaker, Sudhir. *Frederick W. Taylor: A Study in Personality and Innovation.* Cambridge, Mass.: M.I.T. Press, 1970.
Katz, Harry C., Thomas A. Kochan, and Kenneth R. Gobeille. "Industrial Relations Performance, Economic Performance, and QWL Performance: An Interplant Analysis." *Industrial and Labor Relations Review* (October 1983): 3–17.
Katzell, R. A. et al. *A Guide to Worker Productivity Experiments in the U.S., 1971–1975.* New York: New York University Press, 1977.
Kendrick, J. W. "Total Investment and Productivity Developments." Paper presented at the Joint Session of the American Finance Association and the American Economic Association, New York, December 30, 1977.
Kilborn, Peter T. "American Savings Less Now than Before the 1981 Tax Act." *New York Times,* September 6, 1983, p. A-1.
Kirkland, Lane. Address to Brandeis University's National Fellows Conference, October 18, 1980.
Kochan, Thomas. *Collective Bargaining and Industrial Relations.* Homewood, Ill.: Richard Irwin, 1980.
———, Harry Katz, and Nancy Mower. "Worker Participation and American Unions: Threat or Opportunity?" M.I.T.: Alfred P. Sloan School of Management, Working Paper no. 1526–84, 1984.
———, Robert McKersie, and Harry Katz. "U.S. Industrial Relations in Transition: A Summary Report." M.I.T.: Alfred P. Sloan School of Management, Working Paper no. 1617–84, 1984.
Kuttner, Bob. "Savings, Investment, and Distribution: Lessons From Abroad on Capital Formation." In Robert S. McIntyre, ed., *Growth with Fairness.* Washington, D.C.: Institution of Taxation and Economic Policy, 1983.

Landefeld, J. Steven, and Kan H. Young. "The Trade Deficit and the Value of the Dollar." *Business Economics* (October 1985): 11–17.
Lawrence, Robert. *Can America Compete?* Washington, D.C.: Brookings Institution, 1984.
Leinster, Colin. "Can Pan Am Survive?" *Fortune,* April 15, 1985, pp. 49–50.
Leontief, Wassily. "Technological Advance, Economic Growth, and the Distribution of Income." *Population and Development Review* (September 1983): 403–10.
Lerner, Barbara. "American Education: How Are We Doing?" *Public Interest* (Autumn 1982): 59–82.
Levitan, Sar, and Clifford Johnson. *Beyond the Safety Net.* Cambridge, Mass.: Ballinger, 1984.
———. "The Future of Work: Does It Belong to Us or to the Robots?" *Monthly Labor Review* (September 1982): 10–14.
———. "After Hard Times—What Hope for Labor–Management Cooperation?" *Daily Labor Reports,* September 17, 1982, pp. E-1–E-3.
Levitan, Sar, and Robert Taggart. *The Promise of Greatness.* Cambridge, Mass.: Harvard University Press, 1976.
Lewin, Tamas. "Worker-Held Enterprises." *New York Times,* April 17, 1984, p. 28.
Lewis, Paul. "A Fight on Trade in Services." *New York Times,* October 2, 1985, p. D-1.
Lippman, Thomas W. "Preaching Gospel of Productivity: The Sermon Works at Westinghouse." *Washington Post,* March 21, 1982, p. F-1.
Lipsey, Robert E., and Irving B. Kravis. "The Competitive Position of U.S. Manufacturing Firms." *Banco Nazionale del Lavoro Quarterly Review,* 1985, pp. 127–54.
Long, Russell. "Unions and Employee Ownership." *Congressional Record* 129, no. 60, (February 2, 1982), part 2.

McBride, Lloyd. Statement to the Industrial Union Department's Industrial Policy Conference, Baltimore, July 21–22, 1983.
Marsh, T. R., and D. E. McAllister. "ESOP's Fables: A Survey of Companies with ESOPs." *Journal of Corporate Law* 6 (1981): 551–623.
Marshall, Ray. "Government, Markets, and Consensus-Building Mechanisms." *National Productivity Review* (Autumn 1982): 445–50.
———. *The Negro Worker.* New York: Random House, 1967.
———. "Selective Programs and Economic Policy." *Journal of Economic Issues* (March 1984): 117–42.
——— et al. *An Economic Strategy for the 1980's.* Washington, D.C.: Full Employment Action Council, National Policy Exchange, 1982.
Meidner, Rudolf. *Employee Investment Funds.* London: Allen and Unwin, 1978.
Melman, Seymour. "Managers' Debacle." *New York Times,* November 4, 1983, p. A-27.
Meltz, Noah M. "Labor Movements in Canada and the United States." In Thomas A. Kochan, ed., *Challenges and Choices Facing the American Labor Movement,* Cambridge, Mass.: M.I.T. Press, 1985.
Mills, D. Quinn. "A New Cooperation Sweeps Detroit." *Wall Street Journal,* October 17, 1984, p. 18.
———. "Reforming the U.S. System of Collective Bargaining." *Monthly Labor Review* (March 1983): 18–22.
Mills, Ted. "U.S. and European Approaches to Improving Labor Productivity and the Quality of Worklife." Washington, D.C.: American Enterprise Institute, 1982.

————. "Altering the Social Structure in Coal Mining: A Case Study." *Monthly Labor Review* (October 1976): 3–10.

Miner, Thomas. Memorandum of understanding to Marc Stepp, September 16, 1982.

Miyazaki, Yoshikazu. "Japanese-Type Structure of Big Business." In Kazuo Sato, ed., *Industry and Business in Japan.* White Plains, N.Y.: M. E. Sharpe, 1980.

Morrison, Julian. "When Employees Get a Piece of the Action." *Nation's Business,* December 1983, pp. 20–24.

Murrin, Thomas J. Remarks to the American Society for Quality Control Congress, Detroit, May 3, 1982.

National Center for Productivity and Quality of Working Life. *Directory of Labor–Management Committees.* Washington, D.C.: Government Printing Office, 1978.

New York Stock Exchange. *Building a Better Future: Economic Choices of the 1980s.* New York: NYSE, 1980.

————. *U.S. International Competitiveness: Perception and Reality.* New York: NYSE, 1984.

Norsworthy, J. R., and Craig Zabala. "Worker Attitudes, Worker Behavior, and Productivity in the U.S. Automobile Industry, 1959–1976." *Industrial and Labor Relations Review* (July 1985): 544–57.

Obey, David. "Economic Policy and the American Economy: Lessons from the Past and Challenges for the Future." Remarks to the U.S. Congress Joint Economic Committee's symposium on the fortieth anniversary of the Employment Act, Washington, D.C., January 16, 1986.

Okun, Arthur. "The Invisible Handshake and the Inflationary Process." *Challenge* (January–February 1980): 5–12.

Organization for Economic Cooperation and Development (OECD). *The Industrial Policies in Japan.* Paris: OECD, 1972.

Ornos, Peter. "Hi-Tech Wizard Sees Brave New World in '90's." *Washington Post,* March 6, 1983, p. A-1.

Paul, Mark. "Fremont Deal Could Hurt U.S. Industry." *Oakland Tribune,* April 15, 1984, p. 15.

Piore, Michael J., and Charles F. Sabel. *The Second Industrial Divide: Possibilities for Prosperity.* New York: Basic Books, 1984.

President's Commission on Industrial Competitiveness. *Global Competition: The New Reality.* Washington, D.C.: Government Printing Office, 1984.

Rees, Albert. "Improving Productivity Measurement." *American Economic Review* (May 1980): 340–42.

Rehn, Gosta. "Swedish Active Labor Market Policy: Retrospect and Prospect." *Industrial Relations* (Winter 1985): 62–89.

Reisman, Barbara, and Lance Compa. "The Case for Adversarial Unions." *Harvard Business Review* (May–June 1985): 22–36.

Richardson, David. "U.S. International Trade Policies in a World of Industrial Change." Paper presented at conference sponsored by the Federal Reserve Bank of Kansas City, August 24–26, 1983.

Rosen, Corey, and Katherine Klein. "Job-Creating Performance of Employee-Owned Firms." *Monthly Labor Review* (August 1983): 15–19.

Rostow, W. W. *The Barbaric Counter-Revolution: Cause and Cure.* Austin: University of Texas Press, 1983.

Sachs, Jeffrey. "Real Wages and Unemployment in OECD Countries." *Brookings Papers on Economic Activity* 1, 1983, pp. 255–304.

Salpukas, Agis. "The Long Fight for TWA: Unions Decided the Winner." *New York Times,* August 31, 1985, p. A-1.

Sawyer, Kathy. "Communication Workers Act to Ease Impact of Future Shock." *Washington Post,* March 29, 1983, p. A-3.

Schultz, Theodore W. *Human Resources.* Fiftieth Anniversary Colloquium of the National Bureau of Economic Research, Atlanta, 1971. New York: Columbia University Press, 1972.

Schultze, Charles L. "Industrial Policy: A Dissent." *Brookings Review* (Autumn 1983): 3–12.

Schwarz, John E. *America's Hidden Success.* New York: W. W. Norton, 1983.

Scott, Bruce. "Toward Greater U.S. Competitiveness." *New York Times,* November 25, 1984, sec. 3, p. 3.

————. "National Strategy for Stronger U.S. Competitiveness." *Harvard Business Review* (March–April 1984): 77–91.

Seidel, Hans. "Incomes Policies in Austria." *Challenge* (September–October 1981): 58–60.

Serrin, William. "Bold G.M. Pact Draws Praise, and Some Caveats." *New York Times,* August 3, 1985, p. 6.

Servan-Schreiber, John J. *The American Challenge,* Ronald Steel, trans. New York: Atheneum, 1979.

Shaiken, Harley. *Work Transformed: Automation and Labor in the Computer Age.* New York: Holt, Rinehart & Winston, 1985.

Shioji, Ichiro. "Productivity and Labor–Management Relations." Paper sent to author, 1985.

Simmons, John, and William J. Mares. *Working Together.* New York: Knopf, 1983.

Sommers, William P. "Are We Still Managing Our Way to Economic Decline?" Unpublished paper, Booz, Allen and Hamilton, 1985.

Southern Labor Institute, *Now Is the Time.* Atlanta: SLI, 1986.

Stein, Herbert. "Don't Fall for Industrial Policy." *Fortune,* November 14, 1983, pp. 64–78.

————. "Industrial Policy à la Reich." *Fortune,* June 13, 1983, pp. 201–8.

Stepp, Marc. Speech to Society of Automotive Engineers, February 29, 1984.

Suzuki, Yoshio. *Money and Banking in Contemporary Japan: The Theoretical Setting and Its Application.* New Haven, Conn.: Yale University Press, 1980.

Taira, Kogi. "Economic Growth, Labor Productivity and Employment Adjustment in Japan." Paper presented at annual meeting of the Industrial Relations Research Association, 1982.

Tanaka, H. William. Statement before the Joint Economic Committee, 97th Congress, 1st Session, July 28, 1981.

Taylor, Frederick W. *Scientific Management.* New York: Harper Bros., 1947.

Terleckyj, N. E. *Effects of R & D on the Productivity Growth of Industries: An Exploratory Study.* Washington, D.C.: National Planning Association, 1974.

Thurow, Lester. *The Zero Sum Solution.* New York: Simon & Schuster, 1985.

Tomaskovic-Devey, Donald, and S. M. Miller. "Can High-Tech Provide the Jobs?" *Challenge* (May–June 1983): 57–63.

Trost, Cathy. "Labor Letter." *Wall Street Journal,* September 17, 1985, p. 1.

United Auto Workers Research Department. "Choices for American Industry: Autos." 1985, unpublished UAW paper.

U.S. Congress Joint Economic Committee. "Monetary Policy, Selective Credit Policy and Industrial Policy in France, Britain, West Germany and Sweden." Washington, D.C.: Government Printing Office, 1981.

U.S. Department of Commerce. *Japanese Technology Evaluation Program Report on Opto- and Microelectronics.* Washington, D.C.: Government Printing Office, 1985.

——, Bureau and Economic Analysis. *Survey of Current Business.* Washington, D.C.: Government Printing Office, February and September 1981.

——, International Trade Administration. *U.S. Competitiveness in the International Economy.* Washington, D.C.: Government Printing Office, October 1981.

——, National Technical Information Service. *The Impact of Labor Unions on the Rate and Direction of Technological Change.* Prepared for the National Science Foundation, Policy Research and Analysis, by the Institute of Labor and Industrial Relations, University of Michigan–Wayne State University, February 1979, PB-297-084.

U.S. Department of Labor, Bureau of Labor–Management Relations and Cooperative Programs. *U.S. Labor Law and the Future of Labor Management Cooperation.* BLMR no. 104, 1986.

U.S. House of Representatives, Committee on Energy and Commerce. *The U.S. in a Changing World Economy: The Case for Integrated Domestic and International Commercial Policy.* Staff report, 1983.

——. *Industrial Import Shock: Policy Challenge of the 1980s.* Staff report, August 1985.

Vogel, Ezra. *Japan as Number One: Lessons for America.* New York: Harper & Row, 1980.

Walton, Richard E. "How to Counter Alienation in the Plant." *Harvard Business Review* (November–December 1972): 70–81.

Watts, Glenn E. Remarks at the Third Annual Labor–Management Conference, University of Wisconsin, Milwaukee, November 16, 1983.

——. Statement to the Economic Policy Council of the United Nations Association, Washington, D.C., June 11, 1982.

Weiler, Paul C. Speech before the National Academy of Arbitrators, May 30, 1985. *Daily Labor Report,* June 11, 1985, p. E-3.

Weiss, Andrew. "Simple Truths of Japanese Manufacturing." *Harvard Business Review* (July–August 1984): 119–25.

Weisskopf, Thomas E., Samuel Bowles, and David M. Gordon. "Hearts and Minds: A Social Model of U.S. Productivity Growth." *Brookings Papers on Economic Activity* 2, 1983, pp. 381–451.

Whyte, William F. et al. *Worker Participation and Ownership.* Ithaca, N.Y.: ILR Press, Cornell University, 1983.

Wood, Robert C. "Japan's Industrial Vision." *Asia* (January–February 1982): 8–9.

Yankelovich, Daniel P. *New Rules: Searching for Self-Fulfillment in a World Turned Upside Down.* New York: Random House, 1981.

——. *Putting the Work Ethic to Work.* Washington, D.C.: Public Agenda Foundation, 1983.

INDEX